EX LIBRIS

Given By
Lauren
Prager

LIBRARY
BOOK

by
Alexandra
Brown
1983

24.6.87

·THE·CHILDREN'S·
·HISTORY·OF·
CIVILIZATIONS

·THE·CHILDREN'S· ·HISTORY·OF· CIVILIZATIONS

GIORGIO P PANINI

HAMLYN

Published 1986 by
Hamlyn Publishing
Bridge House, London Road,
Twickenham, Middlesex, England.

© 1983 Arnoldo Mondadori Editore S.p.A.
Milan, Italy

© Copyright 1986 English language edition Hamlyn Publishing
a division of The Hamlyn Publishing Group Ltd

ISBN 0 600 31075 2
Printed in Italy

Frontispiece: Ancient Egyptian statue being taken
apart by archaeologists. When the Aswan Dam on
the River Nile was built and Lake Nasser created,
many ancient treasures were drowned. However,
part of this precious heritage was saved by much
patient work transporting and reassembling
various objects out of reach of the lake's waters.

Contents

Introduction

The history of mankind is an enormously complex field of study. There are a great many starting points from which to begin sifting through the vast amount of information that has been collected about the activities of our ancestors. This book is concerned with the cultural history of early man and the subsequent development of the first cultures that are now recognized as civilizations.

Culture is not an easy term to understand, but essentially social scientists – those engaged in the scientific study of all aspects of human behaviour – see it as the factor which above all else distinguishes man from other animals. Man has much the same physical abilities as his near relatives the African great apes, and many other 'higher animals' for that matter, although his large brain and sensitive, agile hands can be said to have given him an advantage. However, no other animal has been able to manipulate its environment to satisfy its needs so successfully and it is his use of culture which has enabled man to do so.

Broadly speaking a culture is the way of life of a group of people. It includes material culture and non-material culture. Material culture refers to all the tools, objects, buildings and discoveries which people make and use and which form the basis of their way of life. These profoundly influence the non-material culture which is all the standardized forms of behaviour, ideas and beliefs of a people; it includes everything from methods of growing wheat or making pottery to religious rites and the ways in which the ruler is chosen.

An important aspect of culture is that it is accumulated knowledge which is learnt and passed on from generation to generation. Animal behaviour is instinctive and is inherited as biological traits. Some of man's basic behaviour such as eating and sleeping falls into the latter category, but so much more (such as language, technical skills and morals – all that which is culture) is dependant on the accumulated experience of generations and can only be passed on by instruction and imitation. As a consequence culture is very fragile and could easily be lost if a society were to break down. One can easily see that technical skills would be lost if the specialists in them did not teach younger people, and the same applies to more general aspects of culture. In fact, some ancient craft skills have been lost because they became obsolete and no-one bothered to learn them.

We have already mentioned language with regard to culture. Language, while being part of culture, has played a vital role in the transmission and the increasing complexity of cultures. It enables information to be passed from one individual to another quickly and easily. Writing has further enhanced the power of language by making information permanently available to others.

Civilizations, as we have already mentioned, are particularly advanced types of culture. They are generally recognized as those cultures which include the use of writing, the presence of cities, have highly organized systems of government and in which there are many specialist jobs. Of course, to reach this degree of sophistication, a culture must have the means (technology) to enable it to produce enough food to support those not occupied in food production. It must also have the means to transport and store food for those living in cities.

However, these criteria for civilizations are not rigid, and as this book illustrates, cultures which did not have writing or cities have been sufficiently important to warrant being discussed as civilizations.

Our knowledge of man's early history is the result of much painstaking research by historians and archaeologists. The first historians relied on oral traditions and the few written documents available. But all the evidence of prehistoric man has been derived from archaeological study, as of course these people had no written language. Even those ancient civilizations which did possess writing have often left little more than memorial inscriptions.

Archaeology is the scientific study of the material remains – tools, weapons, household goods, buildings, graves, and even fossils – of people from the past in order to learn about their lives and activities. Until the discoveries of many of the ancient civilizations by archaeologists in the 19th century, there had been virtually no evidence of their existence other than in the accounts of Greek and Roman historians. The painstaking excavation, examination and cataloguing of the remains of cultures and civilizations all over the world have given us a remarkable insight into man's early history. This is a process which is continuing and as new evidence is discovered, so our understanding of human history is changing. In particular, understanding of the ancestry of man has been undergoing considerable modification in recent years with the discovery of new fossils.

This book begins by studying the evolution of man and culture. The progress from the use of the first stone implements to modern space travel and computer technology represents an enormous leap in knowledge and skill. And yet the first hesitant steps to developing a simple Stone-Age technology, used in conjunction with hunting wild animals and gathering plants for food, took by far the longest. This period of man's cultural evolution is known as the Palaeolithic, but it is worth mentioning that while it does generally coincide with a particular period in time, it really refers to a type of culture. In fact, there are still people in the world today who have a Palaeolithic culture. That is they live on what their environment provides rather than using it to produce what they want.

The next important step in man's story was the development of agriculture. Man took the bold step of using the environment to produce the food he wanted, both crops and animals. This – the Neolithic period – encouraged the establishment of more permanent settlements and saw the discovery and use of such things as pottery and metals.

We then move on to a consideration of the environments which produced the first great civilizations. This is followed by a look at the particular circumstances which led, and in some cases, forced, the peoples of these regions to develop the highly complex organizations of civilization. For example, it sometimes happened that conditions in the environment were so difficult that in order to survive a community had to adopt complex methods to produce sufficient food. These methods involved a high degree of co-operation and when successful formed the basis of civilizations.

A more detailed examination of the civilizations of the Near East follows. Of particular importance here are those civilizations – in Egypt, Mesopotamia, and the Indus – which were dependant on rivers. Our attention is next focussed on Europe where a multiplicity of peoples lived without any overall organization, but who were capable of producing enormous stone monuments for religious and astronomical purposes, as well as being advanced in the use of pottery and metals.

The remainder of our study is taken up with a detailed account of the ancient civilizations of Crete, North and South America, China and Japan, Persia, Assyria, Babylon, the New Kingdom of Egypt, the Phoenicians and the Etruscans in Italy.

Successful cultures are those that are well adapted to their environment – their people are able to produce enough food to live comfortably and raise healthy children. However, it can happen that circumstances in the environment change – a disease wipes out a culture's main crop, or a neighbouring people steal their livestock. Thus a culture can rapidly become unsuccessful and be extinguished. In a successful, well-adapted culture, new inventions, ideas and ways of doing things will often be rejected because they are not necessary and upset the relationship of the people with their environment. However, when a people is faced with extinction, these new inventions, ideas and ways of doing things may be absolutely vital if they are to adapt their culture sufficiently to enable them to survive in their new circumstances.

It is this process of adaptation to new circumstances which is at the heart of cultural evolution. It is a process which, as we shall see in the following pages, produced the great civilizations of the past. It also produced modern civilization and we can see it taking place today as man continues to face new problems threatening his survival. It is hoped that this book's study of man's early cultural evolution and the rise of the first civilizations will help us to put our present problems in perspective.

1. The Roots of Civilization — Paleolithic and Neolithic Man

The First Men

Present-day man, or in the language of zoological science, *Homo sapiens sapiens*, represents the particular stage we have reached in a process of evolution which began many millions of years ago. This process is similar to the countless other evolutionary processes which have produced today's plants and animals and are the basis of the story of life on this planet. The story has un-

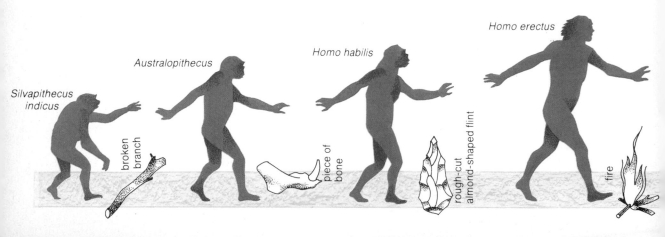

Silvapithecus indicus — broken branch — *Australopithecus* — piece of bone — *Homo habilis* — rough-cut almond-shaped flint — *Homo erectus* — fire

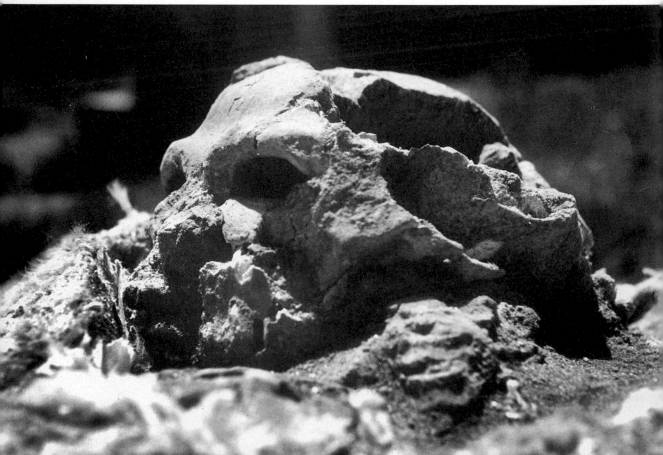

rolled not as a steady development but as a long series of bursts, phases during which creatures adapted to the various situations around them and responded to the problems which, one by one, their environment placed in their path.

Evolution, as Charles Darwin perceived and explained over a century ago, is based on the ability, common to all organisms, to change and diversify so as to survive and gain a slightly better life. Those creatures least well adapted to their situations do not survive because they are unable to have many offspring, with the result that their decreasing adaptability is not passed on to their descendants. On the other hand, an individual which has adapted well finds survival easier, and is able to have many offspring who will inherit the adaptation which is so obviously favourable. This is the principle of natural selection which is a fundamental element of evolutionary theory.

Man first emerged from a huge group of mammals known as primates. Among this group are the apes, all of which are tail-less and resemble us quite closely. The African great apes (gorillas and chimpanzees) belong to the same group of animals as man. For the last five to ten million years or so one particular branch of this group, the family of hominids, has been gradually evolving; we represent the stage it has currently reached.

Homo sapiens neanderthalensis

Homo sapiens sapiens

bolas

bone harpoon

Opposite above: The story of the hominid family's evolution goes back at least five to ten million years. The oldest form we know is *Silvapithecus indicus*; the latest (ourselves) is *Homo sapiens sapiens*. In this diagram the main species and sub-species of the family are shown with particular objects which they made and used and which are associated with them. The story of mankind is also the story of technology. These ancient objects represented a response to the needs for which they were made. Neanderthal man made things from stone, bone, ivory, animal horn and other softer materials which have not been preserved, producing a whole range of tools comparable to those found in any repair workshop today.
Opposite: Skull of *Homo sapiens neanderthalensis* found in the Shanidar caves in Iraq in 1951.
Right: Site in Ethiopia, a region of Africa which has produced important remains and evidence of the first forms of the genus *Homo*.

Even this brief mention of the principle of natural selection shows, in rather simplified terms perhaps, a fact which is indisputable. Any evolutionary history like this one is a history of failures, accidents and deaths. For every one who survives, there are many that die.

The individuals who are cross-fertile (those who are able to have offspring who in their turn are able to have more offspring) make the species a constantly changing and dynamic entity. Despite the variety of places in which we live and the differences in our appearances, we are all members of the human species.

Culture and Evolution

The cost of evolution is the continuing death of those who are less well adapted and do not 'make the grade'. Over the five to ten million years of the hominids' evolution, in the timespan between *Silvapithecus indicus*, the first of the primates which can be identified as a hominid, and ourselves, man has become different not only from the other animals, but also from his ancestral hominids. This divergence has become more marked during recent eras, and particularly over the past half million years. About two million years ago, a creature of the genus *Homo* was chipping away at a stone near the shores of the huge expanse of water which is now Lake Turkana in Kenya; this creature was being closely watched by a similar one who tried to imitate it using another stone. We are all descendants of those hominids who learned how to chip pebbles by watching one another.

The leap we have made in terms of capabilities and skills from those first primitive tools to today's computers and space-rockets is a truly great one, and apart from developing our physical faculties, we have also evolved cultural ones. Culture in this context refers to all the knowledge that is accumulated by a group of people and which is passed on to successive generations. Many animals learn; they imitate other members of their species and acquire ways of behaving which will help them survive. This happened with the hominids, too, but at one stage in his development, man acquired the ability to communi-

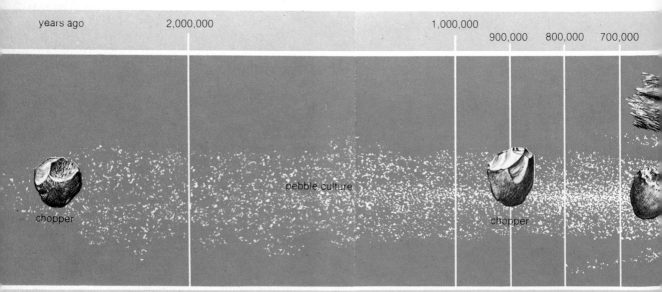

years ago   2,000,000   1,000,000   900,000   800,000   700,000

chopper

pebble culture

chopper

LOWER PALAEOLITHIC

cate in a very efficient way. Gestures were followed by grunting noises, then mimicry and finally words. The amount of information which could be passed on from one individual to another was far greater than with any other animal. This was reflected in a saving of lives: the heavy toll exacted when everyone had to learn by experience was dramatically reduced. One member of the species could now say to another, 'If you walk too close to the edge of a cliff, you'll fall over it', rather than letting the connection between these two facts

cutting edge

cutting edge

uncut side
of the stone

Right: Almond-shaped tool (above) from the Abbeville culture and another (below) from Saint-Acheul, a suburb of Amiens, both in north-east France. These weigh about 310 grams (9.3 ounces) and 290 grams (8.7 ounces) respectively. For its weight, the Acheulean (as objects from Saint-Acheul are known) tool is considerably larger. Being thinner, it is also easier to grip firmly in the palm of the hand.

Opposite: Time chart showing the development of the main objects of the Lower and Middle Palaeolithic periods. Also shown are the main cultures which correspond to these objects and the techniques used for making them. The word Palaeolithic (literally meaning Old Stone Age) refers not only to the objects themselves, but also to the whole way of life associated with them.

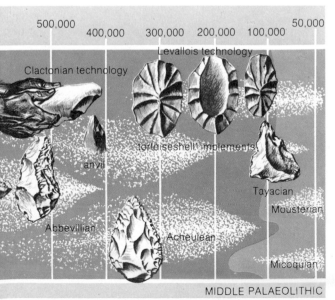

500,000   400,000   300,000   200,000   100,000   50,000

Levallois technology

Clactonian technology

'tortoiseshell' implements

anvil

Tayacian

Mousterian

Abbevillian   Acheulean

Micoquian

MIDDLE PALAEOLITHIC

cutting edge

cutting edge

be learned by seeing a number of one's companions falling over the edge!

The cultural component vastly accelerated man's evolution. Over a very short space of time compared with normal biological evolution, man succeeded in gaining mastery over a great many elements of his environment.

Very often during man's cultural evolution people were able to break out of the structures of their culture and recreate a new one. This happened every time a new discovery was made or tool was invented which resulted in new ways of doing things. Sometimes this evolutionary process produced a stable situation in which the culture and its environment were well matched. However, the most successful cultures were those which remained flexible and were capable of adapting to their environment even if it changed from time to time.

Sometimes a culture would become very complex and efficient and became what we call a civilization. However, if its organization was too dependent on one particular factor, such as the annual flooding of a river (as was the case in Egypt), any change in that factor could be disastrous for the civilization. So we see that even highly-organized, complex civilizations can still be very fragile.

Given this understanding of culture and the way it develops let us return to the relationship between man and his environment by looking at our forebears.

Creating a Material Culture

For man the hominid, culture became a vital means of expressing himself as a species. There are two types of evidence as to man's distant past. One is physical evolution (for example skull fragments which give us an idea of the changing volume of the skull and therefore the changing size of the brain). The other is the remains of his 'material culture'. The term 'material culture' refers to the means and objects used to establish a basic equilibrium between man and his environment and create a certain way of life. The making of objects is the framework of a material culture. This sounds very complicated: what we are really talking about are the weapons, pots, jewellery, tools and so on which were used by different peoples as the basis of

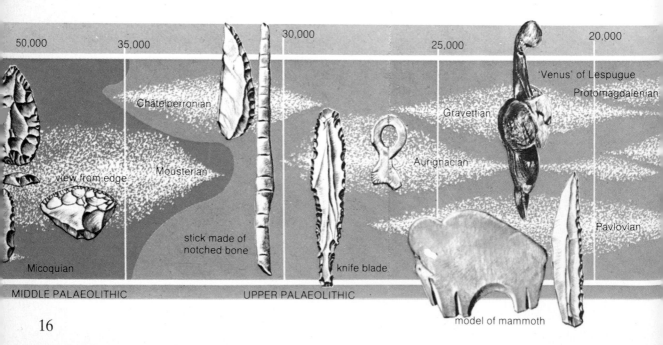

50,000   35,000   30,000   25,000   20,000

Châtelperronian

'Venus' of Lespugue

Protomagdalenian

Gravettian

Aurignacian

view from edge   Mousterian

stick made of notched bone

Pavlovian

Micoquian

knife blade

model of mammoth

MIDDLE PALAEOLITHIC   UPPER PALAEOLITHIC

incised awl

awl

bone needle

incised bone harpoons

their way of life, and which have been left behind as evidence of it.

However, this evidence of a material culture does not always correspond to a particular point in the history of humankind. If one type of relationship with the environment works particularly well, and therefore helps a group of humans to survive, it may continue for centuries. For example, many groups of Australian aborigines still have a material culture based on the use of

Opposite: Time chart showing the main objects and cultures of the Middle and Upper Palaeolithic periods. The timescale is different to that of the chart on pp 14–15. It will be seen that many objects were made of materials other than stone during the Palaeolithic period (including bone, animal horn and ivory). At the end of the Upper Palaeolithic, the Mesolithic (or Middle Stone Age) cultures took over.

Left: Pointed tools, bone needles and harpoons from the Magdalenian period in Europe (about 12,000 to 10,000 years ago). During the last phases of the Upper Palaeolithic period, when Magdalenian culture was prevalent, many paintings and drawings appeared on cave walls.

Below: Horse painted in the cave of Las Chimenas, near Santander in north-east Spain. Signs representing spears and lances can be seen on the animal's body. These pictures probably played an important part in the magic of hunting; whatever happened to the paintings would also happen by magic to the animals which man was hunting.

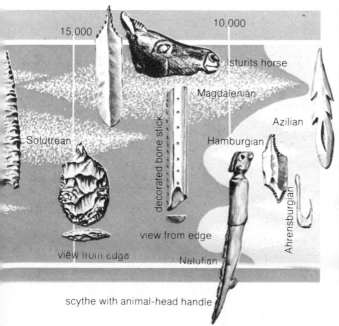

15,000

10,000

Isturits horse

Magdalenian

Azilian

Solutrean

Hamburgian

Ahrensburgian

decorated bone stick

view from edge

view from edge

Natufian

scythe with animal-head handle

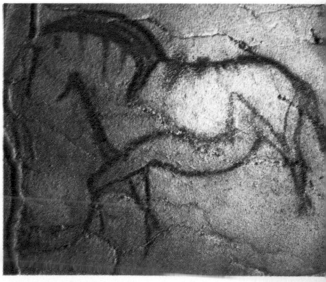

17

chipped stones. As we will see, this type of culture belongs to the period of man's history known as the Palaeolithic period, and, in most areas, became outdated thousands of years ago. However, in some isolated areas of Australia, the Palaeolithic way of life is still acceptable and this is how the aborigines live, though to other cultures they are a curiosity. Arrowheads have been found, which have been made, not by chipping stones, but by using Coke bottle tops: material fragments which obviously belong to another way of life. And indeed it is a characteristic of the Palaeolithic way of life that it uses any raw materials which may happen to be available.

Cases of cultures which have escaped the main tide of civilization in this way are rare, however. The overall view we obtain by gathering many, many shreds of evidence from every corner of the globe is that most 'primitive' material cultures are actually part of an ordered series of events. Man makes objects, and always has done, in order to solve two aspects of the problem of survival which all animals share: one is defence against predators and other enemies, and the other is the attainment of goals. Goals consist primarily of acquiring food on which to subsist, shelter and warmth, as well as acquiring or making goods to achieve these ends.

The diagrams on the previous pages show the main cultures which arose after man first began making objects around one million years ago. Remember that these are simply trends and there are always exceptions to them.

Stone Tools

Let us try to improve our definitions, moving step by step, as though slowly cutting out a stone tool.

Culture is a particular way of making objects, a particular way of producing

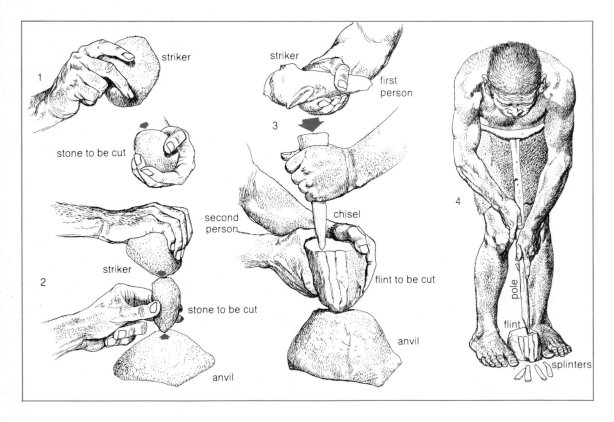

food and material goods using other objects. Throughout the very long Palaeolithic period (the 'Old Stone Age'), man acquired food by hunting and by gathering such things as vegetables, small animals, insects and shellfish. Strictly speaking, we could therefore say that anyone who obtains food in this way is Palaeolithic, even though they may not use stone implements. Fishing is a Palaeolithic activity; so is gathering mushrooms or collecting blackberries to make into jam.

If, however, we can distinguish a number of different cultures within the broad spectrum of the Palaeolithic period, it is because the evidence of them so far discovered (in most cases chipped stones) shows that there were various phases and ways of making stone objects. The results were different too. In particular we can see a steady improvement in the quality of these implements, and it is fair to say that there was technical progress between one phase and the next.

Opposite: Prehistoric peoples had different ways of cutting stone. Each method corresponded to a particular technology and often led to the creation of an object which belonged to a well-defined culture. 1. Direct impact – one hand held the stone to be cut and the other hit it using another stone, the striker. This produced large fragments and a roughly cut tool. 2. Cutting by bilateral impact – the stone being cut was placed on top of another, larger one (the anvil) and hit with a striker. This gave fairly neat cuts. 3. Indirect impact – one person held the stone on the anvil while another hit it with a chisel, which need not necessarily have been a stone one. This gave neat cuts. 4. Cutting using body weight – a single person placed his chest on a pole sharpened at one end. This force could be directed quite accurately and produced very well-made stone knife-edges.
Below left: Two fairly rough tools, probably from the Clactonian culture (diagram p 14). These were made by hitting a large stone resting directly on an anvil and were found at Hassi Fokra in Algeria.
Below: This scraper is from the Mousterian culture, and is the equivalent of a modern-day pen-knife used for cutting or scraping rigid surfaces.

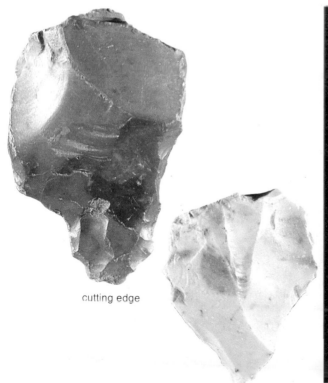

cutting edge

cutting edge

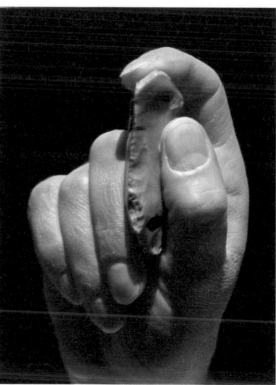

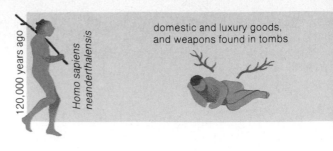

120,000 years ago

Homo sapiens neanderthalensis

domestic and luxury goods, and weapons found in tombs

Right: Comparison between *Homo sapiens neanderthalensis* and *Homo sapiens sapiens*. Neanderthal man survived about 90,000 years; *Homo sapiens sapiens* has been on this planet for approximately 35,000 years. The artefacts found buried with Neanderthal skeletons were those of the Mousterian culture. There is also important evidence of magical and religious rites accompanying the burial of the dead.
Below right: Skeletons of the two best-known sub-species of *Homo sapiens*. *Homo sapiens fossilis* is virtually the same as *Homo sapiens sapiens* (the present form); the skeletal differences are no more than we would expect to exist within a generic subspecies, but there are important anatomical differences between *Homo sapiens neanderthalensis* and *Homo sapiens sapiens*.

What are the qualities of an effective stone tool? Firstly, it can be used for cutting, striking or scraping. Like a knife, it must therefore have a point and a sharp edge, this edge being as long and straight as possible. It must also be possible to resharpen it if it gets damaged. The first men probably made their tools only when they needed to, for example when they went out hunting, and probably threw them away when they were completely worn out. This is why chipped stones are so common in the areas where the earliest human beings lived (*Homo habilis*, *Homo erectus*, see diagram pp 12–13).

In later ages, the tool would have been refined by being better looked after and sharpened using minute strokes from another stone. Even later we find large, flat cutting tools which have been made with some precision using pre-cut tools. This was *Levallois* technology (or material culture), so called after Levallois-Perret, a suburb of Paris where the first examples of these tools were found.

Throughout the first part of the Palaeolithic period (the Lower Palaeolithic as it is called) the main tools we find are *amigdala*, or 'almonds', so called because of their characteristic shape. These tools had many uses. The raw material was always stone – primarily flint, a rock composed of

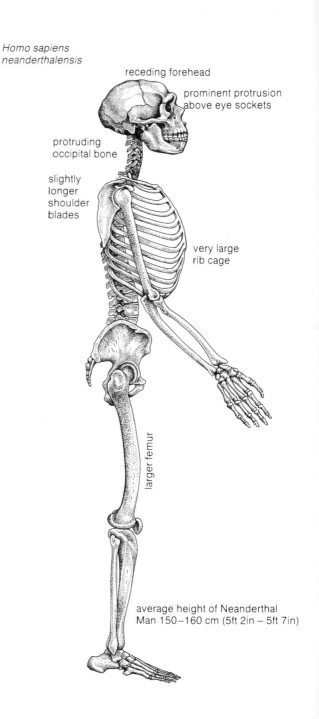

Homo sapiens neanderthalensis

receding forehead

prominent protrusion above eye sockets

protruding occipital bone

slightly longer shoulder blades

very large rib cage

larger femur

average height of Neanderthal Man 150–160 cm (5ft 2in – 5ft 7in)

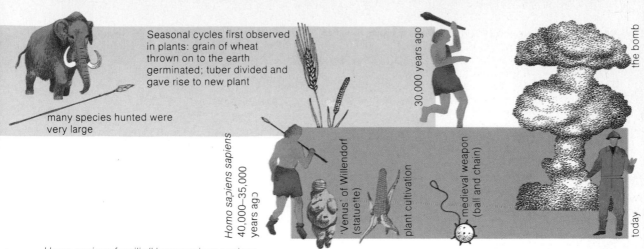

Seasonal cycles first observed in plants: grain of wheat thrown on to the earth germinated; tuber divided and gave rise to new plant

many species hunted were very large

30,000 years ago

the bomb

today

Homo sapiens sapiens 40,000–35,000 years ago

'Venus' of Willendorf (statuette)

plant cultivation

medieval weapon (ball and chain)

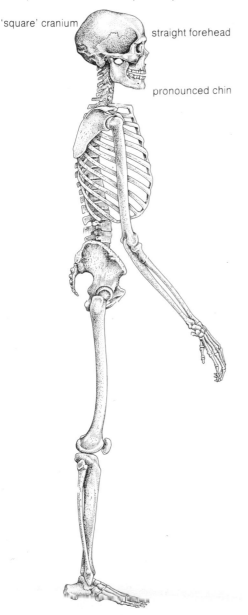

Homo sapiens fossilis/Homo sapiens sapiens

'square' cranium

straight forehead

pronounced chin

minute crystals – which is hard but easily chipped. It is more than likely that other materials, particularly wood, were used. Objects made of these materials have not been preserved, however, because they are less durable than those made of stone.

Neanderthal Man

The first real boom in the production, diversification and quality of man-made objects occurred in the Middle Palaeolithic period, dominated by the 'Mousterian' culture (from Le Moustier in the Dordogne region of France). This culture is a typical example of that of Neanderthal man, a form of *Homo sapiens* which flourished between about 100,000 and 35,000 years ago.

The way tools were made from the original block of stone varied a great deal. The most common shapes were points, almonds and scrapers. The finishing touches – the smallest cuts – are very precise and the cuts are long and straight. The tools are not heavy so they must have been very manageable, and Neanderthal man was skilled at obtaining the maximum number of tools, as well as the longest cutting edge possible, from a very small piece of flint. We have also found tools made of bone, and the wood-working industry

21

1. Their huts were made of wooden palings (or bone or mammoth tusks) on top of which animal skins were sewn together. 2. According to the anthropologist F E Koby, the scratches sometimes found on the enamel of Neanderthal teeth show that they ate their meat by cramming it into their mouths and cutting off the remaining piece with a stone knife. Some Eskimos eat in this fashion today. 3. Simple clothes would almost certainly have been made, given the harsh climate of Europe. Their manufacture demonstrated Neanderthal man's use of abstract thought to shape the clothes to the body. The fact that the objects they made tended to be symmetrical shows that they were able to imagine ideal shapes and then hew them from the material.

Below: Artist's impression of a scene from Neanderthal daily life, portraying these people as semi-herders. Such a relationship may never have existed between man and animal, but it is possible that even as early as this, man was selectively protecting the animals used as prey by, for example, not killing young or female animals and not disturbing them during the mating season.

must by now have been flourishing.

Also common are the stone balls which, tied together by a cord of vegetable fibre, formed the throwing weapon known as the bolas. This was still being used not so long ago by cowherds in the South American pampas for catching cattle; the bolas was thrown between the animal's hooves and became entangled between them, thereby tripping the animal and hindering its flight.

A particular technology was taught, transmitted and remained part of the cultural heritage of the group. In the case of Neanderthal man, archaeological finds show that different kinds of tools were made (and presumably used) on a single site. This shows that Neanderthal man's technology was not dependant on a single object: his culture encompassed a huge variety of

products and the technology used to produce them must have been very effective.

Compared to the 'one-track' (or single-object) culture of previous forms of humankind, Mousterian culture shows that Neanderthals could deal with a great range of, sometimes, critical problems. The results of this are clear to see. Neanderthal man was the longest-lasting stage in the development of *Homo sapiens*. If being around for a long time is an indicator of success, it is fair to say that *Homo sapiens neanderthalensis* (as Neanderthal man is known zoologically), having lived on this planet for almost 70,000 years, is several lengths ahead of ourselves, *Homo sapiens sapiens*, who have been here for a mere 35,000 years.

The Neanderthal Way of Life

How did Neanderthals live? We can answer this question in a single word: comfortably. Let us look at the way we reconstruct details of how they lived, based on the evidence we have available.

Their bones were powerful ones, with plenty of muscle. These *Homo sapiens* generally must have been healthy because they ate well. However, they may have had problems with the cold climate and the use of animal skins as clothing, as some skeletons show traces of rickets which may have been caused by lack of exposure to sunlight (Vitamin D, which helps prevent rickets, is built up in the body by solar radiation on the skin).

The Neanderthal way of life was Palaeolithic. They hunted large animals, probably by ambushing them along their migration trails and possibly following herds of large herbivores, such as deer, cattle and bison. The meat

tiny grooves on front teeth

axis of symmetry

axis of symmetry

was cooked on glowing stones inside an oven. Vegetables, roots for example, and fruit would have been eaten. Certainly these people lived in close contact with nature. Watching plants and their reproductive cycles, the strange way in which certain roots multiplied must have been obvious; they must have noticed, too, that how quickly a seed germinates depends on the kind of soil it is placed in.

The environment in Europe was a very cold one: Neanderthal man lived mainly on the tundra bordering the great glaciers which expanded during the Würm period of glaciation (the last of the five stages of the Great Ice Age). They wore clothes, garments stitched together from the skins of animals they had killed. Clearly this operation depended not only on the use of other tools specially adapted for the purpose

(awls and cutting blades). It also involved the use of mental abstraction in measuring the body to fit it with clothes. The use of cord made of animal tendons or vegetable fibres to sew animal skins together enabled them to create strong, waterproof garments. For many tasks they used their teeth. Microscopic examination of their teeth has shown that many of their incisors have tiny scratches – possibly due to their habit of putting large chunks of meat in their mouths and cutting off the surplus with a flint blade – but undoubtedly also because they used their teeth as a built-in, multi-purpose tool.

Thinking of Tomorrow

The first stone implements and the first deliberately chipped flints are evidence

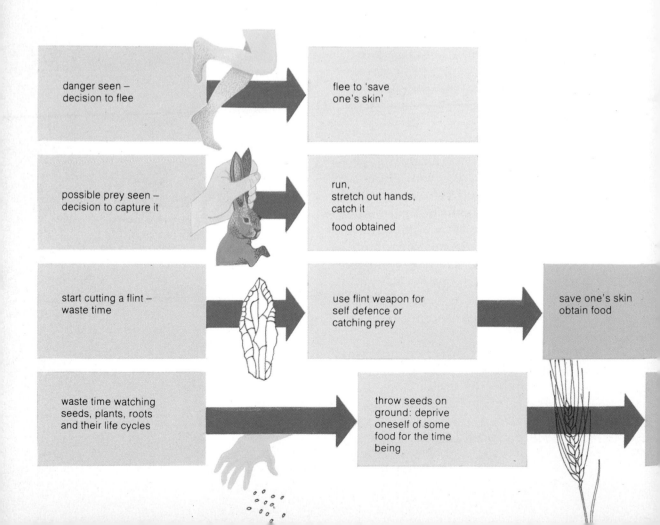

danger seen –
decision to flee

flee to 'save one's skin'

possible prey seen –
decision to capture it

run,
stretch out hands,
catch it

food obtained

start cutting a flint –
waste time

use flint weapon for
self defence or
catching prey

save one's skin
obtain food

waste time watching
seeds, plants, roots
and their life cycles

throw seeds on
ground: deprive
oneself of some
food for the time
being

of the rise in the hominid family of a vitally important thought process which today we would describe as 'the awareness of time'.

Almost all animals carry out acts which have immediate results: running to escape danger or catch their prey, grasping it, killing it by gripping it with their teeth. All the hominids carried out this process. Then some of them took to cutting flints, an obvious waste of time for anyone who thrives on immediate results. You cannot eat cut flints and they are not, in themselves, a protection against enemies. Anyone cutting flints must therefore have thought, 'They're no use to me at this precise moment, but I'll be able to use them soon'. This thought may also have been prompted by the knowledge that day follows day: that the sun will rise again tomorrow. With this awareness of time came a new

Opposite: Diagrams showing how mankind gradually developed the ability to think of the future and acquired an awareness of time, thereby progressing from closely watching natural events to using them to satisfy the basic need for food.
Below: Map showing, in blue, the areas covered by glaciers during the last Ice Age (the *Würm* period). The coastlines which existed approximately 20,000 years ago are also shown. It can be seen that the amount of land covered by sea was greater than that today; there were also many 'land bridges' across which animals migrated, followed by man who hunted them.
Bottom: Time chart showing warm and cold phases occurring since the Mesozoic era. The phase we are currently passing through is dry, warm in summer and sometimes very cold in winter, but with very little precipitation. This chart is not drawn to scale – earlier periods have been telescoped.

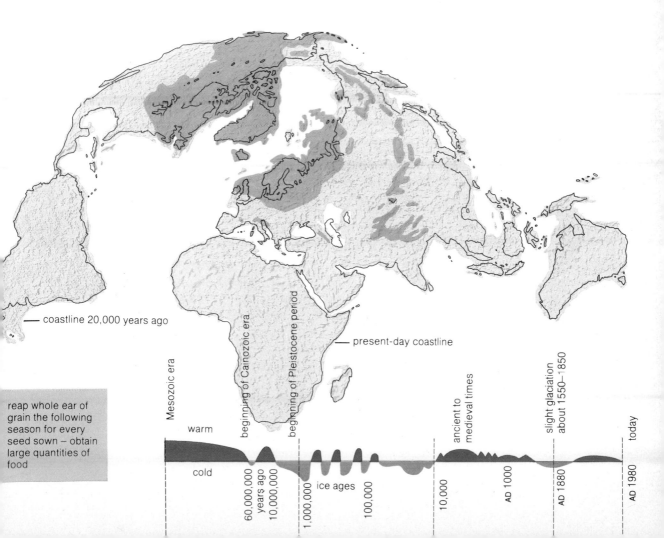

coastline 20,000 years ago

present-day coastline

reap whole ear of grain the following season for every seed sown – obtain large quantities of food

Mesozoic era

beginning of Cainozoic era

beginning of Pleistocene period

ancient to medieval times

slight glaciation about 1550–1850

today

warm

cold

60,000,000 years ago
10,000,000

1,000,000 ice ages

100,000

10,000

AD 1000

AD 1880

AD 1980

way of thought, the capacity to abstract, to plan something before doing it.

It now became possible to hunt in a group. Man was able to foresee the need to carry out a certain action or actions now, even though their results may not occur for some time to come. We have also touched on another important use of abstract thought: the mapping of the shape of the body so as to make clothes for it. The awareness of symmetry, evident in so many of nature's creations and not least in the human body itself, may also be seen as an example of man's ability to think abstractly. This awareness was reflected in the almond-shaped stone implements made by man.

Other things which were possibly first noticed by the Neanderthals include the cycles of nature: animals tend to reproduce at a certain time of year, and after a fixed period of time roots and seeds developed into new plants. The awareness of the passage of time must have been an extremely useful means towards obtaining food.

Development of a Non-material Culture

But man did not stop here. Using his thinking capacity, he could imagine unfamiliar combinations of events: for example, if a buried root could spring to life as a new plant, why should a dead companion placed in the earth not also come back to life?

The first deliberate burials seem to have originated in Mousterian culture. It is therefore quite certain that Neanderthal man believed in the possibility of reviving dead companions. But he could see that intervening in these strange, invisible processes in this way was a risky business. It was useful to have one's chief back, or one's young son, but it was also dangerous to increase the number of members in the the group. What would happen, for example, if the dead came and started making demands on the food supply? It was therefore sensible to provide them, in their bed of earth, with rations and weapons for hunting; and perhaps, too, it would make sense to tie them up so that they did not go wandering around too much and possibly rob others of some of their vital energy. So the abstract idea of a life after death arose in direct contradiction to the apparent finality of death; and alongside this belief there arose a fear of vampires and ghosts which return to haunt the living.

Cave-dwelling bears too (which were enemies because they were predators, but at the same time friends because they too were hunting animals) became objects of worship. This conclusion has been drawn from the large number of bear skulls which have been found neatly piled up in caves.

An important element of man's culture was therefore developing: the idea of being able to influence the invisible forces which man imagined existed alongside the physical reality which he could see with his eyes. Death worship and magical and religious ceremonies must have begun about the same time. We can see from the evidence of this important phase – physical objects such as bones and utensils – that man was starting to work with ideas, beliefs and ceremonies. In fact, he was evolving a non-material culture.

Towards the end of the Middle Palaeolithic period, Neanderthal man was replaced by a new form. This is the sub-species to which we ourselves, *Homo sapiens sapiens*, belong. The oldest remnants are classed as belonging to *Homo sapiens fossilis*, but in fact there are very few fundamental differences between the skeleton of modern man and the oldest *Homo sapiens fossilis*.

During the last phase of the Palaeolithic period (the Upper Palaeolithic), between 35,000 and 10,000 years ago, man began reproducing nature. He drew figures on the innermost, and therefore most private, walls of his caves, scratching them out with stone, ivory and bone. Clearly man, now master of a great many technical skills, was creating scenes which would help him in his hunting when used with the appropriate magical rites. Whilst the physical tools he used in the hunt were being constantly improved and refined, man also regarded it as an investment in time to make use of the instruments and weapons of magic. Painting or scratching pictures of horses, buffalo and mammoth helped him, he believed, to hunt horses, buffalo and mammoth more easily and in

Above: The figures painted or drawn on cave walls by Palaeolithic peoples are thought to have been part of magic rituals connected with hunting. This would explain the many pictures of potential prey (wild bulls, horses, mammoths, bears, reindeer, even fish, as well as lions and wolves). Representations of human beings were rare, however, possibly because it was thought dangerous to leave a picture on the wall which an enemy could have used to harm the person depicted.

The meaning of the figures in the painting shown here, photographed in the caves of Lascaux in the Dordogne region of France, is obscure. The man sprawled on the ground appears to be wearing a mask with a beak; possibly he was a sorcerer who had been felled by the bull. The bird looks like a chicken on a stick. The practical use of some of the objects that have been found, such as the so-called 'staff of office' made of animal horn shown above, also from the Dordogne, is not known. Were they sceptres or instruments for some magical rite?

27

greater numbers. By harnessing the invisible forces they believed existed, people could assist the production of food. This interpretation of cave art in magical terms is supported by symbols representing spears above the animals in some pictures; sometimes, too, there are signs that clay pellets were thrown at the animals in the cave drawings.

Adapting to Changing Environments

When speaking of the 'economy' of a given group of humans we mean all the processes which ensure the production and distribution of the materials which satisfy man's basic needs. For example, the economy of a small group of people may be based on milking cows, but it would include all the associated activities such as making the milk into cheese and butter, transporting it to a market to trade it for such things as butter-making tools and winter feed for the cows when there isn't enough grass. So, the way of life of any population of people is strictly geared to the environment in which it operates. Thus, a change in environmental conditions (such as a drought killing off the cows in the example above) can directly condemn the population to death.

It can also happen that a population is able to evolve a new economy, a new system of production, which can actually turn this change in environmental conditions to its own advantage. Situations like this occurred much later during Middle Neolithic period (which followed the Palaeolithic) and at the end of the Upper Palaeolithic.

Neanderthal man evolved various ways of adapting to the very hard climate of the Würm period of glaciation: hunting techniques improved, eating habits changed, and perhaps also a certain number of physical character-istics evolved, such as slightly more fat under the skin and lighter skin colouring to absorb the sun's rays better. During the final stages of glaciation, the herds of predators thinned out and many of the areas around the glaciers became uninhabitable because a gradual rise in temperature which melted the ice caused frequent flooding. It is possible that some groups of Neanderthals remained isolated in regions where resources were becoming increasingly scarce. As a result, and possibly also through the influence of the new populations of *Homo sapiens sapiens*, the sub-species *neanderthalensis* became extinct.

So, around 30,000 years ago, *Homo sapiens sapiens* began to spread throughout the globe, probably showing characteristics which worked in his favour during the late Ice Age. Probably having evolved in milder climates and therefore being darker-skinned, he may have become used to moving home as and when the need arose and without any difficulty. So while the cold gradually loosened its grip, man gained a foothold in fresh environments and increased in numbers, spreading throughout the world (with the exception of the Antarctic).

As we have already seen, the Upper Palaeolithic was a period of steady progress in the technology of hunting, fishing, and the ability to make objects, and there was an ever-closer interweaving of the real world and the world of magic. The awareness of the seasonal cycles (and other phenomena such as the ebb and flow of tides) was becoming greater. People also adopted varying lifestyles and different economies (from living in tents and moving from place to place in search of food, to living and working in permanent settlements), so diets differed too (see diagram p 30).

Man Produces his own Plants and Meat – the Dawn of the Neolithic Period

About 10,000 years ago in certain areas of the Near East, *Homo sapiens sapiens* took an enormously important step forward. He turned changes in the environment to his own advantage, throwing handfuls of seeds on to the earth and replanting tubers. He also began deliberately protecting certain animals. These were all actions which gave no immediate reward, but allowed him to obtain more in the long run. Man's diet changed, and there were also important changes in the way social groups were made up (see also pp 43–4). The economy changed and the number of human beings increased.

It was a combination of all these factors which triggered the rise of civilization. Man the hunter and gatherer became man the farmer. This step was the beginning of the Neolithic period of human culture. It did not happen at once, but the various factors emerged one by one in different places at different times, taking many centuries to come together and form what we now recognize as Neolithic culture. And the

wild forms
of grain plants

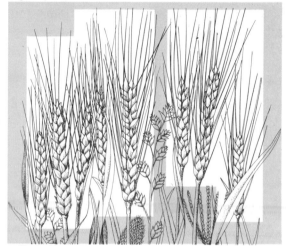

cultivated forms
of grain plants

Above right: Man first became an agriculturalist by harvesting various wild grains and replanting seeds obtained from them. The plants selected were those with the most ears of grain and which could be used as food. The first grains man cultivated were barley and various types of wheat.

Right: Magnified section of a flint from a prehistoric scythe. Implements like this were made from a series of small flint blades set along a crack in a piece of wood or bone, which acted as a handle, and were held in place using bitumen or vegetable resin. The flint has clear grooves and has been worn down by the action of passing it through plant stems with a high silica content such as those of the grass family.

changes which resulted in Neolithic culture set in motion the long chain of events which led eventually to the great civilizations of the ancient world.

This chain of events was the result of a lack of equilibrium between man and his environment. Generally speaking, a species of animal prospers when its food is plentiful; the number of individuals increases and they are healthy and robust. But a situation of equilibrium arises when the number of individuals per group does not increase beyond a certain point because various external factors, such as natural enemies and shortages of food, restrict its growth.

Human populations are no different from other animals in this respect. However, in some places Neolithic culture set in motion various mechanisms, not all of them natural ones, which prevented man from establishing such a state of equilibrium with the environment.

Step by Step

During the Neolithic period man became very different indeed from his fellow creatures. The story of civilization is a story of the various imbalances which it gradually created and the discoveries man made in his attempts to conquer the various difficulties he

Opposite: Shepherd and his dog tending a flock of sheep in the Abruzzo region of central Italy. The main products of a pastoral economy are milk (and therefore cheese), meat and wool. The animals also fertilize the fields with their manure.
Below: The Neolithic way of life was characterized by the fact that man produced, using plants and animals, a significant proportion of his food instead of simply hunting and gathering as in Palaeolithic times. There are many possible combinations in which vegetables and/or animals can be used; the table shows the main ones as well as the resulting type of diet. There is no one combination which is better than all the rest; the correct one is that which makes the best use of the resources of the environment. The choice of a system of production becomes crystallized as a tradition, itself a major component of culture.

Settlements, sources of food and diets

TYPE OF SETTLEMENT

Seasonal shelters used by nomads	Tents and shelters used by semi-nomadic people	Tents and occasional shelters used by nomads	Semi-stable settlements with huts	Stable, static settlements	Villages and towns

VEGETABLE SOURCES OF FOOD

Mainly gathering fruit, tubers and large seeds	Semi-selective gathering including small seeds	Gathering in some areas	Selective gathering of tubers and cereals	Sowing of tubers and cereals	Sowing, harvesting and preservation of crops, especially cereals

ANIMAL SOURCES OF FOOD

Hunting large animals, fishing	Hunting, gathering shellfish, insects and crustaceans	Protective animal breeding (pastoralism)	Some selective hunting, fishing	Animals protected in pens	Animal rearing in pens and castration of male animals

DIETS

Mainly protein diet	Balanced but poor diet	Mainly protein	Balanced diet	Mainly carbohydrates	Slight preponderance of carbohydrates

faced. One step at a time, man adopted animal breeding and growing crops, uniting the two with extremely successful results.

He was however forced to live first in villages, then in towns; he had to build storage space in which to keep his goods, and he had to invent methods of defending villages and towns from attacking enemies. These ideas were passed from one area to another, one environment to another, in a continuous assault on the forces of nature.

One step at a time is how civilizations grew up. However, every civilization, beginning with a particular combination of environmental factors, followed a course of action which depended upon the way in which people organized their work to produce food and material goods.

Cereals and the Beginning of Agriculture

One very important feature of the Neolithic period was the discovery of pottery. As early as the Upper Palaeolithic period, man had used clay to model statuettes which were then baked in the fire to harden them. However, this method of treating clay to make terracotta vessels does not appear to have occurred until the Neolithic period, during which containers for food, and particularly for drying out seeds or roots and cooking broths, began to be produced.

The plant products most widely used in the Palaeolithic period were those which contained highly energy-giving substances, such as sweet fruits (figs and dates) containing sugar, or roots con-

Below: Map showing where the cultivation of various plants probably first took place. In some places the varieties we know and use today gradually took shape through the repeated crossing of plants which had already been semi-domesticated with others which were still wild; this happened in

the case of wheat, for example. The transition from wild to domestic varieties was reflected in changes in the size of the useful parts of the plants. The remains of cereals found in excavations of prehistoric settlements are generally those with the largest ears and the most grains (see p 65).

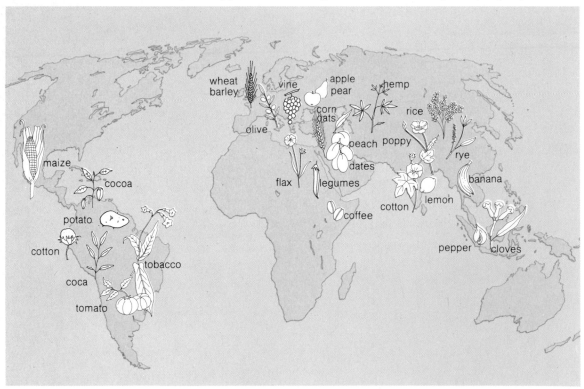

taining starch. Roots, for example, could be cooked in the embers to make the starch more digestible. We all know how much more palatable a baked potato is than a raw turnip.

Below: Terracotta model of a farmyard cart with spokeless wooden wheels pulled by Indian buffaloes. The yoke (reconstructed) allowed the combined strength of two animals to be used. The model came from Mohenjo-daro, an Indus Valley site in Pakistan (see also diagram on p 149).
Bottom: Map showing where the domestication of various animals probably first took place. The bones found in excavations give a fairly precise indication of when the animal they belonged to was domesticated (domestic animals tend to have weaker bones).

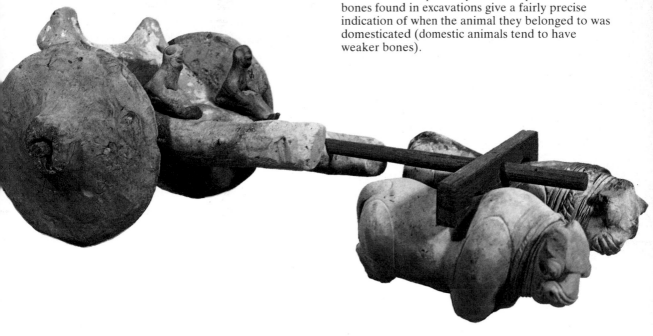

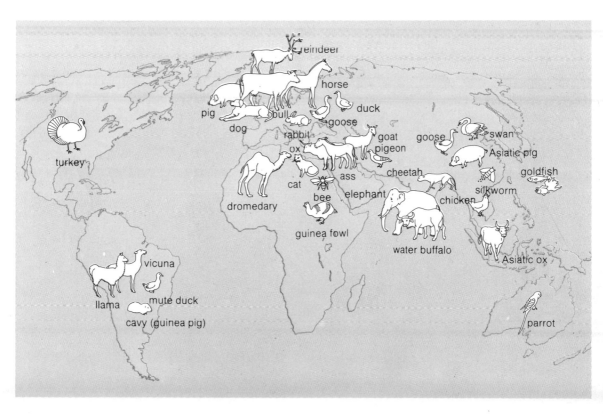

The large-scale cultivation of cereals (grain plants such as wheat, oats, rice or maize) also began during the Neolithic period. Man discovered that, from one root or piece of root, he could grow two more; but he also noticed that from a grain of barley or wheat, a whole ear (40 or 50 grains) could be obtained.

These plants suddenly became a miraculous way of combating hunger. The grain, containing starch and other useful substances, could also be cooked: not on a fire, which would burn it, but by boiling. This idea naturally led to the production of bowls and pots, which were essential if the grain was to be kept away from damp which would cause it to sprout and start growing. Let us now look more closely at the various stages of the development of agriculture.

years ago			10,000
tundra (semi-frozen marshland, bushes, grass)			
northern regions – coniferous (evergreen) forests			
temperate zone – deciduous forests (trees lose their leaves)			
steppes (extensive grassland)			
sub-tropical areas (including Mediterranean region)	hunting harvesting		cereal growing hunting
South-east Asian region			
Pacific islands			

spear thrower increases the speed of the spear and therefore its force

spear thrower

spear

wooden shaft

flint spearhead

grass crops cut by hand

shelter in rocks

PALAEOLITHIC PERIOD

Experts have long debated why man first became an agriculturalist in the semi-arid regions of the Near East. This question can be answered to some extent by looking at the environment of this huge region. On the slopes of the mountain ranges south of the Black Sea and the Caspian Sea, as well as on the foothills of the Zagros Mountains (in what is today western Iran), barley and

Below: Chart showing how systems of production established themselves and gradually spread across the climatic zones of the Earth. The arrows show probable movements of people.

Bottom: Comparison between the production systems of the Palaeolithic period (left) and the Neolithic (right). Tools used by men and women to produce or kill food are in blue. Note particularly the spear-thrower held by the Palaeolithic man; this tool artificially increased the reach of his arm.

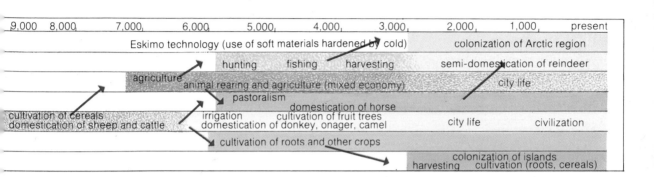

9,000	8,000	7,000	6,000	5,000	4,000	3,000	2,000	1,000	present

Eskimo technology (use of soft materials hardened by cold) — colonization of Arctic region

hunting — fishing — harvesting — semi-domestication of reindeer

agriculture — animal rearing and agriculture (mixed economy) — city life

pastoralism

domestication of horse

cultivation of cereals — irrigation — cultivation of fruit trees — city life — civilization

domestication of sheep and cattle — domestication of donkey, onager, camel

cultivation of roots and other crops

harvesting — colonization of islands — cultivation (roots, cereals)

use of agricultural tools

huts

domesticated animals

dog

scythe made of flint blades

hoe

NEOLITHIC PERIOD

wheat grew wild (see illustration p 65). As early as the Palaeolithic period, people were starting to make use of the seeds of these plants as food.

Later, as they came down into the valleys (perhaps following migrating animals) they saw how the region's rivers (called wadis) filled with water during the short rainy seasons, later to almost disappear in a dried-out slurry of mud and pebbles. Land watered by these wadis would soon grow a thin covering of vegetation. In particular it is likely that some of the seeds which man was already using in the hills (where the rain was slightly more plentiful) would have grown here as well. The ebb and flow of water and its consequences encouraged man to store seeds away from the water, and to put them back in the earth when the water returned to bring them to life.

To summarize: with the availability of suitable plants, man could make seeds multiply at will by shrewdly observing and making use of a regularly varying environment.

Organizing Food Production

The various communities of the Neolithic period tried out different ways of producing the goods to sustain their way of life. The best solution must have been to make each part of the process fit in totally with all the others. Merely raising animals without cultivating the fields would lead to wastage on a huge scale. For example, the manure produced by animals which enriched the soil would go unused. Furthermore, the stems and leaves of cereals and the leaves of many root crops could not be eaten by humans. They would therefore have been thrown away and would not have served their function of fertilizing the soil between one harvest and the next.

Opposite: Artist's impression of how the discovery of pottery might have been the result of clay on the floor or clay utensils being accidentally baked in a cooking fire.
Below: On the left is a vase from the Sasso culture (found at Sasso Furbara, a site on the Via Aurelia 60 kilometres [37 miles] north of Rome in Italy), and on the right is the mouth of a vase from the Ripoli culture, found in Ripoli di Corropoli in the province of Teramo in Italy. These are about 6,000 and 5,000 years old respectively.

Some quite clearly defined cultural trends can be seen in the way the use of pottery spread. For example, there was a tradition of pottery with incised linear bands in the Danube area and elsewhere in Europe. The Sasso culture was part of this tradition. The Ripoli culture, however, was part of the huge group of cultures found mainly along Mediterranean coasts and which used painted ceramics. Both vases originate from Avigliano Umbro in Italy; they may have reached these two sites by traders, or simply through imitation.

How did man choose what plants to cultivate? Root crops gave a fairly modest rate of return. Many fruits (such as figs and dates) took up a great deal of space because only so many trees could be fitted into a given area of land. Preserving fruit and roots was a problem as well, as they tended to rot. This brought about another discovery, that of alcohol.

Cereals on the other hand were small plants (a dozen could be grown in a space the size of a hand); they were dry, so they could easily be preserved; and they had a very high rate of return (that is, each grain produced a large number of grains). When man made the choice, it was heavily in favour of cereal crops. In the Near East, apart from barley and wheat, rye and oats were cultivated; in the Far East (slightly later) it was millet and rice; and in America maize was grown. The by-products of agricultural production could be eaten by domesticated animals; their bodies rapidly broke down the vegetation and made it into high-quality manure. This was a system of production where everything slotted in neatly.

There were further improvements beside the discovery of cereals. Other plants, such as lentils, peas and beans could be grown on small plots of ground and were rich in protein. They also had leaves and stems which were relished by the animals.

In this scheme of things, everyone had a particular function: human energy was used to the full. Watching the livestock enclosures could be done by children and old people; the children could look after the vegetable patch with the women; the women could lend a hand with the mowing whilst the elderly stood in for them in the kitchen or kept an eye on the infants. Men would tend the larger cattle and work with the young in the fields. Equally they could make earthenware con-

tainers, whose firing was perhaps supervised by the women. Occasionally, the men would hunt a few wild animals. So in a thriving Neolithic community there would have been no strict division of labour. On the contrary, people would have worked together on all the necessary tasks so as not to waste time.

The natural forces of which everyone was so aware were also included in this scheme of co-operation: the earth, which gave life to themselves and their plants, seemed like a great mother figure whose role in the system of cultivation was crucial. Often people would try to fathom her inscrutable 'desires': did she ever get hungry and, if so, what for? Did she get angry with her 'children'? Even in the very earliest Neolithic communities there were priests who attempted to answer these questions.

Opposite: Statue of a clay mother-goddess from Çatal Hüyük, the Neolithic 'holy city' which flourished from about 7000 BC in southern Anatolia in Turkey. The object is only 17 centimetres (7 inches) high, but the overall effect is imposing. The figure with its huge breasts seems to be sitting between two animals (dogs, sheep or cattle?). The realistic wrinkles on the knees and stomach emphasize the figure's fatness; some archaeologists take the object below the stomach to be a baby emerging from the womb. What is interesting are the two strange ridges on the shoulders, which are reminiscent of the puffed shoulders of a dress. Is she perhaps clothed, rather than nude? Note also the head, which has been restored because the original was destroyed; it resembles those found on similar statuettes elsewhere. The head of the animal on the right has also been restored. The cult of the mother-goddess was typical of agricultural communities; to them the earth was the great mother who gave life to the various plants which feed her children.

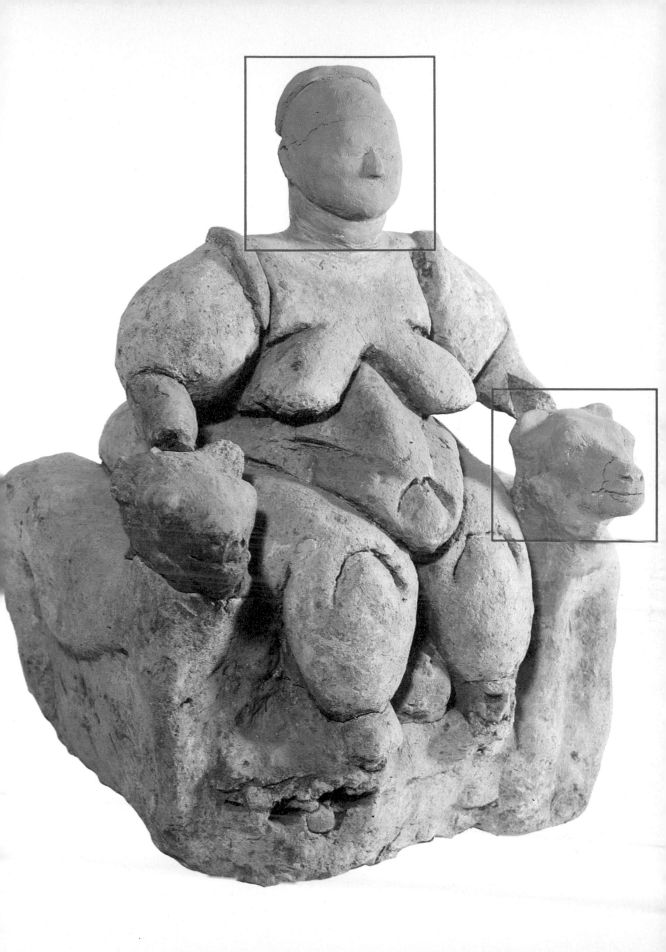

Comparisons

Put simply, Palaeolithic (or Old Stone Age) peoples lived by hunting and gathering. On the other hand, those of the Neolithic period (or New Stone Age) grew crops and tended animals for food. Let us try to compare in more detail the way of life of a Palaeolithic community (for example in the Upper Palaeolithic period) with a Neolithic community (one from, say, the Near East).

We have already seen how blurred the divisions were between people's roles in a Neolithic settlement. If we look at the main objects found in arch-

1

3

2

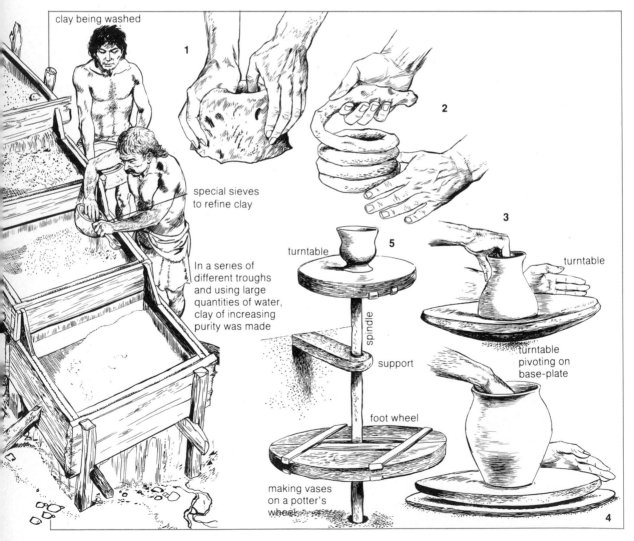

clay being washed

1

2

special sieves to refine clay

In a series of different troughs and using large quantities of water, clay of increasing purity was made

turntable

5

3

turntable

spindle

support

turntable pivoting on base-plate

foot wheel

making vases on a potter's wheel

4

4

5

Left: Objects from various periods (between 6,000 and 9,000 years ago) and various sites in Iraq, all used in ancient Neolithic settlements. 1. Painted pottery vessel used for juices or milk. 2. Pottery bowl with furrows used for winnowing grain. 3. Finely polished stone container. 4. Pottery siphon with handle. 5. Mortar and pestle made from a hollowed-out stone.
Opposite below: Selecting clay and different methods of making jars. 1. Simple hollowing out of clay using the fingers. 2. Building up the walls of a jar using a long sausage-shaped piece of clay; this made deeper containers possible. 3. A potter's wheel. The speed of its rotation fluctuates a great deal and one hand is taken up with keeping the wheel in motion. 4. A potter's wheel in which the turntable is concave and pivots on a base-plate; this gives a greater and almost constant speed of rotation. Also the hand moving the turntable can sometimes be used to shape the vase. 5. A potter's wheel propelled by the feet. It is set in motion by applying the feet to the heavy wheel at the bottom which acts as a flywheel and keeps the speed constant.

aeological digs at the sites of such settlements we find large numbers of containers, sticks used for digging the soil, and scythes made by attaching a series of tiny, sharp flints to a cleft in a piece of wood or bone.

We also find flint arrowheads and hatchets or knives made of finely polished stone. There are sometimes statuettes, too, portraying an 'Earth Mother'. Most of these artefacts were used in the production of food. Only a very small proportion were not: these include bone hairpins, needles, necklaces and buttons. It is also worth noting that, in an area where it was warm enough for clothes not to be essential, accessories and jewellery were probably used very little.

If we look at the artefacts from the site of a late Palaeolithic settlement, we find needles, awls, buttons, hairpins, necklaces of various materials (shells, teeth, ivory, bone, hard stone, amber, quartz and obsidian), finely crafted statuettes and amulets, spear-throwers (see illustration p 34) and clubs made of horn or bone and covered in realistic raised designs; even flutes made of bone have been found. Nor should we forget the statues and bas-reliefs, as well as graffiti and paintings, from this period that have been found (photographs pp 17 and 27).

The contrast is striking. The Palaeolithic cave paintings are those of people dedicated to 'hunting magic'. Probably each of the beads in a necklace was a lucky charm. The fact is that these people spent a very great deal of time making works of art. Why?

The way Palaeolithic people produced things meant they had a certain amount of 'leisure time', to use a phrase much in vogue at the moment. 'Leisure time' is one of the features of the 'affluent society' (the term was introduced by the American economist J K Galbraith) in which groups of individuals have more time than they need to perform essential tasks. So, paradoxical though it may seem, Palaeolithic communities were affluent.

In fact their needs were minimal. There were no complex social mechanisms to operate – hunting, fishing and farming provided food for the group, and the intense cold of Europe allowed them to preserve unused food just as in a deep freeze.

Similar situations do still exist in the few remaining Palaeolithic societies today. People only work for a few hours each day; they have no great needs and are content with what they can obtain by hunting, trapping and cultivation. But they make a thousand and one different 'accessories' such as necklaces, charms and earrings for the decoration of semi-naked or naked bodies.

More Food, More People

Why, then, did man abandon this affluent phase of his existence? Why did he burden himself with the toils of Neolithic life? We have already answered this question: changes in the environment probably no longer allowed man to maintain his former relationship with nature.

The character of these changes (floods, unpredictable wadis, the extinction of some of the large animals that were hunted and the survival of medium-sized herbivores) led man to a solution of the problems they created that was adopted and eventually imposed the world over. During a period which was certainly a critical one

for mankind, what solution could be better than one which offered the chance to produce one's own food and put an end to hunger and starvation once and for all?

Many studies today, including those of anthropologist Marvin Harris, contend that the Neolithic choice contained an in-built problem. The food of Neolithic man was not the same as that of Palaeolithic man. Diets were changing in a radical way and the idea of 'as much food as you like' was being replaced by 'as much carbohydrate as you like'.

The Palaeolithic diet contained plenty of meat, and therefore protein. The Neolithic diet, with its strong emphasis on cereals, was primarily a high-carbohydrate diet of starch and various forms of sugar. In a society which feeds mainly on cereals, the body weight of women tends to be made up of a high percentage of fat: After a pregnancy and birth, the menstrual cycle stabilizes again quite quickly and there is a strong chance of another pregnancy soon afterwards. In Neolithic communities, therefore, women had many babies.

This was not the case in Palaeolithic

As we know, the making of objects was closely linked to people's practical needs; knives, spears, fish-hooks and spear-throwers were all used by Palaeolithic people to obtain food. Similarly in the Neolithic period the tools which were used in the system of production were scythes and pestles. In the Palaeolithic (more especially the Upper Palaeolithic) period, the rich variety and large quantities of man-made objects remind us that these people had plenty of 'leisure time'.

Below: Part of a beautiful spear-thrower with two fighting animals on it. Possibly these realistic figures on a hunting weapon had a magical significance.

Bottom: Some of the day-to-day tasks of peoples of the Upper Palaeolithic period. 1. Scraping animal skins to remove fat and flesh. 2. Sewing clothes using bone needles and vegetable fibres or strips of leather. 3. Making necklaces of pierced shells, teeth or bone fragments using small flint boring tools. 4. Sculpting objects from animal horn, ivory or bone using awls, graving tools and small chisels. 5. Making whistles and flutes using hollowed-out bones with holes pierced in them.

groups, because the high-protein diet allowed women, who were thinner and stronger, to breast-feed children for much longer. The result of this was that the menstrual cycle took much longer (months or even years) to settle down, and another pregnancy might not occur for some considerable time. Therefore few children were born in Palaeolithic societies. It is also possible that Palaeolithic people, being less numerous and living in a family-like clan structure, could accept that some unwanted babies might be disposed of. In the larger Neolithic communities, however, there were basic social rules that would have disapproved of infanticide.

We should now be able to understand that life in Neolithic settlements took a toll on everybody: no one had any leisure time. Man, in his efforts to escape hunger, cultivated only those plants which produced large quantities of fast-multiplying seeds, but these plants increased the number of people and therefore of mouths to feed. This was a vicious circle which compelled people to use all their energies producing food for themselves with hardly a pause for rest.

Paying People to do Special Jobs

At Çatal Hüyük in Turkey, near the present-day city of Konya in Southern Anatolia, there is evidence of Neolithic settlements between 9,000 and 7,700 years ago. Archaeological layers are piled one on top of the other and the oldest relate to a village inhabited by farmers. They grew barley, wheat, peas, and other leguminous vegetables. Almonds, pistachios and rape-seed were all harvested, doubtless in order to extract oil from the seeds. The only domestic animals seem to have been dogs and sheep. The people were active hunters, and the bones of wild sheep, cattle, wild asses, stags, wolves and wildcats have all been found.

Throughout its history, the settlement took the form of a small hill. It is interesting that for over 2,000 years no ceramics (pottery) were produced. Clay was simply dried in the sun. It was used as flooring for the area where markets were held, as well as for walls and houses. Around 8,000 years ago, Çatal Hüyük was already a city, but its houses were all made of clay bricks dried in the sun. As we usually find, a particular environment (in this case, the dry climate) had given rise to a functional solution. This is therefore a preceramic Neolithic period. During the phase of its expansion, this Neolithic city occupied an area of 13 hectares (32 acres).

It is fair to assume that in primitive villages, individual families would have built their own clay huts or houses. It is also likely that these houses would have been scattered here and there over a particular area. In a town-sized conglomeration like Çatal Hüyük this was no longer possible. The buildings were therefore placed so as to support one another, with shared walls between two adjoining houses. A structure of this kind would without doubt have been built in accordance with a 'town plan' rather than being allowed to grow casually. We have proof of this in a fascinating fresco, which is around 8,200 years old, on the inside wall of one of the houses. This consists of a map of the city and is the oldest landscape painting known to man. Apart from the grouping of the houses, we can see on the horizon the crater of the volcano Hasan Daği; this rises more than 100 kilometres (60 miles) from the site but is nevertheless clearly visible and very prominent.

The conclusion must therefore be that there were people who did not

Diets and population growth

PALAEOLITHIC	NEOLITHIC
Hunter-gatherers Nomads living in shelters or tents	Agriculture and animal rearing Stable village life
Mainly protein diet	Slight preponderance of carbohydrate in diet
Little tendency to become overweight; women healthy and strong	Considerable tendency to become overweight; women not very strong
Women able to suckle their children for a long period; menstrual cycle therefore delayed	Suckling finishes early; menstrual cycle stabilizes quickly
Pregnancies do not follow in quick succession	Pregnancies follow in fairly quick succession
Some infanticide tolerated	Abortions and infanticide never seen in villages
Few children	Many children
Static population	Strong, continuous population growth

spend all their time producing food or building their own houses. They had been entrusted by the community with the task of laying out a city which was best adapted to the site it was on.

There are many inspired solutions to this problem. The houses have no doors at ground level; instead there are holes in the roofs or high in the walls. So in Çatal Hüyük people walked on the roofs (all of them flat) using ladders to move up and down between the various levels. To go into a building one had to climb the appropriate ladder. It was difficult to gain entry to a town like this: if the few ladders leading in from the outside were removed, Çatal Hüyük became like a snail withdrawn into its shell. Any enemies or thieves could easily be kept out.

The Role of Priests

Çatal Hüyük is interesting for another reason. Many of its buildings have altars, niches for offerings, fireplaces, relief paintings including human figures and the forms or heads of animals. If cattle were modelled, real horns were stuck into the clay. Some paintings include scenes where people are attired as vultures with masks having beaks and feathers or wearing leopard skins.

Opposite: Table showing the possible connections between diet and population growth in Palaeolithic and Neolithic communities. These links have been put forward using surveys carried out on present-day, so-called 'primitive' societies with similar lifestyles to those of Palaeolithic and Neolithic peoples. A particularly interesting factor in population growth, according to the anthropologist Harris, is that social competition could lead to a reduction in the population as the result of infanticide and abortion. Apparently, in a semi-family situation such as the Palaeolithic clan this killing could be tolerated; but in the more 'public' situation of the village it was frowned upon. Some anthropologists disagree, and stress the possibility that increased contact between males and females in a village situation could equally have led to an increase in the population.

Left: An elaborate, engraved bone hook and eye from Çatal Hüyük. This would have been used to fasten a belt.

Bottom: Cross-section through part of Çatal Hüyük as it might have looked showing a religious shrine and the detail of a wall. There is also an overall view of the town. It had no streets, and movement from one house to another was by walking across the roofs and using ladders.

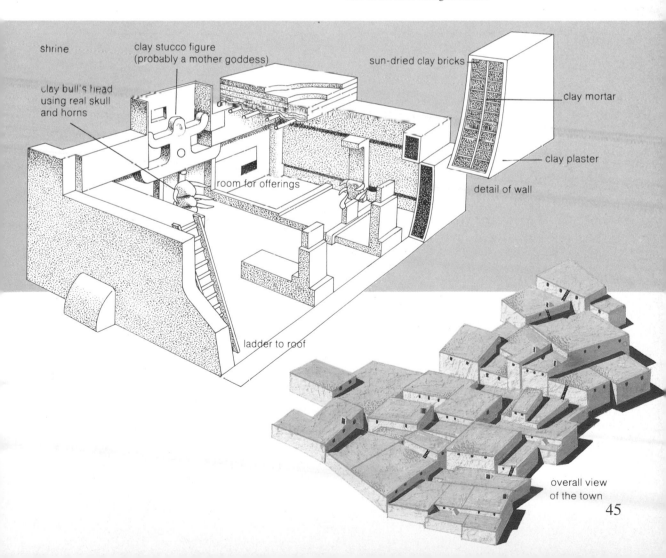

shrine

clay stucco figure
(probably a mother goddess)

clay bull's head
using real skull
and horns

sun-dried clay bricks

clay mortar

clay plaster

room for offerings

detail of wall

ladder to roof

overall view
of the town

45

Bottom: Reconstruction of a house at Hacilar, a town in Southern Anatolia inhabited from about 7000 BC onwards. The roof and dividing walls have been partially cut away to reveal interesting cone-shaped ovens with holes in the top to allow smoke to escape.

Opposite: Vase found in Hacilar shown upright (1) and inverted (2) to reveal its unusual shape and particularly interesting decoration. The almond-shaped signs on the sides of the vase are in fact the eyes of a face, with a protuberance for a nose and two smaller ones for ears. This was possibly a small idol used as a vessel for offerings. It is about 7,650 years old.

Pottery first appeared in Hacilar about 7,800 years ago. The vases were all fairly similar in shape, rounded with wide bodies, fairly narrow necks, and two or four handles through which cords or thongs would have been passed. There was a wide range of decorative styles, usually consisting of geometric shapes painted in a vivid red colour, as in 3. Designs which resemble plaited reeds (4) were also common.

Major sites and cultures of the Neolithic period

Egypt: Badarian, Amratian, Gerzean cultures

Iraq: Giarma (in the Zagros mountains, based on barley and the domesticated goat, between the eighth and sixth millennia BC), Hassuna, Halaf, Samarra

Anatolia: Çatal Hüyük, Hacilar

Mediterranean: Khirokitia (Cyprus)

Greece: Dimini, Sesklo

Spain: Almeria region (villages from fifth millenium BC), Los Milares (fortified village, catacombs and megaliths)

Sicily: Stentinello (village with defensive ditch, incised ceramics), Diana (in the Lipari Islands, produced very elaborate ceramics, traded in obsidian)

Italy: Sasso, Fiorano, Capri (painted ceramics), Serra d'Alto (painted ceramics), Ripoli, Lagozza (very fine ceramics with smooth surface, typical wide shallow cups known as 'streamlined cups'), square-mouthed vase culture

France: Chassey

Switzerland: Cortaillod

Central Europe: *Linearbandkeramik*, Starčevo-Körös (Danube region, sixth to fifth millennia BC), Danilo

England: Windmill Hill (enclosed settlement with raised streets), bell-shaped beaker culture

Ireland: New Grange

Scandinavia: funnel-shaped beaker cultures

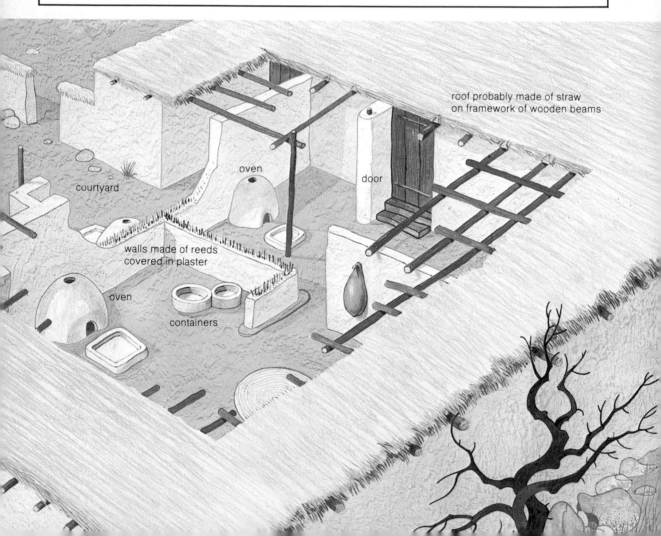

roof probably made of straw on framework of wooden beams

courtyard

oven

door

walls made of reeds covered in plaster

oven

containers

Everywhere we find clay statuettes, particularly ones portraying Earth-Mother figures (see photograph p 39).

Buildings containing such items were 'temples'. There seems to be a disproportionately large number of them considering the size of the city. Clearly Çatal Hüyük must have been a holy city, a city of temples to which people came from far and wide to perform acts of worship, make offerings to the gods and pacify or thank them using the statuettes as offerings.

We have already seen how the 'town planners', the architects, may have been maintained by the community to carry out projects for it. They would have been paid in food in return for creating the practical benefits of a city which was functional, well-built and safe. We can also guess that others, namely the priests, would have been exempted from the duty to produce food in order to do such things as organize religious rites. And others, of course, were employed to decorate the temples and make statuettes as offerings to be placed on the altar by visitors.

The community therefore accepted that it could do without some of its food in order to give it to individuals who did not produce food themselves, but who nevertheless made a contribution towards the community's total productivity. So the difference between the functions is very obvious. Religious ceremonies were based on complex systems of magic; offerings given to the soil made it more fertile and caused Mother Earth to smile more favourably upon her subjects. All this required belief, so people became believers. This meant that almost certainly any village would have had its own priests and wise men. The 'holy' city of Çatal Hüyük shows that 8,000 years ago the services of priests were already very much in demand and organizing ceremonies, as well as speaking to the gods and goddesses, was a thriving business.

Another interesting Neolithic city is that of Hacilar, west of Çatal Hüyük and a few kilometres from Burdur. Here, too, the roofs were used as streets and there were no doors at ground level. Ladders and stairs were used for getting in and out of the buildings. In the courtyards there were grain silos and fireplaces, each shared by several houses.

All buildings were made of clay baked in the sun. Pottery vases first appeared about 7,500 years ago. The flint and obsidian industries flourished (obsidian being the volcanic 'glass' picked or dug up from the slopes of volcanoes). Oats, wheat and barley were all grown, but it appears that animal husbandry was not practised. The inhabitants of Hacilar obtained their meat by hunting. It was a purely crop-growing community. Basket-weaving was widespread but there was only one building set aside for worship. Hacilar was probably a more worldly city than the sacred Çatal Hüyük.

Walls and Sieges

On the site of Jericho (the city mentioned in the Bible, north of the Dead Sea in Jordan), the remains of settlements have been found which go back 10,000 years. The oldest levels relate to a Mesolithic-period (Middle Stone-Age) settlement and indicate a culture standing midway between the end of the Palaeolithic and the Neolithic. This culture was not widespread and is known as Natufian after the Wadi el Natuf near Jericho. There are still traces of a building which must have been burned down on purpose and may have been a temple. Pestles – rough stones, slightly indented on one side and used for pounding grain – have been found here, as have small scythes made of tiny flints mounted in bone.

Cultivation brings about certain changes in plants, since man carries out a process of unnatural selection which favours certain features of the plants he considers desirable. For example, those

cereal plants producing larger ears which contained larger and more numerous seeds and which had softer stems, were cultivated in preference to others. Looking at the cutting edges of scythes from Jericho through a lens, we can see that they have been alternately sharpened and worn down, having been used to cut very hard substances. This effect may have been produced by the stems of wild grasses which, like those of all grasses, are very tough, but thicker than cultivated types.

We can conclude from this evidence that the people of Jericho were harvesters of *wild* cereals, such as barley and wheat. The few seeds which have been found are smaller than those of cultivated cereals, thus supporting this theory. During this period the people were beginning to display the results of

From Palaeolithic to Neolithic

Mesolithic is the name given to an intermediate period between the end of the Upper Palaeolithic and the beginning of the Neolithic period. There was a gradual change in the ways of life of people during this period.

		NORTHERN EUROPE AND ASIA	NEAR EAST
MESOLITHIC		Use of bow and arrow to shoot birds	Hunting of small and medium-sized animals
		Fish-hooks, spears, harpoons	Some occasional river-fishing
		Growing of root crops and sometimes grains	Growing of root crops and particularly grains; use of scythes
		Gathering of insects, shellfish and crustaceans	
NEOLITHIC		Change to Neolithic does not take place; Mesolithic economy very long-lived	Harvesting and re-sowing of cereal crops; agriculture begins. Transition to the Neolithic period takes place; man becomes producer of his own food

Opposite and right: Excavations on the site of Jericho. A number of different human settlements existed here in succession, beginning about 10,000 years ago. During the initial stages, wild cereal crops were harvested. Later, agriculture appeared and later still animal rearing developed. Thus a city with large storehouses for grain, and walls and towers for defence, grew up.
Below: Lid of a wooden box decorated with pieces of bone. This is from a tomb in Jericho dating from about 1500 BC.

a high-cereal diet, especially the high population (see p 42), but they were not yet producing all their own food.

A little later, about 8,800 years ago, there was a proper village of circular or oval huts with floors which were sunk slightly into the ground and covered with a layer of stucco (a building plaster). This stucco contained clay which is still waterproof and in good condition.

Very soon, the inhabitants of Jericho, who were materially better off than the neighbouring communities, dug a ditch into the rock around their city, enclosing an area of 40,000 square metres (48,000 square yards), and built a circle of stone walls. Watchtowers were also built, some of them 10 metres (33 feet) high.

These features show that Jericho was involved in battles: attacks, perhaps sieges, in which people were killed. Some people would have been maintained to build these defensive walls, so vital to everyone's safety.

Particularly interesting here are the 8,000-year-old human skulls remodelled with clay, with shells in the eye sockets to look like eyes. Could these have been the severed heads of

Pottery did not appear in Jericho until quite late in the city's development and initially consisted of painted vases, then later engraved vessels.
Above: Before pottery came into use human skulls were remade with clay to look like heads, sometimes with shells for eyes. These may have been the heads of city leaders or trophies of dead enemies.
Right: Many battles took place beneath the walls of Jericho. The grain wealth of this city had to be protected from other people. Several times the city was attacked and burned, but each time it was rebuilt. The destruction of Jericho chronicled in the Bible (Joshua 6:20) possibly took place during the late Bronze Age about 3,500 years ago.

enemies? Or sacrificial offerings to the gods?

During this period, houses in Jericho were rectangular in plan and made of sun-dried clay: the bricks are shaped like huge loaves of bread and cemented together using a clay-based stucco. Fireplaces were built outside in the courtyards.

By now the practice of agriculture had been fully adopted, possibly with goats being reared and domesticated dogs. Hunting (gazelles and wild goats) was still an important part of the economy. Many of the clay statuettes represent animals and were probably used in some form of worship. Figurines and fragments of large statues of the Earth Mother have also been found.

Why these walls, and why the war? Jericho had in fact accumulated a sizeable store of cereal wealth as well as other goods which could be used in the future. This had to be defended, because wealth brought war in its wake. Producing and storing food also meant that some people had to die to defend it.

Building a Home

The construction of shelters and homes is nothing new in man's history. Both *Homo habilis* and, later, *Homo erectus*, built simple stone structures which may have been covered in branches and twigs. Quite large huts held up by wooden palings (these have obviously disappeared but the holes in the ground in which they were planted still remain) are found throughout the Middle and Upper Palaeolithic periods. Sometimes they were supported by animal bones, particularly those of mammoths. The hunting of large animals also provided skins as a building material. These would have been placed on top of the huts after being tanned, especially during those periods when the climate was at its coldest.

Generally speaking, man used house-building materials which were within easy reach, if not the actual by-products of everyday life such as bones. Straw roofs using the stems and leaves of cereal crops were common in many agricultural settlements. Animal-skin huts, not unlike the tepees of American Indians, were typical of hunting and nomadic villages because they could be put up and taken down again easily.

In the buildings of Neolithic villages we can see the very close relationship which man the agriculturalist had established with the earth. The earth was a friend, a mother, who supplied not only food but the materials for building houses, waterproofing grain shelters or floors, making bricks and

Right: The building of shelters and houses must have been one of man's earliest activities. Materials were those which were easily found in the environment or which were by-products of human activity (for example skins, bones, leather, tendons and fat were all produced as a result of hunting). Almost always these materials had to be treated in some way before being used. Stone was measured and cut, clay was dried in the sun or baked in the oven, skins were tanned and rushes had to be dried out.

sticking them together in a wall. In fact, even today bricks, mortar and cement are made using substances extracted from the earth.

A Mixture of Old and New

Seven and a half thousand years ago at Khirokitia, near the southern coast of Cyprus, there was a huge Neolithic settlement, a proper city. The houses all had circular bases of limestone topped with walls of dried-clay bricks. The roofs were dome-shaped and perfectly whitewashed using a paste of clay and limestone (see illustrations pp 53–5). There were several hundred of these houses, and possibly as many as a thousand. There were no separate groups of houses. The main problem from a 'town planning' point of view was that of being able to move quickly and easily between buildings, so the people of Khirokitia built a huge main street and a series of side-streets running off it. All of these were raised above the ground and made of stone

reed hut built on framework of branches. The reeds were covered with clay or mud to make them stronger and more waterproof

Materials used by man

One of man's main characteristics is his ability to change the form and sometimes also the basic characteristics of objects provided by the environment around him. For example, a piece of wood needs to be cut, sharpened, and hardened in a flame to make it really useful; flint can be chipped to make many different kinds of tools; a rock can become part of a wall if stone tools are used to shape it to fit other rocks; a mixture of clay and water can be made into pottery. The use of fire as a tool to change substances led man to discover the properties of metals which could be softened by fire and moulded into various shapes. And materials obtained from vegetables and animals have always been widely used.

Stone: *Flint* is a rock made of microscopic crystals of quartz. It can be shaped to produce sharp edges and was used by Stone Age peoples to make cutting and other tools. *Limestone* is rock composed mainly of calcium carbonate, and can be used as building stone, or to produce lime for mortar, cement and fertilizer. *Obsidian* is a natural glass produced by volcanoes and was used for tools and ornaments. *Basalt* is a volcanic rock which was used in ancient times for making statues.

Clay: This is a very crumbly material, like soil, which, when wet, becomes smooth and is easily moulded into any desired shape; when it is dried in the sun, it hardens. It can be made even harder by baking it in an oven to produce pottery. Clay can be mixed with limestone or chalk and used as mortar to plaster or water-proof walls and roofs, or to cement the bricks or stones they are made of firmly together.

Materials from plants and trees: *Amber* is resin from ancient conifers which has coagulated and been fossilized as an attractive transparent substance. Sometimes insects were imprisoned in amber millions of years ago and can still be seen in it today. *Bark* was often used to cover the frames of buildings and huts, while softer varieties such as birch could be used to decorate vases. *Timber* of all kinds was used to make buildings, boats, tool handles, spears, bows and arrows and, of course, as fuel for fires.

Materials obtained from animals: *Bone* and *horn* were both used for making tools and ornaments. *Teeth* and especially ivory were used in the making of ornaments, but mammoth tusks were also used as stakes for walls and fences. *Coral* made attractive ornaments. *Wax* was used to make moulds into which molten metal could be poured to produce shaped metal objects.

Metals: *Gold, silver, copper, tin, antimony, arsenic* and *iron* have all been used, either individually or in alloys, to make a wide variety of objects. *Bronze* is an alloy of copper and tin; *steel* and *cast iron* are alloys of carbon and iron.

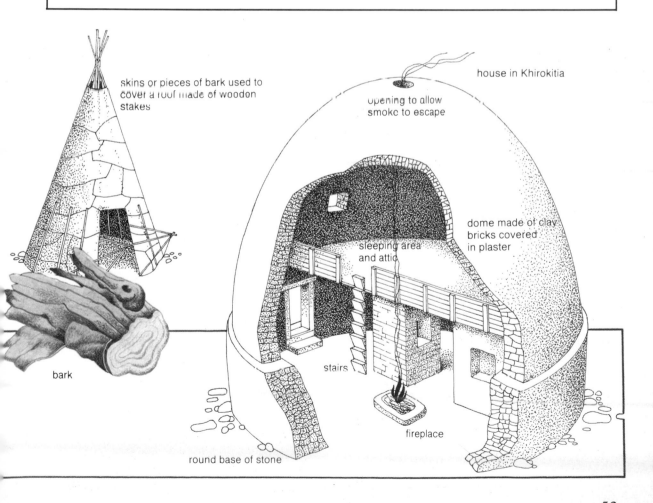

skins or pieces of bark used to cover a roof made of wooden stakes

bark

house in Khirokitia

opening to allow smoke to escape

dome made of clay bricks covered in plaster

sleeping area and attic

stairs

fireplace

round base of stone

ballast. There were no walls around the town.

At Lepenski Vir, a site on the River Danube in Yugoslavia 200 kilometres (120 miles) south-east of Belgrade, there was a Neolithic village consisting of a number of trapezoid-shaped houses. They had large fireplaces and stone-paved floors. The area so far excavated is around 6,000 square metres (6,175 square yards) but possibly half as much again is still buried beneath the river. Today the Danube is wearing away the rock walls and archaeologists have had to dismantle this important site and move it slightly higher up the hill along whose foot the river runs. Particularly interesting are the sculptures frequently found beside fireplaces and which possibly represented gods or ancestors. The oldest remains have been dated to around 7,500 years ago.

Khirokitia and Lepenski Vir are notable examples of the great variety of Neolithic cultures and the way Neolithic people lived.

In Cyprus, the economy was based on sheep and goat rearing (for their meat and milk) and, most probably, pigs.

In some cases the decision to build a town and create an urban culture was very appropriate to the local environment.
Above right: At Khirokitia in Cyprus, the dome-shaped houses were set apart from one another and whitewashed with chalk and clay, partly to reflect the sun's rays; this was a Mediterranean form of architecture and town planning. The raised streets were made of large stones.
Right: A cup and bowl from Khirokitia, which are about 7,900 years old. They are made from andesite, a volcanic rock (pottery was fairly scarce). Notice the little holes in the bowl which were evidently used to thread a thin cord through it.
Opposite below: Map showing the Fertile Crescent, a huge area of the Middle East in which the first settlements of agriculturalists and animal herders have been found. The red line shows the boundaries of the area in which copper was first used.

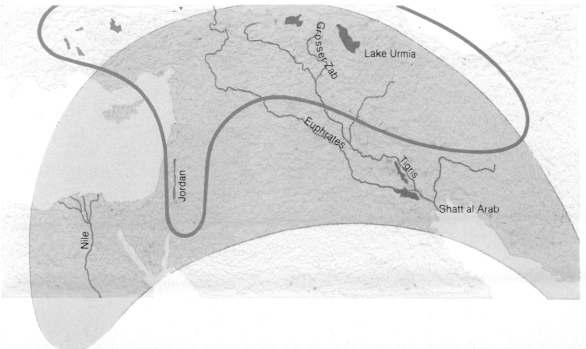

Here again we find scythes made of tiny flints as well as pestles and it is likely that some cereals were cultivated and the rest were gathered from crops which grew wild. Around the settlement there were olive trees growing wild but probably protected by man. Pottery was very rare, but there were many clay charms and statuettes. The most commonly used utensils were made of stone, which was often decorated. Spindles for weaving were also quite common; in Khirokitia, clothes were woven from sheeps' wool.

The Lepenski Vir economy seems to have been primarily Palaeolithic. Fishing and hunting were the main sources of food and possibly the only domesticated animal was the dog. There is no widespread evidence of agriculture. This may have been discouraged by the harshness of the area, consisting as it does mostly of rocks and pebbles. Pottery is abundant, however, and in the most recent periods is decorated in a style found at many other sites up and down the Danube. Goats, pigs, sheep and cattle do not appear at Lepenski Vir until much later. So here too we find a mixture of the old, traditional economy and a new one.

Improving Life

The fact that we find these different economies in areas with different environmental conditions suggests that as he became the producer of his own food, man had to adopt a system that made the most efficient use of the resources his environment made available. The size of the settlements shows that there was a marked increase in

Bottom left: Lepenski Vir is a site on the Yugoslavian bank of the Danube where it forms the border with Romania near the 'Iron Gate', the gorge where the events of the war between the Romans and the Dacians took place (101–102 and 105–106 AD) during the reign of the Emperor Trajan. The excavations carried out since 1967 by archaeologist Dragoslav Srejovič have unearthed a fascinating 7,500-year-old settlement.
Below: The stone sculptures like this one, and those in the illustration opposite, which are frequently found at Lepenski Vir are possibly representations of gods or people's ancestors.
Opposite: The people of Lepenski Vir lived in neatly built houses with stone floors and walls possibly made of wood and animal hides. A simple hole in the roof would have allowed smoke from the fire to escape. There are remains of much pottery, but no evidence of agriculture. The main sources of food were hunting and fishing, so although the culture of Lepenski Vir was Neolithic (as shown by the pottery and neat stone-work), the economy was still Palaeolithic.

population during this period. Many areas of the Neolithic world were beginning to fill with people. These people were forming groups to develop systems of production which enabled them to use their environment more efficiently; from solidarity came strength.

Some of the buildings of a village (temples and grain shelters) showed that people were amassing wealth, and that part of this wealth was considered surplus to requirements and could be 'invested' in useful services. These services could include planning and building a structured town, or building defensive walls and ditches and carrying on wars. Or it could be used for purposes which furthered the beliefs of the community, such as carrying out magical and religious rites. It is not unlikely that temples were often the actual places where wealth was stored. On the one hand it could be placed under the protection of the gods, and even become sacred as a result so that to steal it would be sacrilege; on the other hand it became the obvious place from which priests could take their reward.

The 'person in the street', the actual producer, had by now accepted the idea of doing without some of his or her entitlement in order to create surpluses. The idea of investing these surpluses in other things which were not actually necessities was also catching on.

In the last phases of the Neolithic period, artefacts of every kind have been found which used new materials as well as old materials in new ways. The taming of fire, now used in the making of pottery, was the beginning of man's use of heat to treat the various materials he used. These included the yellow-green or reddish minerals from which the first metal, copper, was extracted. One stone which was widely used was obsidian, but other hard stones were also used to make pendants and beads for necklaces, which were often threaded alternately with shells. Straw and reeds were used for making baskets of all shapes and sizes. Fabrics were made from vegetable fibres (linen) and animal fleeces (wool), so, apart from the spindles needed for spinning the yarn, there were also looms. Pottery was embellished with fingerprints or the edge of a shell whilst the clay was still wet, or it might have been scratched with twigs. Raised designs were made using braided strips of clay and patterns were painted using ochre. Vessels were given handles, partly to make them easier to pick up, but also to improve their looks.

Was the quality of life improving? Possibly it was. Possibly men and women, although continuing to work stolidly and unthinkingly, were beginning to understand the idea of working for the benefit of society at large. Certainly they tried to achieve beauty, both in themselves and in the objects they made.

From a practical point of view, we can see improvements in the way stone was carved. Examples include small, increasingly well-formed flints, polished axeheads and vessels, like those found at Khirokitia, which were patiently rubbed down for hours (see p 54). There were also major advances in drilling and pottery-making tools (see illustration p 40).

Plant-breeding continued, producing bigger ears of grain. From earlier periods when mainly female animals were kept in captivity because they were better-tempered and produced milk, later periods followed when castrated males were kept. These had the advantage of being large but having weaker bones than ordinary males.

The domestication of cattle did not begin until much later, which suggests that people may have tried to domesticate other ruminants such as antelopes and gazelles.

The Development of Trade

It is fair to assume that the large number of Palaeolithic artefacts we have found means that most people had plenty of leisure time. Similar evidence from the Neolithic period shows that man had started to maintain some of his number to carry out the production of non-food goods. So there were specialists from whom ordinary people, the agriculturalists and animal breeders, 'bought' produce. Their exchange of goods would have taken place in the following way: 'I'll give you two baskets

Below: Archaeological studies of the various styles of pottery and technologies are not simply for the purposes of listing and describing them. They provide evidence from the Neolithic period of a vitally important human activity, namely trade. This activity must have developed during the Palaeolithic period and some of the most interesting evidence of this is in the form of tools or fragments of obsidian. Obsidian is a naturally forming 'glass' produced by volcanoes. If we find pieces of obsidian very far from any volcanic areas we can be sure that they were transported there by man for trade. The map below shows some of the main regions where obsidian was (and still is) common. Amber and coral were also traded in Palaeolithic times.

During the Neolithic period, trade in pottery was added to, and sometimes overlapped with the trade in these goods. However, the very widespread use of pottery in Neolithic times was also due in part to 'technical information' or instructions on its manufacture being passed from one community to another. The routes along which pottery was traded were also the routes along which ideas, beliefs and technical skills were passed, being adapted to local conditions as they went.

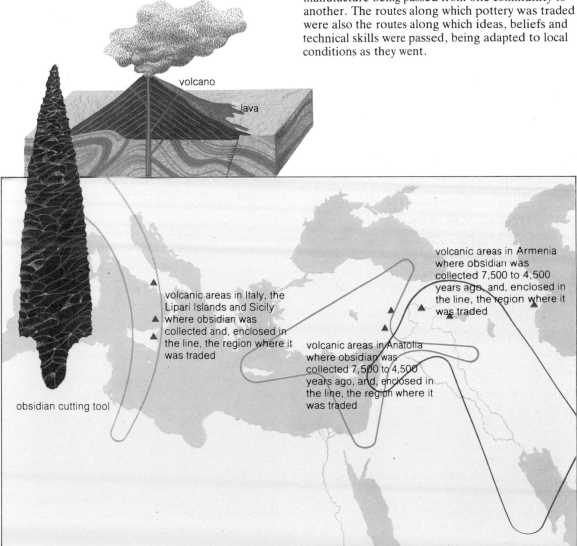

volcano

lava

volcanic areas in Italy, the Lipari Islands and Sicily where obsidian was collected and, enclosed in the line, the region where it was traded

volcanic areas in Anatolia where obsidian was collected 7,500 to 4,500 years ago, and, enclosed in the line, the region where it was traded

volcanic areas in Armenia where obsidian was collected 7,500 to 4,500 years ago, and, enclosed in the line, the region where it was traded

obsidian cutting tool

of figs in exchange for that bowl you've just made and is being fired now;' or, 'Two baskets of grain in exchange for the basket you've just woven.'

This was the birth of 'trade'. Other types of business transactions were starting to take place. Imagine another conversation: 'How much do you want for this piece of material?'

'Ten jars of grain.'

'I've only got two at the moment; can I give you the rest in a month's time?'

At this point the dialogue could go one of two ways. Either: 'All right, I accept, but in a month's time you can give me nine jars!'

'I agree.' (This was how 'credit sales', with the payment of interest, must have begun.)

Or alternatively, 'No, I can't accept that. I must have the grain before you can have the material.'

'In that case I'll borrow the grain from the priest – he's got plenty.'

Then the customer would have gone to the priest and asked, 'Will you lend me eight jars of grain?'

'Yes, but in two months' time you can pay me back ten and meanwhile you can leave a calf here with me so that I can be sure you'll come back in two months!'

'I'll have to accept that: agreed!' Taking the grain, he would have gone to 'buy' his material. This was the beginning of 'secured lending' and the temples, where surpluses were stored, were also most probably the first banks.

It was not only within the village that commercial exchanges took place. Careful chemical testing has shown the complex routes along which obsidian was traded, often very far from the place where it was first mined on the slopes of a volcano. Other tests have been carried out on pottery. Sometimes the spread of a particular type of object or decoration shows that a style had been copied and passed on. In many

Opposite: Reconstruction of a pottery shop in the late Neolithic or early Bronze Age. The potters work using potters' wheels (see also illustration on p 40), while the owner stokes the fire of the oven in which his wares are baked. Note the pots drying in the sun beyond the door. During earlier periods we know that this baking took place around, or in, the fireplace or oven used for baking bread and wafers. Later, the increasing demand for pottery products encouraged some people to spend all their time producing these goods. Obviously the producers of food, the other members of the community, paid for these objects in kind. Thus trade within the village began.

The three ages of prehistory

Christian Thomsen (1788–1865) was curator of the Danish National Museum in Copenhagen. He applied himself to the problem of classifying objects which were found but could not be placed in any historical context because there was nothing by which to identify the culture or community from which they came. Thomsen knew that, in many areas, man had used stone for a long time before turning to metal-working. He therefore decided that it would be very useful to link historical periods to particular types of objects. He thus subdivided the long history of mankind before the appearance of written evidence (prehistory) into three ages. The first was the Stone Age, followed by the Bronze Age which in turn gave way to the Iron Age.

The system Thomsen proposed certainly allows us to place the remains of former cultures into some sort of order. However, it should not be used or interpreted as a fixed, absolute time scale. If we describe an object as belonging to the Stone Age, it has no meaning in terms of dates: the same applies to the Bronze and Iron Ages. This system of classification can only be used if we specify the area to which we are referring because the ages occurred at different times in different places. Many subdivisions for Thomsen's ages have been developed (see table on p 75). For example we speak of the Old Bronze Age and the Late Bronze Age. Perhaps most importantly, the extremely long Stone Age is divided into the Palaeolithic and the Neolithic, with a transitional period between them called the Mesolithic. These terms also refer to particular ways of life and modes of production.

cases it is clear that the objects themselves have been moved great distances and with great care considering their fragility.

Wheat and Bread

There were other abilities which were passed on from one group to another via the networks of trade. New families of plants were bred and spread to areas a long way from where they were first domesticated. The development of a particularly useful plant was often passed on without the whole cross-breeding process necessarily having to be repeated. As we have seen, man, the carrier and transmitter of culture, carried out unnatural selection which led to unnatural processes of distribution. A trader could go out selling pottery and obsidian and come home with a new type of grain or the recipe for a new kind of paint.

It is likely that the selective breeding of some cereal crops, in particular wheat, took place through cross-breeding which was accidental and natural, but which was later produced deliberately. For example, by sowing together in the same field plants whose characteristics they wanted to combine, farmers were able to produce better varieties. The transporting and bartering of seeds was probably a very important factor in this process. Grain as we know it today is the result of commerce.

There was possibly a wild grain similar to a form of wheat called emmer (*Triticum dicoccum*). This most ancient of cereals had grains which were wrapped up inside the head of the plant (in present-day varieties the small sheaths containing the grains [glumes] are open and terminate in the beard of wheat, which is rough and abrasive to the touch because it has little sawlike teeth). With a plant of this kind, it must have been

Opposite: Cultivation in Iran in an arid area where grazing animals on pasture is not possible. It may be that the first attempts at cultivation took place in arid areas which were periodically made fertile by rain or by a river overflowing its banks.
Below: World map showing the distribution of the earliest economies, that is the methods of production chosen by the first people. As can be seen, these areas run roughly parallel to the Equator and correspond to climatic zones. The cultivation of cereals first began in the northern temperate zone (which lies between the Tropic of Cancer and the Arctic Circle).

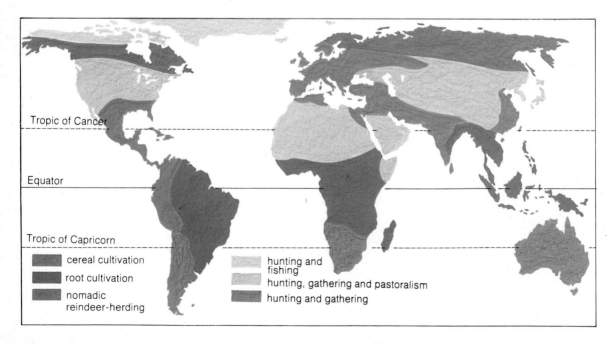

Tropic of Cancer

Equator

Tropic of Capricorn

cereal cultivation

root cultivation

nomadic reindeer-herding

hunting and fishing

hunting, gathering and pastoralism

hunting and gathering

difficult to separate the wheat from the chaff, not least because there was so much chaff. What is more, emmer contains relatively little gluten, the substance which acts as a 'glue' and helps the bread to rise. Dough made from this flour must have produced flat wafers which were baked by suspending them from the inner walls of the oven. The oven would have been a flat-topped cone shape lined with clay (see illustration p 46).

It is possible that the first wheat was crossed with a weed-like grass, *Aegilops squarrosa*, which would have been common in the meadows bordering cultivated fields and is still found wild in northern Iran and Afghanistan. The plants which resulted from this crossbreeding had hard grains with plenty of gluten and smaller glumes. As man grew and favoured this plant he saved more of its seeds and it changed considerably, giving rise to other forms of wheat such as spelt (*Triticum spelta*)

and, more recently, common or bread wheat (*Triticum aestivum*). Other fairly primitive types of grain, some encouraged and cross-bred by man and others by nature, gave rise to a very wide variety of grains.

In the air there are always spores of tiny fungi, invisible to the naked eye. These are yeasts. As part of their life cycle these organisms break up the molecules of sugar and carbohydrates, such as those found in wheat and flour; this reaction gives off the gas carbon dioxide. So if spores of yeast happen to land on dough made from flour containing plenty of gluten, and the dough is later kneaded, the fungi develop. This produces gas inside the dough, which therefore expands and rises. If we now place it in the oven the yeast is killed by the heat and the dough stops rising, but the air spaces inside it remain. When the dough bakes, instead of producing a flat wafer we have a loaf of bread.

The action of yeast produces not only

gas but another important substance – ethyl alcohol. This process of fermentation also allows us to turn substances with a high sugar or carbohydrate content into alcoholic drinks – beers, wines and, if the results are concentrated at high temperature, distilled spirits.

Civilizations and their Geography

We have now briefly sketched some of the main features of the transition from Palaeolithic to Neolithic and the development of the Neolithic way of life. We can now therefore look to see which areas of the world followed these developments through with new solutions to new problems and created not only a new way of working, but a new way of living together.

These new solutions all differed slightly from one another because the areas where they came about were also different. But in time they all became huge productive machines with their own unique characteristics. These were the great civilizations. These did not all arise simultaneously. In some cases they were the result of environmental crises in the region concerned or in neighbouring regions.

Opposite: Agricultural village in Rajasthan, in north-western India, an arid region with large areas of sands with a high salt content. Rajasthan stretches to the south and east of the Thar Desert (Great Indian Desert) on the border with Pakistan. Water is a precious commodity in these communities.

Right: Diagram comparing the dates of the development of Palaeolithic and Neolithic cultures in various regions of the world. These did not arise simultaneously and it is interesting to compare these dates with the map on p 62. For example, we can see that the hunter-gatherer economy of an isolated area like Australia has remained virtually unchanged; no indigenous Australian civilization ever got off the ground. Also shown are the ears of three different types of grain which were fundamental in the growth of civilization: barley and two kinds of wheat, einkorn and emmer.

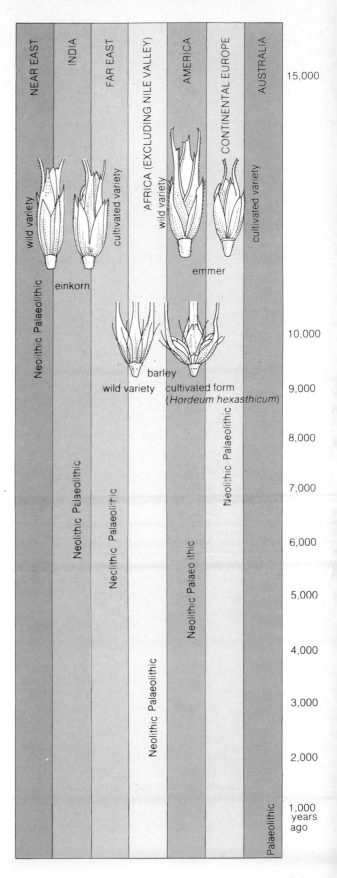

65

2. The Birthplaces of the Great Civilizations

Did they Grow like Mushrooms?

Man, the bearer of culture, of human skills, customs, materials and objects, has always been on the move. Sometimes this was because of a nomadic lifestyle, sometimes it was simply in order to trade. We could therefore ask whether all the civilizations which arose and were dotted around the globe were simply the result of man's wandering from place to place and therefore ultimately originated in one place. Thus it may be that civilizations are like strawberry plants, which grow in various corners of the garden but which are all joined by very long runners along the ground. It could be that we are looking at a single plant and that the history of mankind is that of a single civilization.

Or the complete opposite could be true. Civilizations could be like mushrooms, which seem to grow independently and at some distance from one another without apparently being connected in any way.

Right: Map showing areas under the influence of civilizations during two separate periods, 7,000 and 4,500 years ago. The regions where the most important archaeological finds have been made are also labelled. The expansion of these civilizations was a slow one. In fact, many of the areas which appear empty on this map would have been host to a large number of cultures, but either these left no traces, or their traces have yet to be found. However, it is immediately apparent that areas which did support civilizations often adjoin one another and are mostly within the northern temperate zone of the earth's surface (see map on p 62). Also illustrated are two objects from the historical periods shown on the map.

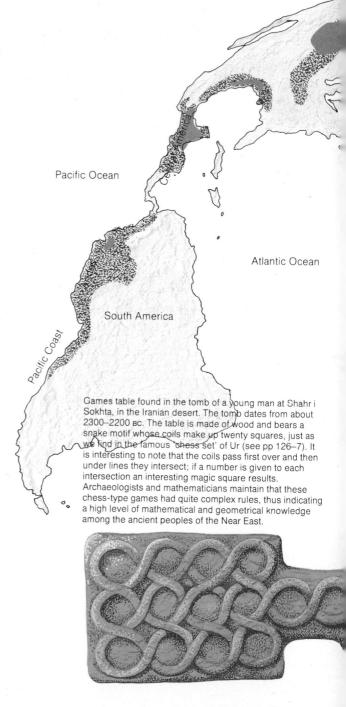

Pacific Ocean

Atlantic Ocean

South America

Pacific Coast

Games table found in the tomb of a young man at Shahr i Sokhta, in the Iranian desert. The tomb dates from about 2300–2200 BC. The table is made of wood and bears a snake motif whose coils make up twenty squares, just as we find in the famous 'chess set' of Ur (see pp 126–7). It is interesting to note that the coils pass first over and then under lines they intersect; if a number is given to each intersection an interesting magic square results. Archaeologists and mathematicians maintain that these chess-type games had quite complex rules, thus indicating a high level of mathematical and geometrical knowledge among the ancient peoples of the Near East.

group of stone figures
representing gods connected
with fertility cults

North America

Japan

Northern Europe

Steppes

Yellow River
region

Central Europe

possible trade routes

possible trade routes

Southern
Europe

Anatolia

Armenia

possible
trade routes

Indochina

North Africa

Mediterranean

Mesopotamia

Indus Valley

Nile Valley

Indian Ocean

Solid brown areas: areas influenced by civilizations
approximately 7,000 years ago

Dotted brown areas: areas influenced by civilizations
approximately 4,500 years ago

Both these scenarios can help us towards an understanding of what actually happened. In the course of time there was obviously contact between the various areas of civilization; in some cases one civilization actually derived from another. But think of mushrooms again. As we know, these organisms are only apparently separated from one another. All we see above ground are the individual heads and stalks of each mushroom. Underground, however, there is a closely woven and extensive network of cells called the mycelium which is the body of the fungus. This is the source of a number of mushrooms and joins them all together. With civilizations, too, there is a mycelium, a single underground connection. As all humans have the same basic needs – eating, reproducing, communicating – each individual civilization therefore develops its own particular way of providing for these needs.

There is one fact which becomes very obvious at this point. At least four of the great civilizations developed on rivers. Having a river as part of its environment apparently favoured the growth of a community. In other cases we can pick out different factors upon which civilizations depended, for example the sea.

Let us then try to gain an overview of the places and their environments where the main civilizations of the past arose.

The Nile

Egyptian civilization grew up in the Nile Valley. The Nile is still the longest river in the world, despite the building of the Aswan dam and the creation of Lake Nasser in 1970 which shortened it by a few kilometres.

It should be mentioned at the outset that only the final 1,000 kilometres (625 miles) or so of the river is the actual cradle of Egyptian civilization. Below this region other cultures developed, including the kingdom of Nubia, which as we shall see had many contacts with Egypt.

Before the Aswan dam was built, the Nile was subjected to quite widespread flooding. The area affected by the flooding was an average of 30 kilometres (18½ miles) wide. Periodically the Nile covered this area with large quantities of water full of organic flotsam, particularly vegetable matter and humus. So when the river flooded, the valley was watered and given new soil containing substances which made the land fertile. Since we know how important water and fertilizer are to agriculture, we can easily see why the area along the Nile has been the home of agricultural communities since man first started cultivating crops. The regularity of the floods and the great size of the river (long stretches of which have always been navigable) are other important factors which led to the dawn of Egyptian civilization.

Later on, we will look quite closely at the rise and subsequent history of this civilization. For the time being we will simply note that the valley of the river Nile is a very unusual environment and we can therefore expect that man's relationship with it would have been unique.

Opposite: An interesting archaeological site near the banks of the Nile.
Below: Nile River near Aswan. We usually tend to think of the Nile and its valley as one long archaeological site covered in ruins. In fact the ruins are dotted along a very great length of river and if one travels down it in a boat, Egypt looks like a series of small or very small villages interspersed with the remains of ancient buildings.

The Nile

The River Nile is approximately 6,670 kilometres (4,170 miles) long. In Egypt the average width of the valley is 30 kilometres (18½ miles). The delta covers more than 23,000 square kilometres (8,880 square miles).

The course of the Nile is all that remains of a huge river basin. We know that in the past (one to two million years ago) the Nile Valley was completely different. There were many tributaries which changed the landscape in ways invisible from the ground but apparent from a great height with the use of special equipment. The course of the Nile therefore became a small thread running between two vast areas of desert. It is possible that the drying out of the surrounding land led to large numbers of people moving to the banks of the river to find food.

The Egyptians had a very simple explanation for the annual flooding of the Nile: the river was a god and the floods were his way of feeding his people and helping them to prosper. The attempts of experts in ancient Egypt to explain the flooding were invariably wrong; they were unaware that the river rose a great deal further south than they thought and that its waters flowed from high snow-capped mountains and an enormous lake.

Mesopotamia

A different situation existed in the region which since Greek antiquity has been known as Mesopotamia, meaning 'between the rivers'. This is the huge area made up of the valleys of the Tigris and the Euphrates, as well as the plains of various heights between the two river basins, in modern Iraq.

The Euphrates is 2,760 kilometres (1,725 miles) long; the Tigris is shorter at 2,000 kilometres (1,250 miles). Both have their sources in the mountains of Armenia, east of Anatolia in Turkey; they draw close to each other at about the latitude of Baghdad and today they join in the area north of the lake Hawr al Ḥammār and follow the same course,

Left: Aerial photograph of an area of Mesopotamia. The Zagros Mountains mark the eastern boundary of Mesopotamia, which is a huge region made up of the basin of the Rivers Tigris and Euphrates.
Above: The Persian Gulf coast. The Shatt al Arab, which flows into this gulf, is a short, wide river formed by the convergence of the Euphrates, the Tigris and other rivers such as the Karun which descend from the Zagros Mountains. There is an old but simple way of remembering which of these rivers is which: 'the Tigris is on the same side as the Tigers', meaning that it is towards India (the home of the Bengal Tiger) and east of the Euphrates.

The Euphrates

The length of the River Euphrates is approximately 2,760 kilometres (1,725 miles). In Armenia, where the river rises, there is considerable rain and snow to feed the river. The long, winding course of the Euphrates and the comparative lack of tributaries means that its flow is much slower than that of the Tigris. The bed of the Euphrates is unstable; flooding can change the course of the river with disastrous consequences for agriculture.

The Tigris

The River Tigris is approximately 1,950 kilometres (1,220 miles) long. It rises in the Armenian mountains and has many tributaries, the biggest of which are the Lesser Zab, the Grösser Zab and the Diyala. It joins the Euphrates in the Shatt al Arab, together with the Karub from the Zagros Mountains. The floods of the Tigris are even more dangerous than those of the Euphrates; to lessen their effect, it is sometimes necessary to breach dykes upstream.

known as the Shatt al Arab, to the Persian Gulf.

The environment here would seem to be a lot more complex than that of the Nile Valley. Historical events followed one another in a continuous chain with more or less separate links, so the overall picture is a lot less simple than that in Egypt. From the physical point of view, too, the various changes which occurred in the environment were of great importance. While the Nile continued to function almost mechanically for centuries without any obvious hiccups, the more complex ecological 'machinery' of Mesopotamia jammed many times and on several occasions underwent far-reaching changes.

Suffice it to say at this point, then, that the region in which both these rivers flow was ecologically unstable, and as recently as 5,000 years ago the two rivers arrived at the sea separately and about 200 kilometres (120 miles) north of present-day Basra and Abādān. It is therefore likely that in the late Palaeolithic period the coastline was even further away, possibly 500 kilometres (300 miles) from where it is now.

Mesopotamia would therefore, in geological terms, be land reclaimed by the action of the two rivers. Landscapes changed rapidly in this region, right before the eyes of man and beneath the blade of his hoe.

The Indus and Yellow Rivers

The Indus River in Pakistan is 3,168 kilometres (1,980 miles) long, and has a huge river basin. In this basin, and particularly along the banks of its various watercourses, a group of imposing cities grew up 4,500 years ago. This was the Indus Valley civilization. Today the soils of the area surrounding the Indus and some of its larger tributaries (the Ravi, Chenab, and Sutlej rivers for example) are dusty, and in some places almost like a desert. Other areas have become swampland. This area, too, seems to have undergone important environmental changes during fairly recent times. These changes were probably caused by man, beginning with the people who built up the Indus Valley civilization.

We know, though, that during the

The Indus

The Indus River is approximately 3,168 kilometres (1,980 miles) in length. The river rises in the mountains of Tibet, flows north-west and then curves down towards the south-west. It then meets a tributary from the west, the Kabul, and the many great rivers of the Punjab join it from the east.

The entire region to the east of the river consists of river plains, but they are comparatively infertile because of the high salt content of the soil. Beyond the river plains is the Thar Desert, also having very salty earth. In fairly recent times a huge network of canals has been built.

The size of the Indus and its tributaries varies greatly according to the season and the melting of snow in the mountains.

The Hwang Ho

In China, the Hwang Ho, also known as the Yellow River, is approximately 4,645 kilometres (2,900 miles) long, generally flowing from west to east. A large part of it flows across fertile loess, but the river and rain tend to erode the soil.

Marco Polo had an interesting comment to make. In his 13th-century account of his travels, we read, 'And when the man had left his castle and went 20 miles to the west, he found a river called the Caramera (this is how he transcribes the Tartar word *Karamuren*, meaning 'black river', but it is certainly the Hwang Ho which he is describing), which is so wide that no bridge can cross it, and it leads to the Ocean (the Yellow Sea). And on this river there are many towns and castles . . .'

Neolithic era and before it in the late Palaeolithic period, the valleys were very rich indeed in vegetation, particularly tall trees.

The Hwang Ho, or Yellow River, in China is 4,645 kilometres (2,900 miles) long. This great river changes many times along its course. Particularly interesting is the area where it has dug a river bed in the layers of sediment called loess. This is a very fertile soil deposited

Opposite: Hills eroded by wind and water at the foot of the Hindu Kush mountains in northern Pakistan. Various tributaries flow into the Indus from the west, one of the most important being the Kabul which flows through the capital of Afghanistan. The Indus rises in western Tibet.
Below: Indus River near Tarbela, 70 kilometres (44 miles) or so north of Rawalpindi in Pakistan. The valley here is already very broad, but confined by mountains. Further down the valley the Kabul River joins the Indus, and it then continues on to a huge plain which is now desert. Much further south it is joined by a number of large rivers from the north east.

during the ice ages by the action of the wind and covering roughly the same area as the glaciers. Loess can be described as an aeolian deposit, from the name of the Greek god of the wind, Aeolus. The term 'loess' itself comes from the Swiss-German word *lösch*, meaning crumbly.

The combination of loess and a large river supplying water gave rise to a number of different cultures, particularly the great An-yang civilization which will be looked at later on. At this stage we need only observe that with these factors problems arise when the river deposits water on soil which is already fertile, and then takes a lot of it away through the process of erosion. This can therefore lead to an unstable ecology.

Europe

In Neolithic times central and southern Europe had no 'great civilizations' and no empires. In many areas there were local cultures, often producing goods of high quality which probably indicate an affluent way of life. But there was no overall organization, no co-ordination of the work being done by different groups.

Many of the local cultures of prehistoric Europe are still shrouded in mystery. Why is this? These cultures did not, in most cases, leave us any form of written evidence. These civilized Europeans of so long ago were illiterate.

Two questions suggest themselves. Firstly, why did so many cultures with a low level of civilization occupy such huge territories? And why did they leave no written records? If we look again at the environments concerned we can give a rough answer to these questions.

There were abundant forests and

many mountain ranges; the plains were not particularly large but were made fertile by the presence of loess and frequent rain. In addition there was often a marked contrast between summer and winter. So Europe had many different environments with their own communities of living things (ecosystems) in fairly isolated areas.

The photographs on these pages show three of the most fascinating sites in Europe.
Left: Stonehenge in Wiltshire, England. This great monument (built overnight, according to legend, by Merlin the Wizard using his magical powers) is about 15 kilometres (10 miles) north-west of Salisbury.
Opposite below: View of the rows of menhirs (long stones) at Carnac in Brittany, about 120 kilometres (75 miles) north-west of Nantes.
Below: Stone village of Skara Brae in the Orkney Islands of Scotland.
Below left: Commonly accepted periods of history and prehistory (see also p 60).

Periods of History and Prehistory

		MATERIALS	ECONOMY
PREHISTORY	STONE AGE	Paleolithic Stone, wood, bone, horn, ivory	Hunting and gathering
		Mesolithic As above	Hunting, gathering and fishing
		Neolithic As above, plus pottery	Agriculture, animal rearing, trade, accumulation of surpluses, villages, towns, social divisions
	METAL AGE	Copper Age As above, plus copper, gold and silver	Various cultures and civilizations
		Bronze Age As above, plus alloys	Intensive trade between cultures and civilizations
		Iron Age As above, plus iron	As above
HISTORY		As above	Regular contacts between different peoples, writing, social divisions, monuments.

In Europe the transition from the Palaeolithic period (which, as we know, left many traces of its culture) to the Neolithic period took place very gradually. There were probably never any large increases in population and changes made by man had little effect upon the landscape. Customs, habits, building styles and techniques could be transferred from one person to another by word of mouth without the need to write them down. Ancient Europe therefore presented a mosaic of different cultures created by different peoples who were aware of each other's existence but preferred to keep themselves to themselves.

The Mediterranean

The Mediterranean (from the Latin meaning 'between the seas') is the biggest enclosed area of sea in the world. We can describe it as enclosed because from the geological, physical and eco-

logical points of view, small openings like the Strait of Gibraltar or artificial channels like the Suez Canal are not important.

In the Mediterranean area many Neolithic cultures developed, as did other subsequent small civilizations. The sea was the one feature which brought them all together. It was a source of food and a convenient, if sometimes hazardous, means of communication.

There was one great empire which arose in this area, that of Crete, the large island south of Greece. Agriculture on the coast was rich and varied, and many naturally occurring trees and shrubs (such as olives and grapevines) could be domesticated. In some areas cereals and leguminous vegetables (such as peas and beans) could be successfully grown, particularly where the rain was fairly regular. This was therefore a different land to most of continental Europe and much of Asia. There was a large variety of products

The Mediterranean

This is the world's largest inland sea. It originated from the Tethys Sea which separated the two super-continents of Laurasia and Gondwanaland early in the Earth's history. The effects of continental drift reduced it to the basin we know today. The final enclosure of the Mediterranean took place as a result of continental drift which created some of Europe's main mountain ranges: the Pyrenees, part of the Alps, the Caucasus Mountains and the Atlas Mountains.

There are no complex currents in the Mediterranean. In the eastern half of the Aegean Sea it is extremely deep.

There is a good supply of fish, though the variety of species is small compared with the oceans. Crustaceans and shellfish are plentiful. The Mediterranean has many islands and straits, which since earliest times have been navigated by man. The first attempts at navigation took place along the coast for the purpose of catching fish; later the sea was used as a major trade route.

Above: Windmills in Crete.
Right: Olive tree in Cyprus.
The great basin of the Mediterranean Sea has its own distinct geological and ecological features. The coastline enclosing it is very long and indented, and there are many large islands (Sicily, Sardinia, Corsica, Crete, Cyprus and Majorca), as well as small ones. Much of the area enjoys a mild climate caused by the moderating effect of the sea. This great mass of water, which has few currents, absorbs heat during the day and releases it at night. Even in winter, the water temperature never drops very low and the coastal regions are kept mild. The daily variation in temperature between the sea and the land causes many gusty winds whose energy can be made use of by windmills or sailing ships. Rain in this area is very irregular, and drought is an ever-present threat.

and people could afford to move around. Trade, a vitally important development in human history, began to take place during the Neolithic period.

North and South America

The two great continental blocks which make up North and South America contain a wide range of environments and landscapes from deserts to tropical and equatorial rain forests, from high mountain ranges to vast fertile prairies.

Man's ancient history in America has still not been properly pieced together. What we do know is that many localized cultures arose which responded to conditions in the environment. There were also great civilizations and empires in both North and South America. This was because some situations made it desirable or even necessary that people work together and co-ordinate their lives so as to obtain better results.

The most important difference between America and the Old World (Europe and Asia) was the complete absence, after about 12,000 to 10,000 years ago, of any very large herbivorous wild animals which could be domesticated.

One great source of wealth arose in the many valleys of the Andes which opened out into the Pacific. This was fertilizer in the form of bird droppings. It is found fairly widely up and down the coast and was the basis of many fairly complex cultures, as well as of the Chimu and Inca empires.

The administration of territories on the edge of the jungle, and sometimes in it, lcd to the development of the Maya civilization in Central America.

The high plains of central Mexico supported cultures which possibly began elsewhere but created such highly organized societies as those of the Toltecs, Teotihuacán and the Aztecs. These were complex groupings of people which sometimes involved large population movements and the use of writing. What is also particularly interesting is that the two great rivers of America, the Mississippi and the Amazon, never sustained any great civilizations.

The Americas

The early civilization and culture of the continent of America were in many ways very different from those which arose in the Old World. In the New World (North and South America) none of the cereals such as wheat, barley, oats or rice were found naturally. However, there was maize. There were no beasts of burden such as horses or donkeys and no cattle which could be domesticated (the American bison was never tamed). There were two very long rivers with huge basins (the Mississippi-Missouri in the north and the Amazon in the south), but the regions surrounding them never presented a combination of circumstances suitable for the growth of great human civilizations. Also important was the fact that 10,000 years ago America was sparsely populated.

Opposite above: Valleys of the Andes sloping down towards the Pacific Ocean in southern Peru.
Opposite below: Chinampas (floating gardens) in Central America. *Chinampas* are islands or peninsulas of cultivated land which were formed when networks of canals were created to drain marshland surrounding lakes. The first were created by the Aztecs, and those at Lakes Xochimilco and Chalco near Mexico City are still used.
Below: Aerial view of the Mompos region on the Rio Magdalena river in Colombia.

3. Organization, Production and Trade

Ancient Egypt's Great Leap Forward

Let us explore more closely some of the facts we have been given. Along the banks of the Nile, particularly on its lower reaches, there was an area of semi-marshland with a great deal of animal life and a fertile soil which supported much wild vegetation. During the Neolithic period various groups of hunter-gatherers lived here. The ecology must have been similar to that of the whole of North Africa, which at

that time was well-watered and fertile. There is widespread evidence that later, starting in the Neolithic period, there were settlements of agriculturalists along the river who still practised hunting but also reared animals and used (and therefore presumably manufactured) linen.

Opposite: Painted vase belonging to the Gerzean culture (from El Gerza in the Faiyum basin of Egypt).
Right: Flint knife with ivory handle made from hippopotamus tusks, also from the Gerzean culture (about 5,600 years ago). The sea battle depicted in the bottom half of the decoration on the handle is particularly interesting, possibly showing a prehistoric invasion of Egypt by Asian peoples.
Below: The Nile near Aswan, showing the typical sailing craft of the river, known as feluccas. The Nile has always been navigable for most of its length, including the final 1,000 kilometres (630 miles) during the season when the river is low. The winds blow from north to south so that boats can be propelled upstream by sails as well as oars.

captured slaves

battle scenes

trophies

bodies thrown into the water

enemies have different hairstyles to those of Egyptians (who have shaved heads)

Several cultures arose in the area at this time: the Badarian, the Amratian, and the Gerzean. The names come from the present-day villages near which excavations have been carried out. There is a great deal of pottery from them with interesting, carefully executed decorations. There are also increasingly widespread indications of the use of copper at this time.

However, these cultures were primarily Neolithic. Copper was not used for making implements and its appearance did not have any noticeable effect on the way things were made or on people's lifestyles.

This takes us to around 3200 BC. Only five centuries later we find the step pyramid of Žoser at Saqqara, a product of a very rational human mind. This is a breathtaking leap forward in technological skill. What happened, then, in the Nile valley between the fourth and third millennia BC?

A civilization was born; Egyptian history had begun. We will enter this history at the point where written records were first made (everything preceding this point being classified as 'prehistory', see table on p 75). There is plenty of written evidence available, such as dedications on monuments, and the names of kings and gods.

Was the development of civilization inevitable?

The culture of ancient Egypt is in some ways an example of how other civilizations arose. It is therefore important to look at what could have happened towards the end of the fourth millennium BC in an attempt to pick out the various factors which lead to the birth of a civilization. As a result, we will be able to draw parallels with other cases and other civilizations.

Firstly, we need to redefine more clearly what we mean by a civilization. As we know, in a Neolithic village or

Opposite above and left: The two sides of the Nar-Mer tablet. This tablet, about 75 centimetres (30 inches) long, is made of slate and was probably used for mixing cosmetics (these would have been stirred up in the small trough formed by the long necks of the lions or leopards). Between the two heads of the cow-goddess Hathor, there is a small square containing a few words which have been deciphered as the name of a person. The whiskered catfish, common in the Nile, represents the sound *n'r* or *nar*; the chisel symbol is *mr* or *mer*. On the same side as the long-necked animals we see the king celebrating a victory, wearing a crown with an ostrich plume, which indicates he was a ruler of Lower Egypt (the delta). He is surrounded by a number of servants carrying trophies or magical or religious symbols. On the right are two rows of enemies who have been bound and decapitated. Below the long-necked monsters, held on a leash by two servants, the king, represented by a bull, destroys a town with his horns and crushes an enemy.

On the reverse side of the tablet, Nar-Mer is wearing the mitre of Upper Egypt and beating an enemy as he holds him by the hair. A servant is holding out his sandals. The falcon is the god Horus (and also represents the king) and is binding some prisoners, possibly marsh-dwellers as symbolized by the papyrus reeds.

Opposite below: Head of a club from the time of the Scorpion King (one of Nar-Mer's predecessors). He is shown wearing the crown of Upper Egypt and holding a hoe, probably as part of a magic ritual.

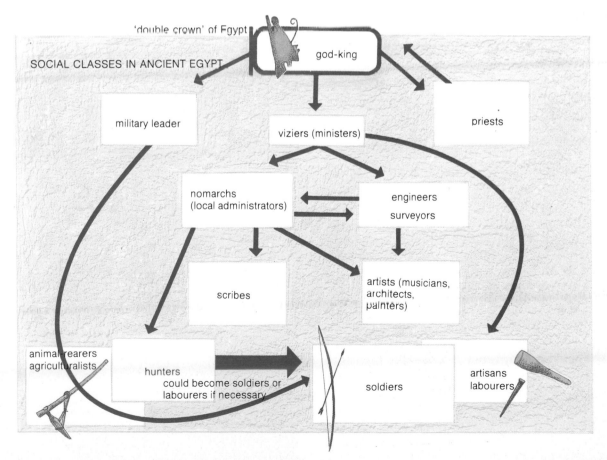

'double crown' of Egypt

SOCIAL CLASSES IN ANCIENT EGYPT

god-king

military leader

viziers (ministers)

priests

nomarchs (local administrators)

engineers
surveyors

scribes

artists (musicians, architects, painters)

animal rearers
agriculturalists

hunters
could become soldiers or labourers if necessary

soldiers

artisans
labourers

town there were 'surpluses'. In most cases there was a certain amount of cereals kept in grain shelters, or often in other types of building where they became sacred and were believed to be under the protection of the gods. Any settlement of this type is likely to prosper without the need to invent new ways of life.

Some sociologists (those who study the development and functioning of human society) believe that the story of civilizations and their birth is basically the story of the choices people have made as to how to use these surpluses. This definition, suggested by the sociologist Ignacy Sachs, can be very helpful. But in many, many cases the rise in technology from a village to a huge state was not simply because people chose to use their surpluses to pay for a fairly restricted group of specialists (such as priests, soldiers, architects and artisans). According to this theory specialists were limited to those really necessary to make the community work better. The remaining surpluses were stored or simply redistributed.

However, it could have happened that a particular set of external events compelled people to make these various choices.

Pressures for change

Let us go back to late Neolithic Egypt. It is very likely that, because of big changes in the climate and ecology, a large part of Africa became inhospitable. A gradual drying of the soil and decline in the flora and fauna drove people towards the banks of the Nile where these changes had had no marked effect.

So this long valley was full of people, and of course they all wanted to live and eat. The fertile soil and water from the river guaranteed food to all agriculturalists, and possibly to all animal-breeders, no matter how many of them

Below: Artist's impression of one of the many ceremonies by which the Egyptian god-kings acknowledged the close relationship between man and the 'black earth' of Egypt. It also gives some idea of the impressive system of waterworks by which the waters of the Nile were put to use and flood damage was prevented. The man in the foreground on the left is leaning on a wooden hoe held together by rope. In the background, on the right, a shaduf is being used. This machine consisted of a pivoting arm with a counterweight at one end and a bucket suspended by a rope at the other. The operator used his own weight to pull the bucket down and fill it with water; when the bucket was released the weight moved downwards and the full bucket could be directed into an adjoining canal or even some way uphill; it was therefore a simple means of raising water.

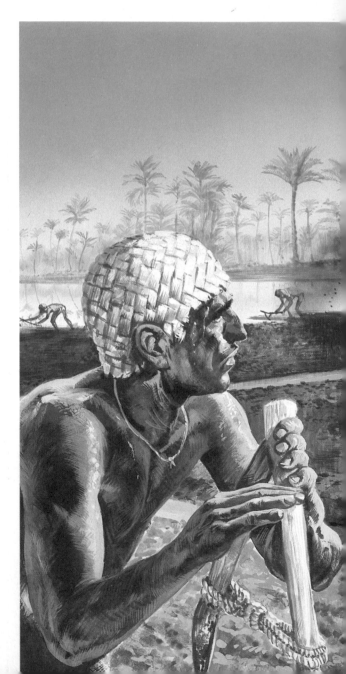

there were. Soon, though, the 'Nile machine' began playing up in a way which, had the communities been smaller, would have seemed less serious.

During the annual floods the river overflowed its banks and inundated wide strips of land on either side. The water, rich in humus and organic substances, created very fertile deposits of mud. When the flood ebbed, and the waters of the Nile returned to their normal level, the land tended to dry out very quickly. It was possible for the floods to have a harmful effect; often some of man's creations – fields and villages – were swept away. Also the large delta at the mouth of the river tended to become waterlogged and the sheer size of the resulting marshes made them difficult to cultivate. The area could become unhealthy and the soil too soft to be of any use for agriculture.

The inhabitants of late Neolithic Egypt therefore took a decision: they would use their surpluses to carry out a huge project. This was a particular type of domestication, not of animals or plants, but of the river itself.

To stop the water returning to the river too quickly, they built networks of dykes and canals. Using simple equipment like the 'shaduf' (illustrated on p 85), they could transfer large quantities of water into these canals.

In this way the area that could be used for cultivation was extended and the mud, so essential for fertilizing the soil, was kept damp. The network of canals and dykes protected it from flood damage. Many areas of the delta were reclaimed by preventing water getting to them so that they could be drained using shadufs and dry out in the sun.

During the first phase of taming the Nile, the problems of the delta and the upper reaches were dealt with separately. Later, people realized that work carried out upstream also benefited areas downstream. They also realized that the river was an excellent means of communication simply because it was so easily navigable. So after this first phase the whole ecosystem, the inter-relating communities of living things and their environment, was treated as a single organism.

The simple social structure which existed in early Neolithic villages was not suited to this scale of work. People who were already used to paying others with surplus goods could now accept that in a situation which threatened to become critical, somebody had to co-ordinate all their work so that the great river could be made to function in the most efficient way. Some people had a good knowledge of the soil structure and the flow of the river and were able to gather together the experiences of the various communities and produce statistics on such things as droughts, floods and crop yields. They also needed someone who could unite the interests of all the different villages into a common goal, that of producing 'black earth' (the fertile soil of the drained lands whose name, *Kemi*, the

---

The first known kings of ancient Egypt

Pre-dynastic: 'The Scorpion', Nar-Mer

First dynasty (about 3200–3000 BC): Horus Aha (Menes, possibly the same as Nar-Mer), Djer, various other kings, Ka

Second dynasty (about 3000–2700 BC): various kings, Khasekhem

Third dynasty (about 2700–2620 BC): Žoser, Teti, Nekbare, Neferkare, Huni

Below: Statue of Žoser, made of limestone about 2700 BC. This imposing piece of sculpture still shows traces of having been painted in reddish-brown, black and white.

Opposite above: The step pyramid of King Žoser and part of the sacred boundary wall of Saqqara, near Cairo. This huge complex was built from square stones by the Žoser's visier Imhotep, who was later accorded the status of a divinity. Imhotep clearly achieved what he had set out to do; generation after generation of people, some of them very famous, have marvelled at this pyramid (and the more famous ones at Giza) built to last an eternity (drawing, *opposite below*). The structure was completed in several stages. The first stage was a great mastaba (a rectangular tomb with sloping sides and a flat roof) which covered the shaft down which the sarcophagus containing the King's body had been lowered.

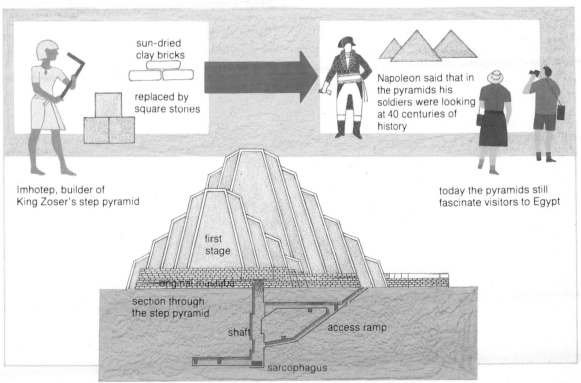

sun-dried
clay bricks

replaced by
square stones

Imhotep, builder of
King Zoser's step pyramid

Napoleon said that in
the pyramids his
soldiers were looking
at 40 centuries of
history

today the pyramids still
fascinate visitors to Egypt

first
stage

original mastaba

section through
the step pyramid

shaft

access ramp

sarcophagus

ancient Egyptians gave to their country) to grow crops for their children and their children's children.

Who could be accepted as lord and master in decision making, imposing rules and making sure they were carried out? Only a king or god could do all of these. And in Egypt, the king *was* also god.

We do know that in earlier periods there were well-recognized leaders in the delta region, where Buto was a sort of capital city, and in the main valley where the capital was near present-day Kôm el Ahmar. When unification of the two regions took place a single god-king for both lower Egypt (the delta) and upper Egypt (the valley) was established. Horus Aha, known in Greek tradition as Menes and possibly the same person as Nar-Mer, was the first god-king and founded his new capital city at Memphis on a site created by diverting the course of the Nile. This was one of the first examples of the Egyptians' skill at hydraulic engineering, that is controlling and using the motion of water. It took place around 3000 BC.

The story of Egypt is continued on pp 110–120 and pp 248–264.

Southern Mesopotamia

What happened on a large scale in Egypt at this time had already occurred in some areas of southern Mesopotamia. Here too we need to look at the causes of these important events.

Almost everywhere in Mesopotamia (that is, throughout the length of both the rivers, from the areas near the mountains to the vast plain) there were agricultural villages. These people had to make use of simple irrigation schemes to supplement the poor supply of rain. They had domesticated animals but were active hunters and traders too.

Above: The earliest settlements in lower Mesopotamia consisted of huts, possibly like the 'floating' houses of present-day Marsh Arabs in Iraq, seen here from the air, situated around the fertile semi-marshland of the area. From the middle of the fourth millennium BC onwards, there were urban centres with great monumental buildings both in the south and along the upper reaches of the Tigris and Euphrates.

Opposite: Reconstruction of the Sumerian temple of Eridu. Now Abu Shahrain on the southern Euphrates, Eridu was originally on the seashore but since it was built the coast has retreated some 240 kilometres (150 miles). Also shown is one of the domed buildings on the upper Tigris, not far from Nineveh, built by pre-Sumerian peoples of Mesopotamia. The holy areas of the city-states of Mesopotamia were believed to be inhabited by the gods to whom they were dedicated. Thus temples were always rebuilt on the same site and grew successively larger.

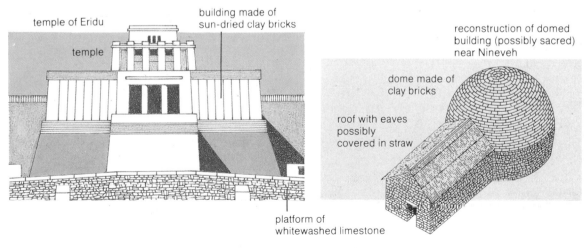

temple of Eridu

building made of
sun-dried clay bricks

temple

reconstruction of domed
building (possibly sacred)
near Nineveh

dome made of
clay bricks

roof with eaves
possibly
covered in straw

platform of
whitewashed limestone

Along the rivers a great deal of trading took place, mainly in obsidian, pottery and minerals for the earliest attempts at metal making. From their centre at el Ubaid, which at that time was on the coast, pottery with simple painted decorations was bought and sold up and down the rivers and the style was copied everywhere. In some of the trading centres there were buildings which were bigger than the houses and huts people lived in, and which were made of sun-dried bricks. These were used as temples for the local deities and possibly also as storehouses. There are important examples at el Ubaid in the south and Tepe Gawra and Tell Halaf in the north.

About 3500 BC, in the area near the sea (which was fertile, but much of which was covered in marshland), life was already different from elsewhere; the settlements were larger and had turned into cities. The public buildings were particularly impressive, and again were made of sun-dried bricks.

These people produced written documents and other evidence which show with a fair degree of certainty that writing was first invented in this region as a way of using signs to provide a permanent record of information. But we will look at this theory in more detail later on (see pp 92–6).

The hybrid Sumerians

During the first half of the fourth millennium BC a new group of people made their presence felt in lower Mesopotamia. These new arrivals may have appeared in small numbers over a long period of time; at any rate they integrated fairly well with the people already living there. The result was a hybrid society who are described by historians as Sumerians.

Let us try to reconstruct, using the information we have, the kind of

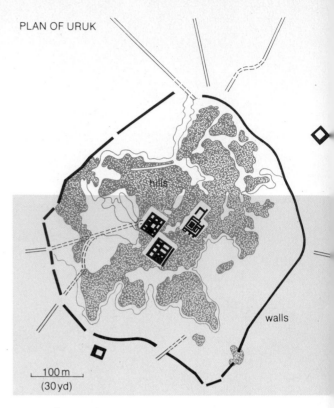

PLAN OF URUK

hills

walls

100m
(30 yd)

Above: Comparison between the layouts of two Sumerian towns: Uruk in approximately 3200 BC, and Ur about 2100 BC, when it was undergoing a renaissance.
Opposite above: Woman's head in marble, from Uruk, dating from approximately 3200 BC. The indentations on the top of the head and above the eyes were possibly filled with coloured plaster or stones; traces of bitumen were also found on it. The eyes would have been hard stones. This is one of the most fascinating relics of antiquity ever found; it is about 20 centimetres (8 inches) tall.
Opposite below: Sumerian frieze showing workers in a workshop. Milk stored in large churns is being poured off and possibly processed to make cheese.

lifestyle this civilization represented and notice the similarities and differences to the way in which Egypt grew.

In both cases it was the arrival of a large influx of people which provided an external impetus for change. In Egypt's case the result can be seen in population terms; the increase in the number of mouths to feed meant that the river had to be used in a more efficient way. The ability to use the Nile as a means of production was already very apparent amongst prehistoric agriculturalists,

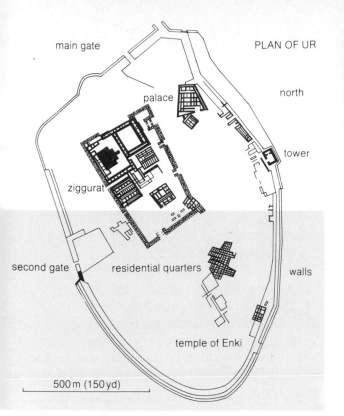

main gate

PLAN OF UR

north

palace

tower

ziggurat

second gate

residential quarters

walls

temple of Enki

500 m (150 yd)

and their success depended on how well this knowledge was put to practical use.

In southern Mesopotamia the soil was less favourable to agriculture. Since it originated in what was fairly brackish marshland, it had a high salt content (see photograph p 70). In a region like this the abundant water supply was useful for plant growth, but if the water was allowed to evaporate or sink into the ground, the salt concentration would gradually build up. This in turn tended to cause aridity. The waters of the Tigris and Euphrates were full of fertilizing substances, but not humus. This was because of the shape of the river bed and its very winding course, especially in the mountainous regions.

So there was none of the constant renewal of the soil which took place in the valley of the Nile. The most successful settlements were small agricultural villages which possessed domesticated animals whose excrement could be used as manure. There was also a great problem with flooding which often had a devastating effect. It was in these regions that the story of the 'universal flood', recounted in the Bible and elsewhere, first appeared, and excavation of ancient settlements has revealed traces of large-scale deposits of material carried and left behind by flooding rivers.

The people of el Ubaid had attempted to tame their rivers by using dykes, canals and land reclamation. But we know that only when the 'new peoples' arrived on the scene were these attempts really successful. It seems that these people had particular technical and organizational skills and were able to apply them to the two rivers. Why was this, and where was it that they came from?

We have no definite answer to the second question, though there are various hypotheses which can be put forward. They came from the north, and knew the upper reaches of the rivers. They knew when they could expect heavy flows of water caused by melting snows, and also when they could expect low rain or snowfall which would lead to water shortages in the valleys. Their language had no native words to describe working on the land or different types of crops, so they had to borrow foreign words from peasants with whom they came into contact. For example *engar*, meaning peasant, and *ishbar*, meaning weaver, are both words which do not fit into the normal structure of the Sumerian language.

The Sumerians had a mania for constructing buildings shaped like artificial hills. It was here that they placed their temples, houses for their gods. So perhaps we can assume that their gods were, or had been, mountain-dwellers.

What conclusions can we draw from this? Probably the newcomers were nomadic and possessed a great deal of knowledge and inventiveness. Possibly they came from Central Asia, crossing the mountains of Armenia or the high plains of Iran and the Zagros mountains. They were skilled traders and were used to dealing both in raw materials and in ideas.

Whatever the origins of the Sumerians, it was only in lower Mesopotamia that a Sumerian civilization was able to flourish.

Speaking and writing

Writing is one of the great unifying forces of humanity. But it is possible that it is not an essential ingredient of a high quality of life or a certain level of cultural attainment. We have already seen that some of the greatest cultures of ancient Europe were illiterate and did not produce written records.

As far as we are concerned, we have a centuries-long tradition of the written word; it is difficult to imagine a world without writing. Writing is part of the way in which we have become what we are today. But we cannot ignore the fact that even today, writing is not the privilege of everyone.

According to Denise Schmandt-Besserat, a French researcher who has applied herself to the problem for

Opposite: Artist's impression of the building of the inner hall in the White Temple of Uruk. Some of its columns have been reconstructed in the Berlin State Museums. Uruk was first excavated by German archaeologists in 1912. The temple was built between 3200 and 3100 BC on the remains of previous sacred buildings (this was because it was holy ground and could not be used for any other purpose). Its shape was similar to those of earlier sanctuaries such as the temple of Eridu shown on p 89. The building was made of sun-baked clay bricks. There were steep flights of stairs up the outside of the base of the building as well as inside it. The wall and column decorations of cone-shaped clay tiles in various colours are particularly interesting. These cones were embedded in mortar so that only their bases could be seen, with the result that the decoration consisted of thousands of little circles arranged mosaic-fashion in geometric patterns. The temple of Uruk (known as the White Temple because it was whitewashed) was probably dedicated to Anu, god of the heavens. The pyramid-shaped base which characterized Mesopotamian temples is known as a ziggurat, and was usually more impressive than the temple itself. That of Uruk was over 12 metres (40 feet) high.

several years, the elaborate writing system of the Sumerians, developed over several centuries, derived from an ancient system of symbolic representation connected with trade.

Traders have always had the problem of proving and guaranteeing to customers that all the goods in a particular consignment have actually been delivered. It is not particularly pleasant for the person sending goods to be told by the person receiving them (or by the transporter or anyone else) that he has given short weight. So an information system grew up between supplier and customer which helped prevent deception.

Traders made a series of tokens roughly similar in shape to the goods being sent. They would then place these tokens in a clay vase and seal it up. On the outside, while the clay was still wet, they would inscribe a few signs repeating in diagrammatic form what was actually on the tokens inside; other signs showed the number of tokens. Today we might call this a consignment note.

The recipient would break open the vase (which archaeologists call by its Latin name of *bulla*) and check that the signs on the outside corresponded to the tokens inside, and then that these signs agreed with the goods themselves.

The fact that we have found large numbers of tokens at various sites, as well as some still unbroken *bullae* where the signs correspond to the contents, strongly supports Schmandt-Besserat's theory.

The signs scratched on the surviving *bullae* are quite abstract, rather than being accurate representations of the goods, and are not dissimilar to the cuneiform characters of classical Sumerian writing. It therefore seems likely that the signs scratched on the clay tokens are a half-way stage between actual drawings of objects on the one hand, and writing on the other.

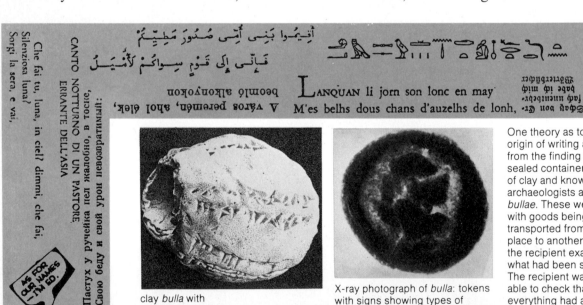

clay *bulla* with cuneiform symbols

X-ray photograph of *bulla*: tokens with signs showing types of goods are visible

One theory as to the origin of writing arose from the finding of small sealed containers made of clay and known to archaeologists as *bullae*. These were sent with goods being transported from one place to another to tell the recipient exactly what had been sent. The recipient was then able to check that everything had arrived.

Right and below: The invention of writing divided mankind into those who could read and write and those who could not. Writing quickly became an essential feature of a water-dependent society and the control of its water resources. Writing is still crucial in controlling modern resources such as electric power.

Bottom: Different examples of written languages, both ancient and modern, and an explanation of the way in which they may have developed.

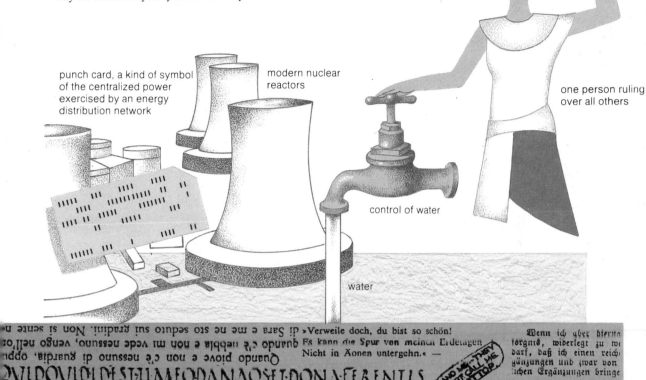

crown: a symbol of power

one person ruling over all others

punch card, a kind of symbol of the centralized power exercised by an energy distribution network

modern nuclear reactors

control of water

water

Bullae contained small tokens which resembled or suggested the shapes of the goods being sold. Symbols were stamped on to the outside of the *bullae* which corresponded with the tokens and therefore the merchandise. Later these symbols may have been simplified to become the wedge-shaped writing engraved on stone with a chisel and known as cuneiform.

how two tokens may have become pictographic symbols and then cuneiform writing

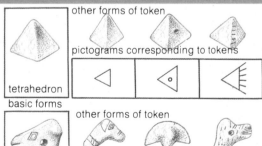

other forms of token

pictograms corresponding to tokens

tetrahedron
basic forms

other forms of token

pictograms corresponding to tokens

animal's head

dog

bull

lion

In fact, tablets bearing pictograms (as the first simple diagrammatic representations are called), *bullae* signs and cuneiform characters have been found on some Sumerian sites. Thus it seems reasonable to assume that writing developed from pictograms via *bullae* signs.

Checking and recording

Given that *bullae* were pictographic tablets, we must realize that the need to check, guarantee and verify goods meant that merchants also had to record the quality and quantity of the goods being sold.

In a large-scale productive society (where a river had been made to work for man, for example) writing became a very basic need. Recording the surpluses received from each individual, giving facts about events such as over or under-production of a crop, and co-ordinating work (such as calculating how many people were needed to carry out a certain task) were some of the duties of someone with the ability to write. So people who were literate, the scribes, were very important, a major cog in the wheel of society.

Of course, though it arose from these very practical needs, writing soon became used for other forms of communication such as inscriptions, dedications, hymns to the gods, poems and simple letters. Today we can sit back and admire these products of a culture, but we must not forget that the written word was, and still is, an instrument of power.

Turn to pp 120–133 and pp 264–272 for later developments in Mesopotamia.

Below: Fourth millennium BC tablet from the Mesopotamian city of Kish bearing the oldest known example of pictograms (pictorial signs or symbols). Another theory about the origin of cuneiform writing suggests that it may have derived directly from ancient pictograms, without the intermediate stage represented by *bullae*.
Bottom: Tablet used about 2600 BC for writing exercises, with some obvious 'spelling mistakes'; it was probably used in a school for Sumerian scribes.

the symbol for king is wrongly written and incomplete. It should look like this

the sign for dust has been turned on its side: it should be written like this

Urnanshe, King of Lagash, son of Gunidu, dedicated [this inscription] to Ninghirsu when he built the temple of Nanshe [a goddess], he built the *igbal*, the *kinir*, the *baga*, the *edam*, he built the temple of Gatundung [another goddess], he built the *tirash*.

Urnanshe, King of Lagash, son of Gunidu, built this temple of Ninghirsu.

Dedications in Sumerian: The words in italics refer to parts of the temple.

Top: Two Sumerian stone seals (right) and their imprints (left). They include the bulls with human heads characteristic of Mesopotamian art.
Above: Two of the oldest known Sumerian texts. Written in cuneiform characters, they are dedications to holy buildings by Urnanshe, King of Lagash (pp 120–7). One is simply the bare bones of a dedication; the other mentions various parts (naves, altars, etc) of a temple. According to a Sumerian legend, writing was invented by Enmerkar, lord of Uruk, when he had to send the king of another city-state a long message which none of his messengers was able to commit to memory.

Civilization of the Indus Valley

There are many problems connected with the study of the birth and development of civilizations.

Let us transport ourselves to the area between south-east Iran, Afghanistan and the Indian sub-continent. In this region, from the middle of the third millennium BC onwards, the Indus Valley civilization grew up. This civilization is younger than those of either Egypt or Sumer. Is it therefore possible that it derived from these older civilizations?

The way the main centres of this society were organized shows that people were aware of, and responded to, the environment in which they found themselves. We will see this on p 144

and after. It is also clear that there were similarities with the organizational structure of Mesopotamia. There is evidence of intensive commercial activity between the Indus Valley and Mesopotamia via the major port of Tilmun on the island of Bahrein in the Persian Gulf. Experts in the past have favoured the theory that one derived from the other, though the great English archaeologist Sir Mortimer Wheeler advised against considering the Indus civilization as a 'Western colony'.

Above: Grey pottery bowl with black painted decorations, from about 3500 BC. This is from Mehrgarh, a site on the Pakistani river Bolan, one of the irregularly flowing rivers running from the mountains of Baluchistan into the Indus Valley.
Left: Two earthenware statuettes (12 centimetres, or 5 inches high) from about 3500 BC, also found in Mehrgarh. The man is wearing a turban and the woman has an elaborate hairstyle and a breastplate.

Left: Vase with a geometrical pattern from Mehrgarh about 3500 BC. This site was inhabited for a very long time; the various cultures were forebears of the Indus Valley civilization (pp 145–9).

Below: On sites such as Mehrgarh, the remains of animal bones from the seventh to the fifth millennia BC clearly show the transition in the Indus Valley from a hunting economy to one based on rearing animals. The blue bars represent the percentage of wild animals hunted and the yellow bars represent the percentage of domestic animals or their wild ancestors used by these peoples.

Today we know that the Indus civilization, like other great river peoples, developed after a thriving Neolithic phase. Settlements like that of Mehrgarh on the Bolan River, inhabited between about 6000 and 2600 BC, show that an economy of agriculturalists and hunters gradually turned into one of agriculturalists and animal herders, and a village turned into a town with buildings made of mud bricks. So it was here that the Indus valley civilization grew up; we should not be misled into thinking that it did so because another civilization first sowed the seed.

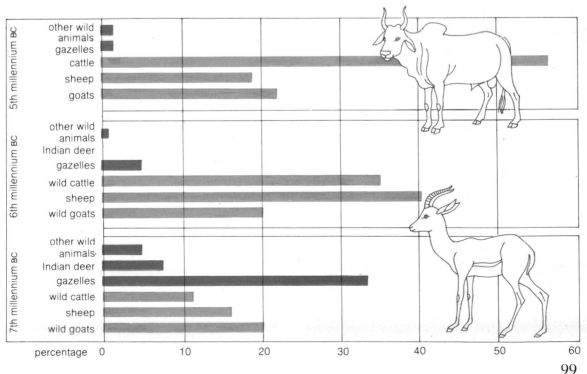

The Far East – A Great Saga

In China, there is an almost unbroken line of evidence for the archaeologist. This begins with the remains of fire places and rough-cut stones from the Lower Palaeolithic period about half a million years ago (the period of 'Peking Man', a variety of *Homo erectus*). It passes through the Upper Palaeolithic (the period about 30,000 years ago of the Ordos culture, which was situated on a huge semi-desert plateau encircled by a giant loop in the Yellow River) to the Megalithic cultures of the coast with sites along the Yellow River and in Korea and Taiwan.

Some Neolithic sites, about 6,000 years old, have been found on the loess-strewn plateaux dotted along the Yellow River. One of the best examples is the Yang-shao culture. Here the economy was based on hunting and fishing, but agriculture was also practised on a semi-nomadic basis. The fertile soil was fairly soon washed away by the waters of the river, thus forcing the cultivators to find new land. This system may seem odd because we tend to associate agriculture with staying put in one place, but in fact these people were itinerant hunters.

Yang-shao ceramics are characterized by certain shapes and decorations. Particularly notable are the vases with three legs which resemble cows' udders. The villages were comparatively large and seem to have been inhabited for longer than those of the Lung-shan culture which followed it. Probably there was a certain amount of co-operation between the various centres of population, both in controlling the waters and also in trading, during this Late Neolithic phase.

About 1700 or 1600 BC the first bronze artefacts were made; already they were quite elaborately crafted. The Shang civilization was born, with Cheng-chou

Above: Two earthenware vases from late Neolithic China (the Lung-shan culture of the later half of the second millennium BC). The three-legged shape has been frequently found and is also used in bronze artefacts. These vases were made on a potter's wheel and are very fine (sometimes only three millimetres ($\frac{1}{8}$ inch) thick). The oldest bronze objects in China appeared around 1700 to 1600 BC.
Opposite above: One of the mainstays of the ancient Chinese economy was the rearing of silkworms to produce silk thread. An indication of how highly they valued silk is given by the fact that the Chinese believed a goddess had invented it. China traded with many areas of the Near and Middle East from very early in its history; it is likely that silk, at first confined to people of very high rank (ordinary people wore woollen clothes or animal skins), became one of the main products traded by merchants. Rice, hemp and corn were also important to the ancient Chinese economy. Similarly, the Phoenicians believed that their major product for trade, purple-dyed cloth, had been discovered by a god.
Opposite below: Vases in a tomb in the Neolithic burial ground at Banpo in China's Shensi province.

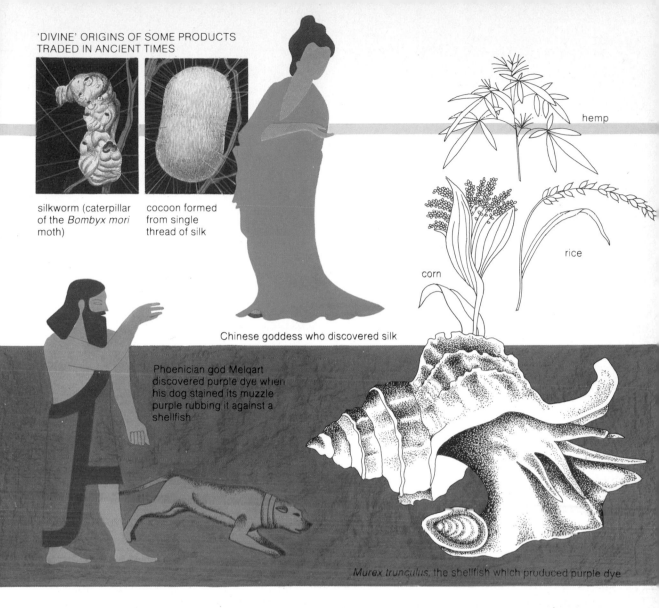

'DIVINE' ORIGINS OF SOME PRODUCTS TRADED IN ANCIENT TIMES

silkworm (caterpillar of the *Bombyx mori* moth)

cocoon formed from single thread of silk

Chinese goddess who discovered silk

hemp

corn

rice

Phoenician god Melqart discovered purple dye when his dog stained its muzzle purple rubbing it against a shellfish

Murex trunculus, the shellfish which produced purple dye

and An-yang as its capitals, and there were probably others as yet un-excavated.

Chinese chronology also mentions an older civilization, the Hsia, but no large-scale archaeological evidence has been found. This was probably a very late and highly evolved Neolithic culture.

The economy of the Shang civilization was based on the cultivation of two cereals – millet and barley. Hemp was also grown. The animals raised included poultry, pigs and also silkworms, cultivation of which goes back to prehistoric times.

Trading flourished (there may have been contact with sites in Turkestan such as Anau and, through them, with Mesopotamia and the Indus Valley), but actual evidence of this is again quite scarce.

During the Shang period the Chinese were already using a form of writing based on pictograms (see pp 222–5).

Japan

Let us move even further east in our search for an understanding of how civilizations begin.

The Japanese archipelago was peopled by groups of humans during the period when there were still land bridges between the various islands and the mainland, such as Korea and Sakhalin. At some sites (for example Iwayaku) Palaeolithic artefacts have been found, mostly simple almond-shaped tools made of stone or obsidian. The latter was a basic raw material in an area which had so many volcanoes.

There was then a Mesolithic phase, characterized by important strata of 'kitchen waste'; their rubbish heaps contain large amounts of shells and fish-bones. There are also large quantities of miniature flints. Finally, about 7,000 or 8,000 years ago, pottery appeared on the scene.

The Neolithic period lasted a very long time in Japan. The pottery of this

period is known as Jomon, which describes the rope-like technique of decoration obtained by applying long, thin, sausage-shaped pieces of clay to the vases. These were not made on a potter's wheel and often have square mouths. The statuettes are interesting, as some of them show a stylized version of the 'slant eyes' characteristic of orientals. The period of Jomon pottery lasted until between 500 and 300 BC, and throughout the period people adhered to an economy based on fishing, with some hunting. Since the environment did not compel them to make changes in their lifestyle, they did not do so. Not until the end of this period do polished stone scythes, pestles and hoes appear to indicate that an agricultural phase had begun.

Around 300 BC the Yayoi phase began when the use of bronze first became widespread, usually for making prestige objects such as religious artefacts. Also in this phase we see the first use of irrigation for growing rice and of terraces for planting it.

See pp 220–35 for subsequent developments in the civilizations of China and Japan.

Opposite (left and right): The inhabitants of the Japanese islands have depended on the sea from ancient times. An ancient Japanese legend says that a god fished Japan out of the sea. For an extremely long time the economy was based mainly on fishing (with some hunting) and was therefore Palaeolithic. Fishing is still one of the main sources of food, although nowadays advanced technology is used.

Pottery appeared over 7,000 years ago, though it did not lead to any changes in the economy. For many thousands of years Japan produced pre-Neolithic pottery. The first indications of agriculture did not appear until 500 BC. A few centuries later cultivation on hillside terraces began, using complex methods of irrigation which moved water from one level to another.

At any given point in Japan's history we can see a close correspondence between environmental features and systems of production. The sea, a major source of food, demanded that an efficient shipbuilding industry be created; the land, which is largely mountainous, gave rise to hill cultivation using terraces (this was particularly suitable for rice, since water could be drained away when it was no longer required).

Below: Two earthenware figures from the Japanese Neolithic period known as Jomon. These were probably idols or representations of gods. The word Jomon comes from a Japanese word meaning 'corded' which referred to the rope-like effect of the decoration on the vases. This was achieved by fixing sausage-shaped pieces of clay to the vases, often producing very elaborate patterns. Jomon vases were square and were therefore never made on a wheel

From the Asian Steppes to Europe

Almost every race believes its land to be the centre of the world. The Greeks were convinced it was at Delphi, where there was a stone known as the omphalos, the navel of the world. All Europeans, divided though they are into many nations, have a tendency to think of the world as being centred on Europe. But looking at the ancient civilizations it becomes evident that there is a great deal of truth in the assertion that Europe is but a minor appendage of Asia, hard though this may seem on Europeans.

The cultures of northern and central Europe are probably all the result of people coming from the east, from the considerably larger area of central Asia. Only a small part of Europe has its own truly indigenous cultures, namely the Mediterranean basin with its many islands and coastal areas.

Agriculture and the domestication of animals both spread into continental Europe from the Near East. Evidently, semi-nomadic peoples from the Near East arrived in Europe in search of new territories and bit by bit transferred these techniques to groups with Palaeolithic or Mesolithic cultures already there. We can follow the traces of this gradual expansion by picking up the pieces of pottery they left behind them. Considering that their likely departure date was the ninth millennium BC and that agriculture spread into the British Isles during the fifth millennium BC, it has been worked out that the average rate of expansion was about 1.5 kilometres (1 mile) per year.

The spread of pottery in Europe

One of the routes by which pottery making spread was along the River Danube and its surrounding area, where straight-banded ceramics (*Linearbandkeramik* in German) have been found. There is also clear evidence that it spread along the Mediterranean coast, particularly that of Italy. There were also important stopping-places on the islands (as evidenced by the dis-

1

2

Metals in Europe's Neolithic period

Those European cultures which practised agriculture and had a thriving pottery industry (in other words, were Neolithic) were often changed quite significantly by the advent of metal making. This spread quickly throughout Europe, not least because of trading. Some Neolithic cultures have interesting 'midway' features as they gradually started using metals to make ornaments and weapons. These cultures are referred to as Chalcolithic or Aeneolithic. They included, for example, the Seine-Oise-Marne group of cultures which inhabited an area bounded by three of the major rivers of northern France; in Italy there was the Gaudo culture at Paestum, near Salerno, the Remedello culture near Brescia, and the Rinaldone culture near Montefiascone in Viterbo. In very many European sites there were Chalcolithic cultures characterized by bell-shaped beakers. These were found at Stonehenge, for example. One of the first Bronze Age cultures of Central Europe was the Unetice. The site of that name is in Bohemia, but the culture extended into Austria, Bavaria, Hungary and Switzerland.

Opposite and below: The objects shown here cover an extremely long time-span. 1. Earthenware container from the Chassey culture, so called because of finds made on a site at Chassey-le-Champ, Saône-et-Loire in eastern France, where a very large fortified settlement was in existence during the Neolithic period and the early Iron Age. The Neolithic artefacts found at Chassey (the oldest dating to 3500 BC) are part of the remains of a huge group of cultures, which also included Italian and Swiss peoples, called the Chassey-Cortaillod-Lagozza group. Cortaillod is a site near Neuchâtel in Switzerland, and at Lagozza di Besnate near Varese in Italy, a settlement which was built on piles has been excavated. 2. Earthenware figurine from the Vinca culture near Belgrade, Yugoslavia, dating from the fifth millennium BC. 3. Second millennium BC amber horse from Scandinavia. 4. Spiral decorations on a stone wall in the megalithic passage grave at New Grange, 40 kilometres (25 miles) north of Dublin in Ireland. It was built about 3000 BC. 5. Earthenware figurine from the fourth millennium BC, found at Becej in north-eastern Yugoslavia.

3

4

5

covery of imprinted and painted ceramics).

There was also brisk trade to the north in obsidian from the southern volcanoes, and in the opposite direction in amber from the Baltic. The paths followed by this particular trade intersect at right angles those of pottery, which was passed from the east to the west and north-west.

One of the last waves of colonization took place even further south than all the previous ones. It was typified by settlements of long wooden huts (for example at Köln-Lindenthal in West Germany) which must have been used for a few seasons at a time and then abandoned. Vases made by these people typically had a funnel shape (in German, *Trichterbecher*).

In southern and central areas many local cultures developed which revealed important advances both technologically and aesthetically. Some Neolithic pottery, such as that of the Chassey-Cortaillod-Lagozza group of cultures, is beautifully shaped and decorated, and the 'square-mouthed vase' culture of northern Italy had a talent for design which can only be described as genius.

Sites in this area were inhabited for longer (particularly those on level ground) and villages are often found built on top of the remains of previous ones, with the result that they form small hills. Some of the fortified villages are particularly interesting because they can be regarded as the first 'towns' in continental Europe. The most important is Dimini, in Thessaly (Greece), whose walls are concentric and made of heaped stones not held together by mortar or mud. There is one main building with a large columned entrance which seems to have been a royal palace rather than a temple.

Neolithic European language

We have already spoken of the evidence provided by pottery, but the spread of civilization in ancient Europe can be followed using another type of evidence.

The people who came from the central Asian and Caucasian regions also imported the Indo-European languages, as we now call them. The term refers to the huge family of languages spoken in the Indian and European regions.

People have long wondered whether the Indo-Europeans were a single race. The great variety of material cultures,

which we see in the various styles of pottery, shows clearly that this was not one people, but many. It is likely, however, that they had a common origin far back in history and that contacts between the various groups were made easier because they had a common linguistic base.

The roots of some very common words such as 'father', 'mother', 'game', 'ten', and 'hundred' are fairly similar throughout all the Indo-European languages. We can easily show this by leafing through a dictionary. Words like *cent* (French) and *cento* (Italian) may seem a long way from 'hundred' (German *hundert*), but

Below: An earthenware vase, painted in several colours, which was found beside the main 'palace' of Dimini (early third millennium BC).
Bottom: Artist's impression of an attack on the walled village of Dimini, near Volos in Greece, 150 kilometres (95 miles) north-west of Athens. The walls of this third millenium BC village were made of limestone blocks without any mortar or other material to cement them together. In the centre of the village there was one building which was bigger than all the others and was possibly a public hall or royal palace.

royal palace   covered portico area

tops of walls were used as a narrow pathway

many gateways possibly protected by sliding grills

not so if we realize that they all derive from the Greek numeral *hekaton*. Likewise the links between 'mother', '*mère*', '*Mutter*' and '*madre*' are obvious; the links between 'foot', '*pied*', '*piede*' and '*Fuss*' come from the Greek '*pous*', but there is also an influence from the word '*fotus*' in medieval Gothic.

The economy of the first Neolithic peoples in Europe was based mainly on agriculture and partly on animal husbandry; fishing and hunting were also important. About 5,000 years ago, in the area which is now the Ukraine in the USSR, the horse was domesticated. This 'discovery' spread fairly quickly to Europe. East-to-west colonization began by way of fertile soils (loess), and also spread to the forests. The tech-

niques of cutting and burning meant that large areas of land were deforested to make way for more agricultural land, which was fertilized by the ashes of the burnt vegetation (see diagram pp 176–7).

Apart from stable settlements, the late Neolithic peoples of Europe built extraordinary structures called megaliths. These 'large stones' (see photograph pp 78–9) truly were built to last. The oldest of these monuments have been dated to before 4000 BC. Their building techniques grew more and more advanced and megaliths continued to be built for more than two thousand years, well into the Bronze and Iron Ages (pp 156–62).

Further developments in the cultures of Europe are related on pp 150–77.

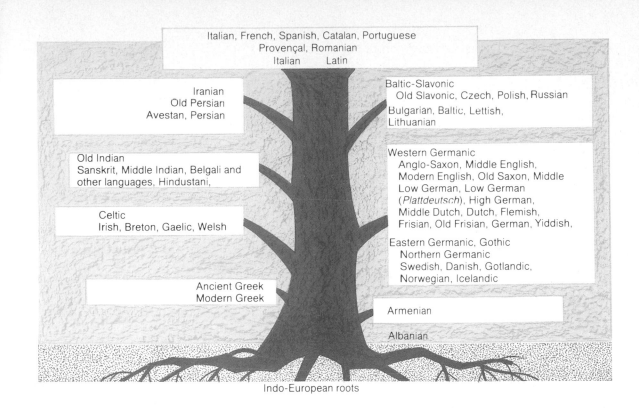

Italian, French, Spanish, Catalan, Portuguese
Provençal, Romanian
Italian   Latin

Iranian
Old Persian
Avestan, Persian

Baltic-Slavonic
Old Slavonic, Czech, Polish, Russian
Bulgarian, Baltic, Lettish,
Lithuanian

Old Indian
Sanskrit, Middle Indian, Belgali and
other languages, Hindustani,

Western Germanic
Anglo-Saxon, Middle English,
Modern English, Old Saxon, Middle
Low German, Low German
(*Plattdeutsch*), High German,
Middle Dutch, Dutch, Flemish,
Frisian, Old Frisian, German, Yiddish,

Celtic
Irish, Breton, Gaelic, Welsh

Eastern Germanic, Gothic
Northern Germanic
Swedish, Danish, Gotlandic,
Norwegian, Icelandic

Ancient Greek
Modern Greek

Armenian

Albanian

Indo-European roots

Living and dead Indo-European languages

Many Indo-European languages are extinct. The oldest known one of these is Hittite (see p 138). The Scythians (see p 245) probably also spoke an Indo-European language, but all that remains of it are a few proper nouns which appear in legends. Another interesting dead language is Tocharian, used in Turkestan (a vast region in central Asia east of the Caspian Sea) from the fifth to the tenth century BC. As a result of incursions by the Turks and Mongols, the people who spoke Tocharian dispersed and the language died out. Other dead languages worthy of mention are Phrygian, from north-western Turkey, and Luwian, spoken by an Anatolian people possibly related to the Hittites.

Above: The 'family tree' of Indo-European languages. Each branch is a group of similar languages often called a family. The tree omits two families of dead languages, Tocharian and Hittite.
Opposite far left: Earthenware statuette from Sesklo, which, like Dimini, is near Volos in Greece. It represents a mother-figure, perhaps a goddess, with a child. It is about 16 centimetres (6½ inches) and dates from the fifth or fourth millennium BC.
Left: An area near the Mediterranean coast of Lebanon. The cedar trees of this area were highly valued and widely traded from very early times.

109

4. Water-dependent Civilizations and Empires

The Egyptian Production System

In Egypt, a single system was chosen in order to govern this enormous land, which in turn made other new developments necessary. When we speak of Egypt, we really mean the land within reach of the waters of the Nile. It was necessary to send and record information, and this led to the introduction of writing (see p 94). Those who had the power to run the system efficiently had to be 'paid' from people's surplus, that is, anything they had left over after they had used what they needed. This quickly led to the rise of a 'managing class', and an army of tax collectors. All these people possessed the art of reading and writing. This organization became expensive to run, and the ordinary people learned the truth: what they had to hand over in order to keep the organization going was not a true surplus, but something they were forced to give. Though the great River Nile

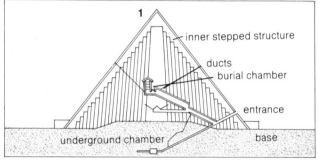

and the black earth worked for the good of all, the ordinary person was perhaps worse off, hungrier, and more worn out than the inhabitant of an 'old-fashioned' Neolithic (late Stone Age) village. But as we have seen, there was no other choice.

The god-king

The king was considered to be a god, and so required the goods and services of one and all, which would have been unthinkable in a simple village-type economy. These divine beings had to be eternal, they had to live forever, just as

Opposite far left: Statue of Khafre (or Chephren in Greek). He built the second pyramid of Giza about 2500 BC.
Below: 1. Section through the Great Pyramid of Khufu (or Cheops). 2. To make the enormous monuments stable, the blocks of stone had to be perfectly cut to size and fitted so that their weight forced them together. As the red line shows, this was done by making the horizontal line of the blocks slightly concave on each side of the pyramid. 3. When the pyramids were built, their measurements were made with rollers. Thus the height and base measurements were worked out in terms of the relation between the diameter and the circumference of a circle. For example the height was an exact number of times the diameter (d) of the roller. 4. The brilliant white limestone slabs on the surface of the pyramids fitted into their own 'slots' so that they did not press down on to one another.
Bottom: The Great Pyramids of Giza.

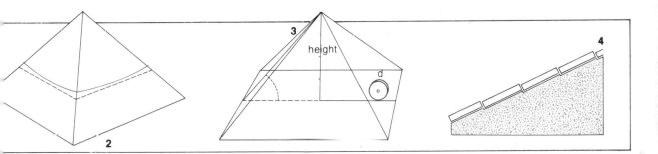

the gods lived forever. Their bodies should not decay after death. This gave rise to the practice of embalming, or treating dead bodies with ointments so that they kept a life-like appearance. This was at first reserved for the king and his immediate family alone. Their houses had to last forever and be incomparably magnificent, and of a size never seen before; they had to look like great works of nature (such as mountains), but more beautiful and god-like because they were planned.

The huge pyramids showed the enormous distance between the god-king and the ordinary person. Naturally, the palaces inhabited by the divine being during his 'real' life had to be splendid and eternal. The material for all these buildings could only be stone, which would last forever. Decoration was sometimes rich, but more often the sim-

ple beauty of pure form was preferred, as in the case of the few lines that outline a pyramid. Or else royal buildings imitated nature in a stylized way. This means that things were made to look more than natural; the columns were like the papyrus and lotus plants, but bigger and more regular than their living models.

So these impressive building works were the result of surplus produce, and above all the work that everyone was obliged to do for the god-king. They were also the result of brilliant management, and everyone admired them. This admiration may have been mixed with reverence and fear, but they certainly felt great pride. Suffering for a living god could even have seemed logical, and to a peasant it seemed to produce definite results.

According to the Egyptians, one of the ways of becoming eternal was to make sure that one's own name continued to be spoken, and was never forgotten. Therefore the kings in whose time the pyramids were built are eternal, because to this day their names have not been lost. According to the physicist and archaeologist Kurt Mendelssohn, the pyramids are not only tombs and monuments to the Egyptian kings. They are monuments to 'the ability to build them', to the 'ability to organize the work of thousands upon thousands of men'. The message of the rulers of those days to us is, 'This is what I have caused to be done!' They have every reason to boast.

Egyptian kings of the Old Kingdom, the First Intermediate Period, and the Middle Kingdom

Fourth dynasty (about 2620–2480 BC): Snofru, Khufu (Cheops), Dedefre, Khafre (Chephren), Menkaure (Mycerinus), Shepsekaf

Fifth dynasty (about 2480–2340 BC): various, Onnos (Unas)

Sixth dynasty (about 2340–2140 BC): various, Pepy II

Eighth to tenth dynasties: nomarchs of Memphis and Heracleopolis

Eleventh dynasty (about 2134–1991 BC): the three Antefs, the three Mentuhoteps

Twelfth dynasty (about 1991–1786 BC): Amenemhat I, others including the three called Sesostris

---

These are the words:
Your heart is your own, O Osiris!
Your feet are your own, O Osiris!
Your arms are your own, O Osiris!

The Heart of Onnos is his own,
The feet of Onnos are his own,
The arms of Onnos are his own,
A stairway to heaven is prepared for him,
   and on it he ascends to heaven.
He rises on a great cloud of incense.
Onnos flies like a bird,
and sits like a scarab
on the empty throne in your ship, O Ra.

Text from the pyramids

Opposite: Egyptian statue of an unknown scribe of the fifth dynasty (about 2480–2340 BC). It is made of painted limestone with inset eyes. The scribe rested a tablet on his knees and unrolled a sheet of papyrus (paper-like material made from reeds) on which to write.

Bottom left: The tomb of Onnos (Unas), the last king of the fifth dynasty. The walls are completely covered with writing. During this period the Egyptian language was written using various signs; these could be ideographic (representing an object or an idea), syllabic (representing a sound), or polysyllabic (representing more than one sound).

Below: Wooden statue of the fifth dynasty dignitary, Kaaper.

Classes of Egyptian society

Egypt was united in order to be a great machine of production, and so needed bureaucrats, or organizing officials, to run it. This they did through writing, accounting, and notetaking. Among the class of bureaucrats were individuals who were nearer to the god-king at the palace. These were viziers, supervisors and courtiers who were princes and nobles.

The class of priests was extremely important. And there were also generals and professional soldiers, a military class. Because Egypt lacked many raw materials, such as minerals, it had to import them. To make sure of a constant flow of imports, it was sometimes necessary to use force, or threaten to do so. An empire that is not completely self-sufficient must fight wars, some of course to defend itself from attackers, but also wars of conquest. When it was necessary, the ranks of the army were filled by the peasants, who were forced to serve as soldiers.

Then there were intermediate ('middle') classes: merchants, whose business often involved fulfilling the orders of the managing class; artisans, including the artists who turned out the many images of the god-king and other gods, and the fine and elegant decorations. We also have the artists to thank for the images that tell us about the lives of ordinary people. These include statuettes, bas-reliefs (pictures cut from a flat stone surface) and paintings.

There was also what might be called an intellectual class. These were people who could read and write and might have been in contact with higher levels of society; some of these writers are very interesting to read. These were not the ones who composed official praises of the ruler, or hymns to the various gods. Instead they described what they saw in words that were extremely 'modern' in feeling; they sang the

114

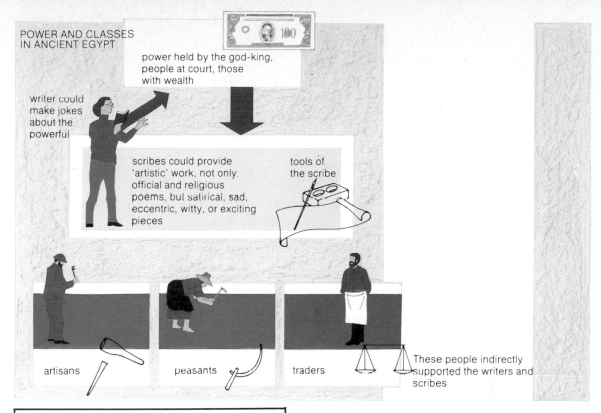

power held by the god-king,
people at court, those
with wealth

writer could
make jokes
about the
powerful

scribes could provide
'artistic' work, not only
official and religious
poems, but satirical, sad,
eccentric, witty, or exciting
pieces

tools of
the scribe

artisans

peasants

traders

These people indirectly
supported the writers and
scribes

The generations perish and pass away,
others take their place, as they did in the time of
    our ancestors:
others who were once kings / rest in their
    pyramids,
they are buried in their tombs, / the nobles and
    the glorious alike.
No one returns from there / to tell us of their
    state,
and of their needs and desires, / to set our hearts
    at rest.
We must wait till it is our turn / to go where they
    have gone.
Think on this:
live for the day's happiness
and do not tire of it.
Behold: there is no one who takes his
    possessions with him;
and no one returns from the place where they
    have gone.

From *The Song of King Antef's Harpist*
(a text from the Middle Kingdom)

Opposite: The ordinary people of Ancient Egypt;
these are statuettes placed in tombs to 'work' for
the dead. They were found at Saqqara and date
from the fifth dynasty. *Above*: a slave washing a
jar. *Middle*: a woman grinding wheat. *Below*: a
man filtering a fermented mixture to make beer.
Right: Relief from fifth-dynasty Saqqara showing
harpist and singers. The gestures indicate a kind of
musical notation. Below are dancers.

115

praises of life, and described the fear of death. In some cases their way of expressing themselves can be seen to have been influenced by a sort of 'fashion'. To be sad might have been a fashion, or to complain about everything might have been another. Things are much the same today in certain intellectual circles.

Finally there were the masses, the most numerous class, who in fact supported all the rest. The Egyptian people for the most part consisted of those who were tied to the black earth: the peasants and herdsmen. When necessary, these people were employed as labourers in the great building works, along with prisoners captured in wars with neighbours. As we have said, they could also be made to serve as soldiers. Egypt was made what it was by these ordinary people.

Civilization breaks down

After more than eight centuries, in about 2200 BC, the Egyptian 'machine' broke down. The masses rose against the central power. This was a revolution. There were massacres and destruction and the descriptions of the downfall of the 'Old Kingdom' of Egypt are full of detail. However, it does not seem likely that this uprising really sprang from among the peasants themselves. As has happened on other occasions since, the masses played into the hands of others, and were used for these people's purposes. Many bureaucrats, who had become powerful as local lords, must have thought that the time had come to overthrow the central power. So why not take advantage of

Left: The end of the Old Kingdom in Egypt was marked by a red revolution. The common people sacked the imperial palaces and destroyed tombs, statues and monuments. However, the bureaucrats (nomarchs) of the various provinces took advantage of the revolt to make themselves into local lords. It was they who benefited most from the revolution.

117

the people's discontent, or even directly provoke it? The next step would have been to point out the 'palace people', the court at Memphis, as the cause of all their troubles. The old king Pepy II (or Phiops II), perhaps more than 90 at the time, witnessed the revolution and the end of an age. He was the last god-king.

The rise of the Middle Kingdom

For about 150 years after the revolution, there were kings without real authority. The capital was shifted from one place to another, and the only truly powerful people were the nomarchs, the governors of the nomes, the administrative regions into which the country was divided. There was frequent fighting among the various regions, and frequent famines. The Nile's 'system' could no longer work without some form of central government. There were also invasions by people from Libya and the countries north-east of the delta. Finally, in the confusion of this phase (usually called the first intermediary period), the nomarchs of Thebes, a city in Upper Egypt, imposed their rule.

Below: A typical view of the banks of the Nile. Transport between villages is often by cart.
Opposite above: Group of statuettes dating from the 11th dynasty. They show cattle being counted for a census. The scribes doing the counting are on the sheltered platform.
Opposite below: Statue of the 12th-dynasty king Sesostris I wearing the crown of Upper Egypt.

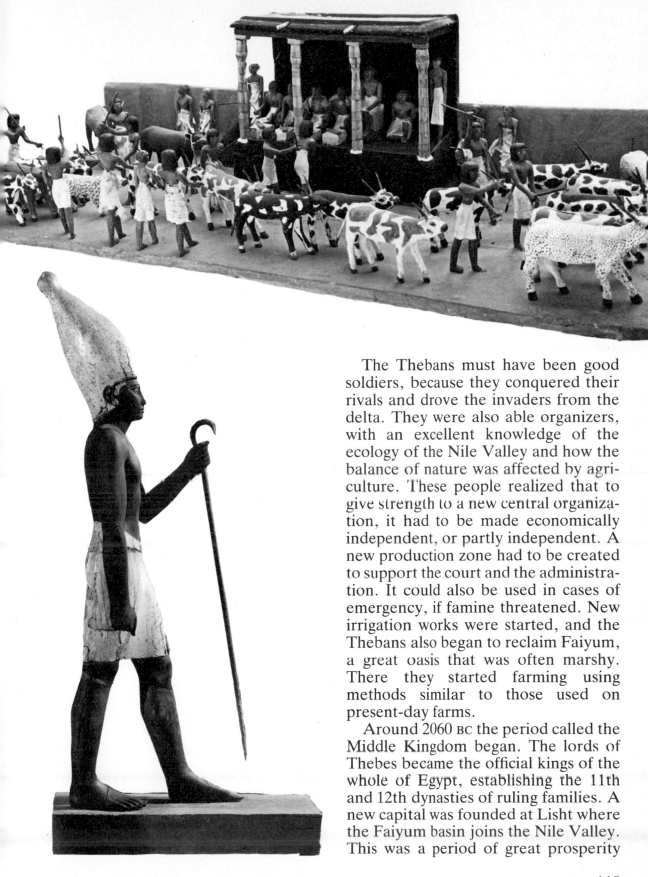

The Thebans must have been good soldiers, because they conquered their rivals and drove the invaders from the delta. They were also able organizers, with an excellent knowledge of the ecology of the Nile Valley and how the balance of nature was affected by agriculture. These people realized that to give strength to a new central organization, it had to be made economically independent, or partly independent. A new production zone had to be created to support the court and the administration. It could also be used in cases of emergency, if famine threatened. New irrigation works were started, and the Thebans also began to reclaim Faiyum, a great oasis that was often marshy. There they started farming using methods similar to those used on present-day farms.

Around 2060 BC the period called the Middle Kingdom began. The lords of Thebes became the official kings of the whole of Egypt, establishing the 11th and 12th dynasties of ruling families. A new capital was founded at Lisht where the Faiyum basin joins the Nile Valley. This was a period of great prosperity which produced many splendid works of art. The 'divine' nature of the ruler was not questioned, but it was felt to be less important. Mummification and elaborate tombs were no longer for the king alone; courtiers and officials could also have these things for themselves. They were not only a sign of a person's importance, but were thought to ensure immortality. Along with these developments went an increase in the power of the priests.

Outstanding characters of the Middle Kingdom were Sesostris I (about 1971 to 1928 BC), an able general who led a victorious expedition against Libya, and succeeded in crushing a new outbreak of civil war. Another was Sesostris III (about 1878 to 1843 BC), often called 'Egypt's greatest warrior', who conquered Nubia in the south and also Palestine, thus ensuring his own fame and the power of his dynasty.

See pp 248–64 for an account of Ancient Egypt's New Kingdom.

Comparisons – Egypt and Mesopotamia

The events in the history of Egypt that we have just described make certain things clear: without a system to organize centrally the great communal work of producing food, there could only be hunger, civil war and destruction in the Nile Valley. When things were running well, enormous extra efforts were demanded for elegant and showy palaces and huge monuments. These periods of prosperity were full of the signs of a civilization rich in inspiration and imagination; they produced the most beautiful statues, paintings, and ornamental objects; they produced poetry, chronicles, hymns, memoirs (people's recorded memories), educational works, and even novels and illustrated humorous stories.

Things were different in Mesopotamia. At first, the Sumerians did not build a vast empire. The geography of the territory was more varied than that of Egypt, with different advantages and disadvantages. It was ruled from various centres, which were 'city-states'. In all of these centres, however, we find the same structure that we have seen in Egypt. A palace (that is, a place that served as a royal house), a temple, a warehouse, and a centre of administration were at the centre of the city. Around the city were the working areas and the houses of ordinary

Right: Impression of a typical Mesopotamian ziggurat. This is partly based on structures excavated by Sir Leonard Woolley at Ur. These tower-like structures were built to be visible from far away. In a country of flat plains, they looked like man-made hills. Perhaps this is evidence that the people who built them originated in mountainous areas, where peaks were thought to be the homes of the gods. They formed monumental foundations for temples placed on top of them.

The ziggurats were made of sun-baked clay bricks covered with bitumen to make them weatherproof. In some cases, the walls of the ziggurats may have been decorated with bricks glazed in various colours. This type of decoration was found in certain buildings in the last Babylonian period. Inset opposite: The ziggurat of Ur, built during the city's third dynasty. Parts of the walls and staircases have been rebuilt, using the original bricks as a result of Sir Leonard Woolley's excavations.

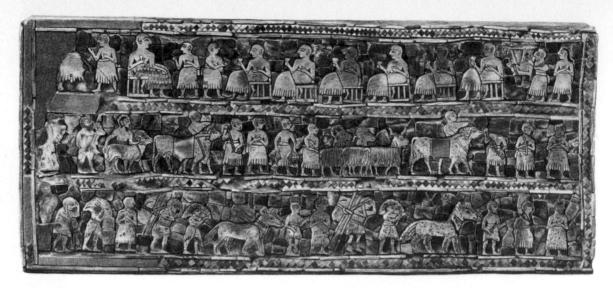

people, made of mud. Further away were the fields, farms, and the few areas where hunting and fishing were possible. There were also harbours and roads.

The king, who controlled everything, was different from the Egyptian god-king. The difference lay in the way people looked at him. In Egypt, the god-king, to exert authority over the great complex, had to be 'most high' or actually divine. In Mesopotamia, the king could remain human, as the territory he ruled was smaller. He acted in the name of the local god, and as an interpreter of the god's will. Through the king, the god transmitted his commandments, which were obviously aimed at making his own land and people 'work' in the best possible way.

Between the ruler and the masses there were various bureaucrats, technicians, priests, and soldiers, as well as artisans and artists. The latter were closely connected with the palace, and their work was produced for it.

Within the different levels of this society, there were people who stood out from the others in being able to read and write: accountants and poets, agricultural experts and historians, even leaders of literary styles, and others like the author of the Harpist's Song (p 115).

Definitions

A useful way of looking at all these factors is that of the German historian Karl A Wittfogel who worked out his ideas in the 1930s, and drew upon the works of previous historians and economists. The inspiration for many studies of societies were the theories put forward by Karl Marx (1818–1883) in the last century. Marx described societies and production methods of what he called an 'Asiatic' type, because of their geographical position. Wittfogel elaborated on this by including within this type 'hydraulic civilizations' and 'empires', because the basic element in these systems was the use and control of the water of a river ('hydro-' comes from the Greek for water). Some of Wittfogel's ideas associated with this definition have been criticized. However, the basic definition remains useful for those who want to understand how ancient civilizations developed and worked, and not just simply admire the pyramids, temples, colossal statues, stepped towers, and great walls.

Hydraulic civilizations developed in areas where rain was scarce, and the water of a river was available. It had to be possible to move the water to the land in order to farm it. In regions

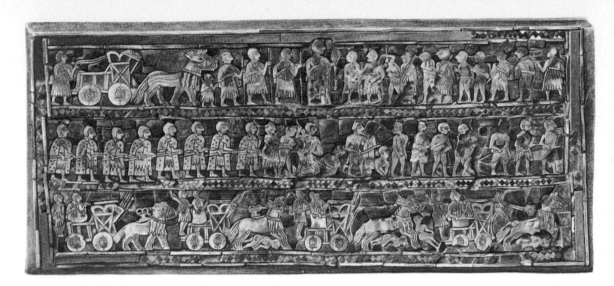

Opposite and above: The two parts of the so-called royal standard of Ur, dating from around 2700 BC. They are probably the two sides of the sound box of a harp, and are decorated with lapis lazuli and pieces of shell. One side (above) illustrates, from top to bottom, prisoners being presented to a king; an infantry battle, and charging war-chariots with solid wheels, pulled by onagers. The other side (opposite) shows, from top to bottom, a feast in honour of the victor; a procession of animals, perhaps for sacrifice, and spoil from a victorious battle being carried away.

Right: Reconstruction of the stele of Ur-Nammu, king of Ur and founder of the Third Dynasty. A stele was an upright stone which bore inscriptions or pictures. The fragment on which the reconstruction is based has been coloured. The original was slightly more than 3 metres (10 feet) in height and 1.5 metres (5 feet) wide. The king can be seen in the coloured fragment, pouring drink offerings before the throne of a god who is holding the 'stick and circle', thought to be symbols of justice. The stele, dating from 2100 BC, commemorates the consecration of a temple founded by Ur-Nammu.

where there was little rainfall, this was the only way. It was done by means of great 'productive installations' (canals, reservoirs and dykes, all structures necessary for irrigation). As rivers could cause great damage by flooding, 'protective installations' (dams to control water level, channels for excess water to escape) were also necessary to prevent disasters.

The complex was fairly large, and may have become very productive, especially compared with neighbouring

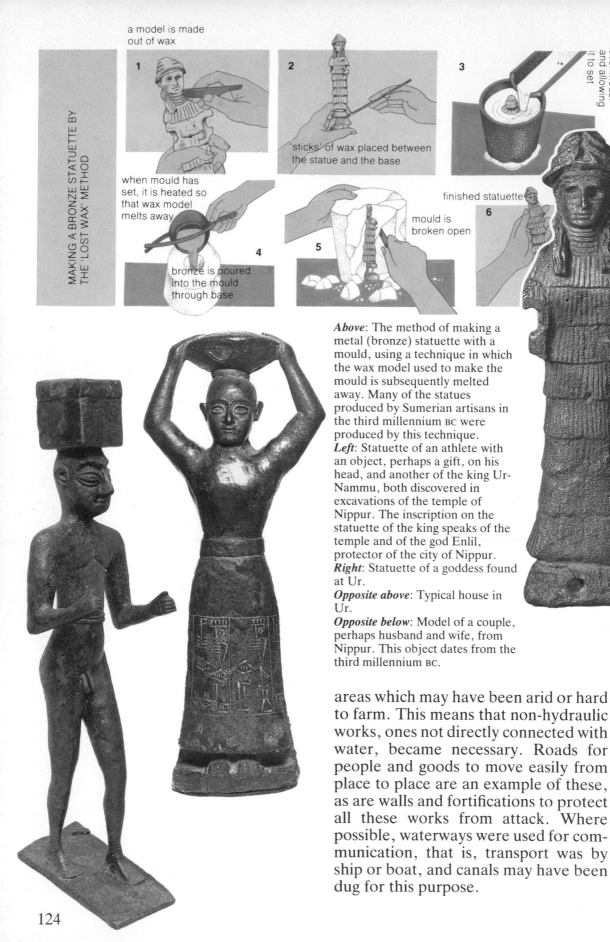

a model is made out of wax

1

2 'sticks' of wax placed between the statue and the base

3 mould is made by pouring clay or plaster over model and allowing it to set

when mould has set, it is heated so that wax model melts away

4 bronze is poured into the mould through base

5 mould is broken open

6 finished statuette

Above: The method of making a metal (bronze) statuette with a mould, using a technique in which the wax model used to make the mould is subsequently melted away. Many of the statues produced by Sumerian artisans in the third millennium BC were produced by this technique.

Left: Statuette of an athlete with an object, perhaps a gift, on his head, and another of the king Ur-Nammu, both discovered in excavations of the temple of Nippur. The inscription on the statuette of the king speaks of the temple and of the god Enlil, protector of the city of Nippur.

Right: Statuette of a goddess found at Ur.

Opposite above: Typical house in Ur.

Opposite below: Model of a couple, perhaps husband and wife, from Nippur. This object dates from the third millennium BC.

areas which may have been arid or hard to farm. This means that non-hydraulic works, ones not directly connected with water, became necessary. Roads for people and goods to move easily from place to place are an example of these, as are walls and fortifications to protect all these works from attack. Where possible, waterways were used for communication, that is, transport was by ship or boat, and canals may have been dug for this purpose.

These great complexes were managed by a whole variety of people, depending on the civilization concerned. However, in everything to do with management an effort was made to concentrate as much power as possible in the hands of one person, or of very few (such as priest-kings or general-kings). Building works were necessary to provide houses for the staff of managers. These buildings were a sign of power, but also, because of their comfort and beauty, they encouraged the officials to work hard to support whoever was in power. Other extra water-related works such as canals and

aqueducts might have been built to supply great houses and palaces with drinking water, and drainage systems created for removing waste.

Architecture in these civilizations tended to be 'monumental', that is, impressive and built to last. It consisted of huge stone buildings, symbols of the greatness of the rulers, with simple lines which were easy even for ordinary people to comprehend. The pyramids are a fine example of this. In Egypt, there are the tombs of the god-kings. In Mesopotamia we find vast foundations on which temples (houses of the gods, and also warehouses) were placed. In South America, as we shall see, pyramids took the form of monumental staircases leading to temples and holy places.

Concentration of power caused what Wittfogel calls hydraulic civilizations to become despotic empires (a despot is a ruler with total power). As these empires arose in various parts of the East the term 'oriental despotism' is sometimes used. The whole economy depended on primary production, that is, the production of food. There were

counters   four-sided dice

O King! Roaring wild bull!
You slay the tongue of wickedness and enmity,
You silence the raging tempest by sprinkling
the water of health!
The ordering of everything is in your hands . . .

From the *Hymn of Ninghishzida* (perhaps a
messenger god like the Greek god Mercury), a
sacred composition for recital, perhaps by more
than one voice, from the Third Dynasty of Ur.

Opposite left: Statue of a singer.
Opposite right: Bas-relief of a lute player.
Below: The famous 'chess set' found at Ur,
complete with counters and dice. These objects
date from the third and early second millennium BC.
The discovery of a similar but more recent object
(see pp 66–7) gave some ideas about the game
played on the 'chess set'. The shape, in relief, of a
snake runs over the later board, touching with its
coils the different angles of the squares in a
sequence based on complex mathematical rules. In
ancient Mesopotamia mathematics and geometry
had many practical applications; why should they
not also have been part of a fascinating game with
difficult rules?

counters

not as many new technical ideas as one
might expect given the large number of
artisans. Not many new ideas were
spread through trade. It has, in fact,
been said that the great water-
dependent empires were nothing but
'hypertrophied Neolithic civilizations,'
that is to say, over-developed Late
Stone Age cultures. Their metallurgists
worked in gold and copper, but the
working of bronze and iron came comparatively late. Also, the use of these
metals in the making of tools such as
sickles, hoes, and ploughs, was very
slow to spread.

Cities and Civilization

The word 'civilization' comes from the
Latin word *civis*, meaning citizen. The
city was a typical and essential feature in
all water-dependent empires; it was not
only the centre of power and organization but of culture and religion as well.
What the city was like depended on its
environment (climate, geographical
position, etc); but there were always
temples and palaces, with nearby an
area that could be called a 'city of the
dead', or necropolis, to use a word from
Greek. The great number of people
crowded together in such a city created
various problems: overcrowding
brought with it the danger of disease
and epidemics. This made technical
solutions necessary: aqueducts and
drainage systems (already mentioned)
had to be built on a large scale, and
there also had to be a system for planning streets and buildings. Many of the
living-places were small and close
together, like those of the workers and
artisans, and formed real human
anthills. Shops and workshops sprang
up next door to the dwellings. All in all,
the way the city was planned and built
made it very clear that its society was
divided into classes.

Languages and Writing

We know that writing was a most important factor in organizing water-dependent empires. For those who study the evidence of ancient remains, every piece of writing has a double value. Firstly, it tells us its message. For example, 'King so-and-so conquered such and such a city or founded such and such a temple'. Secondly, it also tells us something of the history of the language itself, how it developed. We not only look at what is said, but at how it is said. For example, we can study the spread of the wedge-shaped characters used by several ancient Mesopotamian languages known as cuneiform characters, and how they were used to put the different languages of different people into writing. We can see how languages can be divided into linguistic families, like the great group of Indo-European languages mentioned on pp 106–9.

The history of the ancient Near East is also the history of the spread of Semitic languages, and so also of the peoples that used them. The Semitic languages most widely spoken today are characterized by 'roots' formed of consonants, which carry the basic meaning of words; the vowels show meaning

more precisely, as well as the grammatical form. For example, in Arabic, from the root *ktb* (to write) are derived *kitab* (book), *katib* (writer), and also various forms of the verb such as *kataba* (he

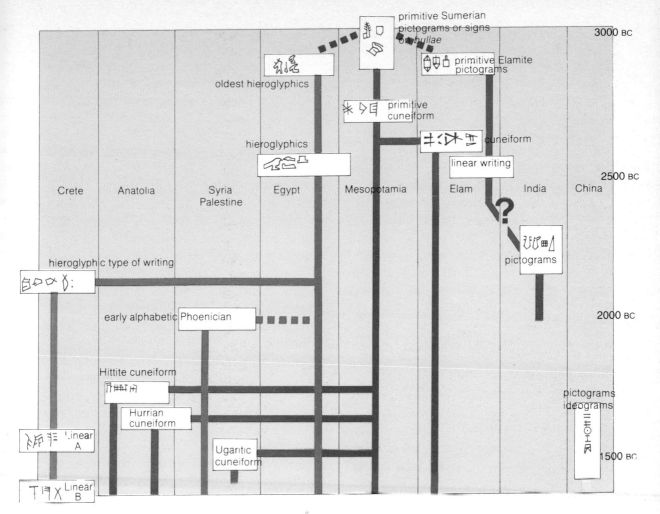

primitive Sumerian
pictograms or signs
on bullae

3000 BC

primitive Elamite
pictograms

oldest hieroglyphics

primitive
cuneiform

cuneiform

hieroglyphics

linear writing

2500 BC

| Crete | Anatolia | Syria Palestine | Egypt | Mesopotamia | Elam | India | China |

?

pictograms

hieroglyphic type of writing

early alphabetic Phoenician

2000 BC

Hittite cuneiform

pictograms
ideograms

Hurrian
cuneiform

Linear A

Ugaritic
cuneiform

1500 BC

Linear B

Opposite above: Fragment of the stele of Ur-Nanshe, king of Lagash, which deals with the consecration of a temple. The written characters tell of the ancestry of the ruler.

Opposite centre: Offering tablet of Ur-Nanshe. The king is always the tallest person in such illustrations. In the upper part, Ur-Nanshe brings a basket of clay bricks on his head; below, the king sits among his children and takes part in the consecration of a temple. Again the text refers to the construction (symbolized by the king carrying bricks) and 'opening ceremony' of a sacred building.

Opposite below: Detail from the stele of Enannatum of Lagash, called the Stele of the Vultures. It is perhaps the most ancient record of an historical

battle, the victory of the king of Lagash over the people of Kish. All three objects opposite date from about 2600–2500 BC.

Above: The possible relations between different forms of writing (and thus the languages) of the Semitic and the Hamitic–Semitic groups. Ancient Egyptian was classed as a Hamitic–Semitic language. Other African languages, often not written, are part of this group. Hittite, also written in hieroglyphics, was an Indo-European language like the Mycenean's Linear B. Alphabetic cuneiform characters were developed in Persia for writing Ancient Persian. Ugaritic was a Semitic language written in cuneiform characters which were eventually used like alphabetic signs. It was a major influence on Phoenician writing.

wrote), or its present tense *yaktubu* (he writes).

Old Semitic languages also gave greater importance to the writing of consonants, though signs indicating vowel sounds also existed in many of them. A particular group of them is that

known as the Hamitic – Semitic languages, which includes various African languages and Ancient Egyptian. Egyptian writing gives no indication of vowels. Sometimes there is a tradition of spelling, for example through Greek, which is used for proper names, names of gods, rulers, and cities. Where there is no tradition of spelling, Egyptologists separate the consonants with the vowel e; thus *mr* (pryamid) is read as *mer*, and *Pth*, the name of a god, is read as *Peteh* or *Ptah*.

Was there, originally at least, a Semitic people? This is a difficult question to answer. Probably, as with the Indo-Europeans, there were only different waves of related peoples. The most ancient centre from which the Semites spread is the area of North-Eastern Arabia. They were groups of nomads who treated the donkey, the onager (a Persian variety of the wild

ass) and the camel as semi-domestic animals. Each group had its own personal beast, in much the same way as the Indo-Europeans used the horse, and took it everywhere with them.

Mesopotamia – Sumer and Akkad

Water-dependent civilizations developed a tendency to increase the area worked, which in turn led to war with their neighbours. Civilization and war: the two seem to go together.

Battles were already being fought at Jericho, as we have seen (p 55). But these wars may have been defensive; the goods stored up in the city had to be defended. With the water-dependent civilizations however, offensive wars, wars of conquest, became necessary. In thousands of inscriptions, the kings boast of victories and massacres, nearly always in the name of some god.

Around 2500 BC, the city-state of Ur stood out from among the various Sumerian centres. The famous royal tombs date from this period (the standard, the chessboard, pp 122–3, 126–7, and the harps and jewellery of Queen Shubad). What happened when people tried to set up their own little empires fits in well with the theories about civilization that we have looked at. In order to work better, the Mesopotamian city-states not only extended their territories, but also tended to centralize buildings to do with power and organization, such as the temples, palaces and offices.

While Ur established itself in the south, the power of the city-state of Lagash (today Telloh) grew in the north-east. The 'stele of the vultures' is the first monument to commemorate an historic event. The stele (or carved stone slab) is so called because the conquerors are shown massacring their victims like birds of prey. It illustrates the

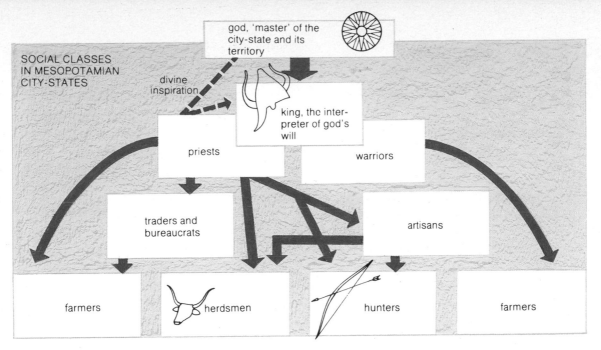

SOCIAL CLASSES
IN MESOPOTAMIAN
CITY-STATES

god, 'master' of the city-state and its territory

divine inspiration

king, the interpreter of god's will

priests

warriors

traders and bureaucrats

artisans

farmers

herdsmen

hunters

farmers

Above: Social structure of Mesopotamian city-states, particularly of Akkad. (Compare it with that of Egypt, see p 83).
Opposite: Embossed bronze head of an Akkadian ruler, probably Sargon I.
Left: Stele of Naram-sin. Approximately two metres (six feet) high, the stele shows this Akkadian king at the head of his troops. Details to note are the standard-bearers, trumpeters, the fallen enemy, and the realistic representation of trees and hilly landscape.

victory of Lagash's King Enannatum over the lords of Kish, another centre further to the north. The conquest of Lugalzaggisi, prince of Umma, by the Semitic Akkadians 200 years later, also started in Lagash. Lugalzaggisi founded the first of the great Mesopotamian empires, conquering Ur, Uruk, Larsa (today Senkere) and, it seems, pushing as far as the Mediterranean (about 2360 BC).

The Semites seem to have slowly taken over in many areas of Mesopotamia during the ancient flowering of Sumerian civilization. In 2350 BC Sargon I, the Semitic ruler of Akkad (the site of this city has not yet been found), conquered the whole of Sumer (southern Mesopotamia), pushed east into Elam (southern Iran), and west towards Syria and Anatolia

(Turkey). Thus, he became 'the lord of the four quarters of the Earth'.

The Akkadian soldiers used javelins and bows and arrows, and they travelled very quickly. The Sumerians, whose soldiers were more slow-moving with their heavy lances and large shields, were crushed.

The empire of Sargon I operated in a way that was typical of despotism (see p 126). The greater the territory, the higher the king needed to raise himself. Sargon made himself a god-king. The languages of both the Akkadian and the Sumerian inscriptions came to be written in the cuneiform characters of the Sumerians.

The grandson of Sargon, Naram-sin, put down various rebellions, and extended the empire still further; he succeeded in adding to it important centres in Syria, among them Ebla (Tell Mardikh). The economy of the Akkadian empire must have been a dynamic one; the movement of raw materials and manufactured goods suggests a great deal of trading.

With the death of Naram-sin, the empire collapsed, and there was an interlude of a century during which power was held by a Persian people, the Gutians. Then the Sumerians had their revenge. Southern Mesopotamia became powerful once more, and the so-called Third Dynasty of Ur was established. The old city was made splendid with a surrounding wall, two harbours, and the highest ziggurat in Sumer (see p 121). Here also the kings became divine. However, the power game was very difficult to play, with as many losers as winners. In the west arose the important centre of Mari (today Tell Hariri), on the right bank of the Euphrates, near the modern border between Syria and Iraq. Lagash flourished once more under the notable priest-king Gudea. According to tradition, he 'worked for peace'. In reality

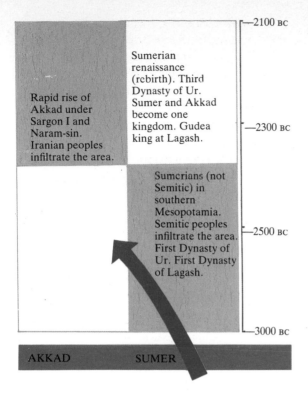

AKKAD	SUMER

Rapid rise of Akkad under Sargon I and Naram-sin. Iranian peoples infiltrate the area.

Sumerian renaissance (rebirth). Third Dynasty of Ur. Sumer and Akkad become one kingdom. Gudea king at Lagash.

Sumerians (not Semitic) in southern Mesopotamia. Semitic peoples infiltrate the area. First Dynasty of Ur. First Dynasty of Lagash.

—2100 BC
—2300 BC
—2500 BC
—3000 BC

> Ningirsu, I will build your house;
> but your exact command has not yet come to me.
> The thoughts of your heart swell like the sea,
> they murmur like a meadow,
> they murmur like running water . . .
> O Hero! Your thoughts are as
>   deep as the sky:
> Son of Enlil, lord Ningirsu,
> What am I to you?
>
> From the *Dream of Gudea*,
> a Sumerian text

Opposite: Statue of Gudea of Lagash, from about 2290–2255 BC. It is 105 centimetres (3½ feet) high. The ruler and law-giver was also a great supporter of trade: under his rule there was a new flowering of southern Mesopotamia after its domination by Akkad.

Left: The histories of Sumer and Akkad. The rise of the kingdom of Akkad did not mean the end of the southern city-states, but only a temporary eclipse of them. However, there is no doubt that Akkadian culture was greatly influenced by that of Sumer, and could be called its 'daughter culture'.

Below: Vase from Susa, an important centre in Elam, dating from about 2000 BC.

Lagash was a most efficient centre of trade; minerals, semi-precious stones and timber (cedars of Lebanon) were moved everywhere through it, as far as the Indus Valley, via Bahrein in the Persian Gulf.

The histories of later Mesopotamian civilizations are described on pp 264–72.

Forgotten Empires Rediscovered

So many attempts were made to build empires within the enormous area of the Near East, that historians have generally limited themselves to a few key events that can be traced and ordered in time, one after the other. This is true in the case of Sumer and Akkad, where the events, especially in school books, are freely simplified; no mention is made of subsidiary but related events which help to give meaning to the main events. This method of tracing history takes no notice of the many parallel, but often very different,

civilizations that developed at the same time as these more notable ones. So it happens that certain events in the period being studied turn out to have no explanation, or only vague and general explanations, such as 'pressures from neighbouring peoples'. What is more, certain centres may be wiped out where history is concerned. They are mentioned less and less, and end up by being forgotten. So it is possible that an archaeological find can present us with the awkward reality of an empire we never knew existed.

Here we shall only mention Alalakh (today Tell Atchana in Turkey) and Ebla (Tell Mardikh in Syria), which were very important at the time when Sumer and Akkad were flourishing. Alalakh was brought to light by Sir Leonard Woolley in the 1930s and 40s, and Ebla by Paolo Matthiae in the 1960s and 70s. The discovery of Ebla in particular has given us an enormous number of inscribed tablets: an archive (state documents), libraries with school texts, dictionaries, and even descriptive atlases. It is as if, out of the silence of the millennia, a voice had been raised telling numerous stories. The Ebla texts are mostly written in a 'new' Semitic language called Eblaic. This is similar to others already known, but it has its own forms, so the dictionaries are precious. The finds from these sites show that Alalakh and Ebla had trading and diplomatic relations with the whole known world of those days. The traces of a sack (destruction by enemies) at Ebla confirm that it was in fact conquered by Naram-sin of Akkad. Traditional dates and those given by archaeology turn out to agree.

Iron and Horses – Instruments of Hittite Conquest

Using Wittfogel's ideas, we have explained the workings of the water-dependent empire, and have looked at some notable examples of it. We have pointed out how such organizations tended to become despotic, that is, ruled by people with absolute power. We also use the word 'empire' for other organizations such as a city-state in which works like irrigation, dams, aqueducts and so on were unimportant. But does it make sense to give the word a wider meaning?

We shall now look at a civilization with many individual characteristics which have little to do with the problems of water, and perhaps we can sketch out some kind of answer. This is the Hittite civilization which flourished between the third and second millennia

Left: A large tablet from Ebla, the ancient city-state in northern Syria discovered in the 1960s and 70s by Paolo Matthiae. The texts of the great archive of this city were written on clay tablets. The fire that destroyed the building where the tablets were kept hardened them considerably by baking them. The writing is cuneiform. This tablet lists the names of several sites in the ancient Near East; it is a 'descriptive atlas' of the area as it was in the third millennium BC.
Opposite: One area brought to light during the excavations at Ebla. The city was literally buried, like so many other sites in the ancient Middle East, in a tell or mound (hence the modern name of the site, Tell Mardikh). It is not mentioned in historical records, so its existence was forgotten.

134

BC in most of Anatolia in Turkey and northern Syria.

Before 2000 BC Indo-European peoples mixed and fought with the people already living in central Anatolia. One of the first capitals was Kushshah; there Labarna made himself king of the 'Hatti'. The Hittites always called themselves 'the people of Hatti', perhaps the name of the original tribe, and the name *Labarna* came to mean the same thing as 'king'.

In the 17th century BC under Hattusilas I, the successor of Labarna, the capital became Hattusas (near the modern Turkish town of Boğazkale). The Hittite expansion lasted almost three centuries, forming the so-called Old Kingdom. Some very important centres in Mesopotamia (including Babylon) and Syria (Ebla) were temporarily conquered and united.

Internal crises (civil wars and murdered kings) were overcome through the establishment, by King Telepinus in about 1460 BC, of an interesting system of rules governing the succession to the throne.

In a new phase of their history called the Hittite Empire, the Kingdom of

Below left: Seal made of silver, and its impression. The Hittite inscriptions around the outside of the seal are written in cuneiform characters. The small 'figures' in the centre are usually named hieroglyphs because of their similarity to the signs used in Egyptian writing. The inscription reads: 'Tarriktimme, king of the land of Erme'.
Below: Bas-relief cut out of natural rock in the open-air cliff sanctuary of Yazilikaya near the Hittite capital Hattusas. On the rock wall the figures of 12 gods have been carved, six of which are shown here. This carving has been named 'the racing gods'.
Opposite: Later civilizations owed their use of iron, the light chariot with spoked wheels, and the domestication of the horse to the Hittites.

seal

impression made
by seal

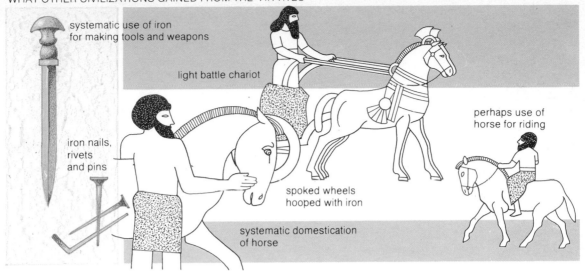

systematic use of iron
for making tools and weapons

light battle chariot

iron nails,
rivets
and pins

perhaps use of
horse for riding

spoked wheels
hooped with iron

systematic domestication
of horse

Mitanni was defeated. This was a sort of buffer state which flourished in northern Mesopotamia between Anatolia and Assyria. The latter, however, proved too tough to crack, and the Hit-

tites turned their attention to the Syrian coast, conquering Alalakh among other centres. Here they were faced with the empire-building and conquering intentions of the Eyptians, and a great but indecisive battle was fought at Kadesh, on the River Orontes (in 1296 BC, see p 261).

Thus the Hittites were a people that grew great at the expense of others, by conquering other nations and making them its subjects. Was it an 'empire'? To find an answer we shall look at how Hittite society was organized.

The king, priests and military leaders had more or less similar roles as their equivalents in the water-dependent societies, but the Hittite king did not call himself a god. There were also skilful artists and scribes.

Of greater interest to us are the artisans who were highly skilled in metallurgy. They knew how to work iron better than anyone else in the ancient Near East. The Hittite conquest of the Anatolian territories and of various other areas rich in minerals were therefore significant. This was the earth 'worked' by the Hittites, just as we talk of 'working' mineral deposits today.

The peasants were obliged to supply

137

food for the whole social organization and labour for public works such as walls and buildings; prisoners of war also played a large part in this activity. But when they were not working in the fields, and when there was no building programme (and that was for most of the time), the peasants were forced to work in their homes producing iron ingots or finished iron objects. Another intermediate class of Hittite people was engaged in trade, not for themselves alone, but under the precise orders of the rulers.

The Hittites sold iron to their friends and prevented their enemies from having it, and thus were able to push up its price by limiting its supply. They had iron weapons, knew how to put iron hoops round wheels, and invented the war-chariot, as they had well-trained horses (being Indo-Europeans). Everything and everyone depended on decisions, for the benefit of the whole community, taken at the ruling centre, Hattusas. For these reasons, we can call the Hittite civilization an empire. Some experts call societies in which the central power controls production and trade with a heavy hand, 'Sub-Asiatic'.

Today we have a clearer picture of the workings of other centres already mentioned; Ebla and Alalakh were empires because they had a very exact production programme ordered from above. What was given most importance in this production system, other than food, was trade. Not, of course, trade by individual merchants.

People of the region, especially the Semites, had a tradition of being on the move, travelling in caravans (that is, in groups with all their goods and animals). Places like Ebla and Alalakh were 'crossroads' very well suited for trade. They were all empires with despotic central rule. Rather than simply working the land, they 'worked' the needs of other people.

Borrowed writing

The Hittites spoke and wrote an Indo-European language. This can give us the feeling that we are dealing with relations, or at least next-door neighbours. When this ancient language was deciphered, the experts had a starting point to help them; among the groups of signs representing words, there seemed to be links that suggested a grammatical system of the Indo-European type.

How did the Hittites write down their language? In two ways: firstly using cuneiform characters (Sumerian-Akkadian and Assyro-Babylonian), and secondly, perhaps later, using designs which suggest Egyptian hieroglyphics. The Hittites' use of cuneiform characters could be compared with the

use made by the Japanese of Roman letters for writing down their language. It is quite a complicated matter, and needs some explanation.

A word could be written in Sumerian, Babylonian, or Hittite using cuneiform characters corresponding to the sounds in question. However, the characters, as well as representing sounds (thus being termed phonograms or 'sound-words'), could also be interpreted as ideograms ('idea-words'), that is, as entire words.

The reader was probably always able to catch the meaning of the writing in the 'right' language; still, to help understanding, the scribes would add other signs, for example endings typical of Hittite grammar, to the groups of characters.

Telepinu cried, 'I shall no longer concern myself with those who depend on me!' . . . And fog covered the windows, and mist invaded the house, and the logs went out in the fireplace. The gods themselves choked on their altars . . . The sheep neglected its lamb, and the cow its calf. Telepinu went and took with him the wheat, and the life-giving breeze. He took away all that the land, the meadow, and the steppe needed.

[The god of vegetation, Telepinu, became angry and disappeared from the world, with dreadful results.]

Telepinu went away and lost himself in the steppes: fatigue overcame him. The wheat and the spelt no longer grew. Cattle, sheep and mankind no longer multiplied.

The plants dried up, the trees withered, and sprouted no new shoots. The pastures and the springs ran dry. The land was stricken with famine, and gods and men were dying of hunger. The great god of the storm gave a banquet and invited a thousand gods. They ate, but their hunger was not satisfied; they drank, but they did not slake their thirst . . .

[The gods searched for Telepinu, and found him, but could not persuade him to return. A ritual invented by a human was then performed.]

Telepinu returned once more to his own house, and cared for his land once more . . .

From the *Myth of the Vanished God*, or *of Telepinu*, an Hittite text.

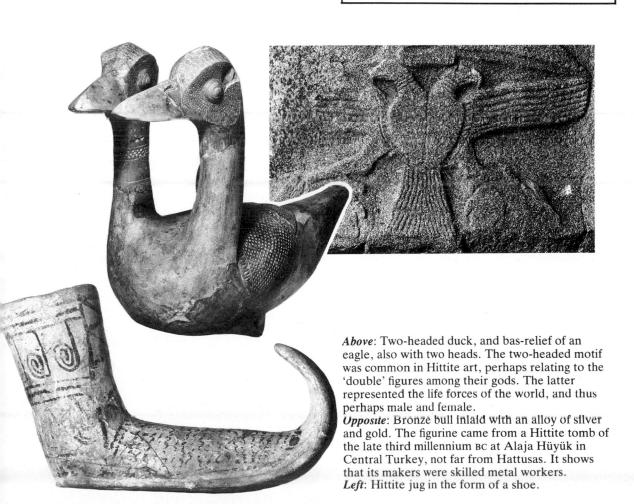

Above: Two-headed duck, and bas-relief of an eagle, also with two heads. The two-headed motif was common in Hittite art, perhaps relating to the 'double' figures among their gods. The latter represented the life forces of the world, and thus perhaps male and female.
Opposite: Bronze bull inlaid with an alloy of silver and gold. The figurine came from a Hittite tomb of the late third millennium BC at Alaja Hüyük in Central Turkey, not far from Hattusas. It shows that its makers were skilled metal workers.
Left: Hittite jug in the form of a shoe.

The Hebrews

In the complex picture of ancient history, a series of events stands out from all the others and seems to have a character all of its own. This is the history of the Hebrew people. Many factors combine to give this impression. Here we shall look at what the history of Israel and that of other Near Eastern peoples (particularly the Semites) have in common.

But let us first look at why the history of the Hebrews seems different. Basically it depends on the type of historical source used. While for other historical peoples we refer to a great variety of written documents (inscriptions, treaties, contracts, inventories, hymns, prayers, poetry, and tales), for the Hebrews we have a single document of truly exceptional size and complexity,

namely the Bible. It is a collection of historical reports (for example in Exodus), laws, prayers, poetry and hymns, predictions (in the books of the prophets), and of laments for the past, a subject and style that was fashionable throughout the Near East (see p 114). This huge collection of texts from different periods and authors has been treated in an unusual way. It has become part of the modern Western world's cultural heritage. People have read a great deal of moral meaning into it, using it as the basis for teaching what is right and wrong. With many of the 'facts' reported in the Bible, it is often difficult to separate their moral value from their historical accuracy. In recent

times, help has come in the form of archaeological evidence. Great floods, the walls of Jericho, and the temple of Solomon have been clearly identified in excavations.

Groups of nomadic shepherds made semi-permanent homes in Palestine in the second millennium BC. The different groups took on independent identities (hence the 12 tribes). There was no king, let alone a god-king. It was rather the god who took on the qualities of king. He lay down very strict laws, and these laws become the basis and the symbol of the unity of the people. The Hebrews' one form of worship and one god (monotheism) could be explained as an extreme expression of the

Opposite: Statue of the Alalakh king Indri-Mi on his throne, dating from 1500 BC. Alalakh was a city-state in what is now Turkey. Indri-Mi wears the type of head-dress used by the kings of Mitanni, a state in northern Mesopotamia that was in constant conflict with the Hittite Empire. In fact Indri-Mi made himself the vassal (or subject-king) of Mitanni in order to gain their protection against Egypt, which was expanding towards northern Syria; he also hoped to gain the protection of the Egyptians against Mitanni! These complicated political games are revealed in the long inscription in cuneiform characters that covers the front of the statue.

Below: A group of terracotta statuettes, probably images of goddesses of fertility. They date from the second millennium BC, and come from northern Syria. This region was the main route from Mesopotamia to the Mediterranean, and so was used by caravans and migrating peoples. The ancestors of the Hebrews were certainly among groups of semi-nomads who arrived on the eastern Mediterranean coast by way of northern Syria.

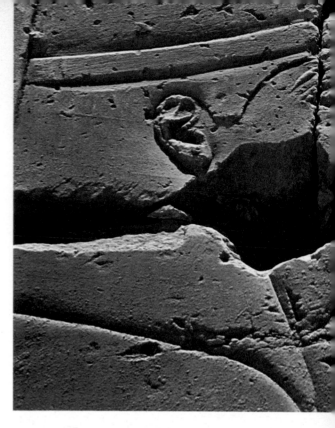

Many Books in One

The Bible consists of various texts by different authors from different times. The Hebrew Bible (the Christian Old Testament) is called the *Tanach*, from the three initial letters (t, n, and k) of its main sections: *Torah* (the Law); *Nebi'im* (the Prophets); and *Ketubim* (the Hagiographa, or the Writings). The Law comprises five books, Genesis, Exodus, Leviticus, Numbers and Deuteronomy, attributed to Moses but probably composed at different times. They form an account of events from the beginning of the world until the return of the Hebrews to Palestine from Egypt. The Prophets are divided into the Former Prophets and the Latter Prophets. The Former Prophets are the historical books. They relate the history of the kingdoms of Judah and Israel. The Latter Prophets contain laments about the sad conditions of the day, and threats against enemies. They also include the anouncement of the coming of the Messiah. The books of the Hagiographa comprise poetical texts such as the Psalms and the Song of Songs, and writings on morality and wisdom. See the illustration below.

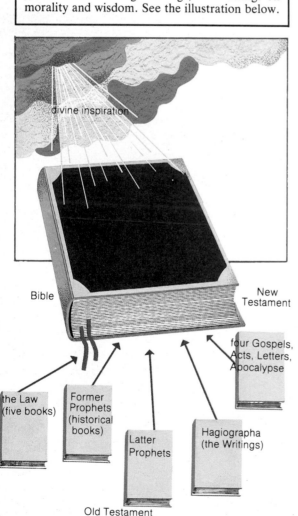

divine inspiration

Bible

New Testament

four Gospels, Acts, Letters, Apocalypse

the Law (five books)

Former Prophets (historical books)

Latter Prophets

Hagiographa (the Writings)

Old Testament

tendency (typical in Mesopotamian city-states) to possess a single local god that ruled and guided them with strict laws.

The Hebrews' contacts with centres and peoples that we know about through other historical and archaeo-logical documents make our ideas about their history more certain. Thus it is very likely that Abraham, originally from Ur, was an important 'caravan chief' who travelled throughout Mesopotamia. It is possible that Joseph was one of the many prisoners taken back to the land of the Nile after being captured by the Egyptians during their wars in Palestine and Syria. There he could well have won favour with the king, thanks to his wisdom. The king was perhaps unable to manage the mass of prisoners, and Joseph helped him to get the best possible work from them. The Exodus (the Hebrews' escape from Egypt), and thus the historical figure of Moses, could be dated from about 1250

BC (towards the beginning of the period known as the New Kingdom in Egypt).

Around 1030 BC Saul became the first of a line of kings. A king was probably necessary in order to deal with the attacks of other Palestinian peoples, such as the Philistines and Ammonites.

The nearest the Hebrews got to establishing an empire was during the reign of Solomon (966–926 BC). Great wealth had been built up, showing that caravan people and nomads could become excellent merchants. There were contacts with other powers through marriages with foreign princesses. Jerusalem imitated the other cities of the region, and the great monumental structures of the temple and the royal palace were built. The territory was divided into twelve provinces, each of which had to support the king's court for one month of the year. There was a strong army, but it was difficult for a shepherding-caravaning-trading people to create a vast and solid empire.

Above: Detail of a bas-relief at the Temple of Karnak in Egypt in which a group of Semites is portrayed. These were prisoners carried off to Egypt during the many expeditions of Rameses II against Palestine and Syria. Hebrews were captured and taken to Egypt on several occasions. The Exodus (the Hebrews' escape from Egypt), organized by Moses, can be dated to about 1250 BC.

With the death of Solomon, unity ended and two kingdoms sprang up: the kingdom of Israel in the north, with its capital at Shechem, then Samaria, and the kingdom of Judah in the south, with its capital at Jerusalem. The messages of the prophets had a moral importance, but also a political significance. Their point was that nothing was better than the unity of the people under their one god.

In 587 BC Nebuchadnezzar II, king of Babylon, conquered and destroyed Jerusalem after a siege of a year and a half. The Hebrews (Israelites and Judeans) were deported to Babylonia (see p 271); this was the beginning of the diaspora (the scattering of the Jews).

The Indus Civilization

The Indus civilization flourished in what is now Pakistan for about a millennium, from 2500 to 1500 BC. About 20 centres have been investigated so far. The main ones are Mohenjo-daro (meaning 'city of the dead' in the local language), Harappa and Lothal. What we know of the most recently discovered centres shows that they had features that were typical of the better known large cities.

Building was carried out in accordance with strict and rational city planning. Wide streets crossed at right angles, marking out great islands of dwellings or other buildings. Secondary streets provided ways to individual dwellings. Generally there was a sort of citadel, a raised area with defensive walls and sometimes towers. These citadels rose above the remains of more ancient civilizations.

A perfect network of drains corresponds to the network of streets, the pipes being ceramic. At Mohenjo-daro there is a building that was certainly used as a swimming pool or public bath house. Many of the larger houses are two-storeyed; they have a courtyard, a water tank, several rooms, and a lavatory. In these cities everything was made of clay bricks cooked in wood-fired ovens.

There can be no doubt about the durability of the Indus civilization's bricks. They have not only survived to our own times, but were used in huge numbers by the British towards the end of the last century to build the bed of the Karachi–Lahore railway.

Enormous efforts must have gone into the making of so many bricks. Some years ago, when this feature of the Indus civilization was becoming clear, a joke was told among the archaeologists. A little boy in ancient Harappa came home and said, 'Ma! I'm hungry! Give me a bit of bread!'

'No food today,' the mother replied. 'I'm cooking an ovenful of bricks.' The joke may contain a grain of truth; as we shall see, these people did in fact suffer hunger because of the bricks.

Especially in the case of Harappa, one gets the impression of an industrial city where the essential products were objects, ceramics and of course bricks. The basic economy was linked to agriculture; wheat, barley, vegetables and rice were grown, and it seems that rice was 'domesticated' for the first time in this region. Also notable was the cultivation of cotton, which must have been something of a speciality and thus a material for trade as finished cloth (perhaps coloured with vegetable dyes). Among the main domestic

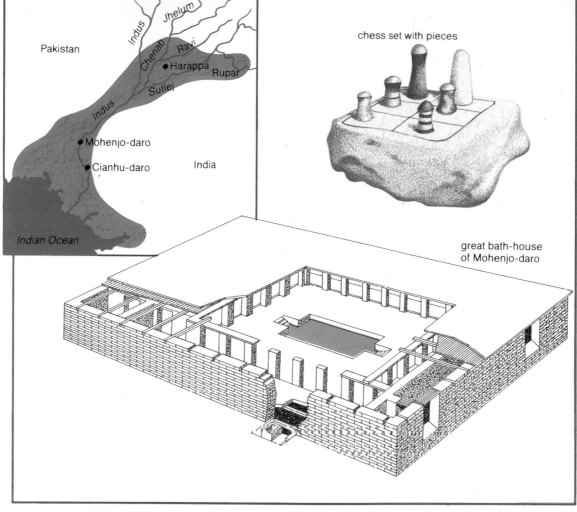

chess set with pieces

great bath-house
of Mohenjo-daro

Above: Map showing the area of the Indus
civilization (about 2000 BC) and some of its main
centres; a chess set from this civilization, and a
reconstruction of the great bath-house of Mohenjo-
daro. The walls and columns of the latter building
were made of baked clay bricks. It was 40 metres
(130 feet) long and had cubicles for private bathing.
Heat was produced under the floor.
Opposite: Ceramic objects produced by Indus
civilization centres, probably for trade. The figurine
in the form of a bull has a moving head. The small,
tightly stoppered jar could have been a cage for
insects or a container for aromatic herbs.
Left: A typical Indus seal, this one depicting a
rhinoceros. The signs at the top are perhaps
characters of the local writing, or a series of
symbols representing a particular craftsman. It is
thought that such seals were used to make marks on
clay stoppers or other soft surfaces to show that
goods had been guaranteed or checked.

145

animals was the Indian buffalo, which we find represented on many of the typical seals.

More than once in this book we have tried to relate certain features of a particular way of living to environmental conditions. What were the conditions in the valleys of the Indus and its tributaries 4,500 years ago? They were certainly different from those of today. Here, as in Mesopotamia, the desert has gained the upper hand, but with a difference: between the Tigris and the Euphrates the tendency to become arid was already clear in the past, whereas the region of the Indus became dry and sandy much later.

In the past, the valleys of the Indus and its tributaries like the Kabul and Sutlej had thick forests. There was plenty of rain. 'Earth-built' architecture, that is, bricks made of dried mud, would have been easily washed away by rain and floods. We must remember that the trees of those forests played a very large part in the creation of the Indus civilization. The trees provided fuel to make innumerable bricks; they provided a source of profitable trade in the form of timber, so prized in Mesopotamia; and by burning the forests the area under cultivation was enlarged.

This deforestation of the land had dramatic results. Disastrous floods became more and more frequent because rain drained off the bare hills much more quickly than before. In order to prevent these disasters, more protective building works were needed, so more wood for bricks was needed, and so more trees were cut down. It was a vicious circle. Certain areas such as Harappa may have had to make more bricks than they needed for themselves; these were then transported to other centres were they were urgently needed for repairs.

Primary (or food) production, brick production, the manufacture of marketable goods, and commerce were all

Opposite: Circular structures commonly found in courtyards of houses at Mohenjo-daro. They may not be the openings of wells, as used to be thought, but ingenious storage places for vases or jars with pointed bottoms.
Below: Part of a statuette found at Mohenjo-daro. It may be the figure of a mother-goddess, but the head-dress with the hollow in it suggests that the object might have been used as an oil lamp.

Bottom: Statuette from the Indus civilization. The arm rings, waist band, narrow waist and large breasts are to be found in later Indian art, thus indicating the possible influence of the Indus civilization on Indian culture. These objects may have been traded over a very wide area, and the Indus people's Indo-European successors took over the styles and tastes of the civilization they destroyed.

organized by a central authority. The rivers were an important means of transport and communication; at Harappa there are the remains of docks and roads linking the river harbours with the great granaries.

So far, no tombs of kings have been discovered. There are a few statues, sophisticated jewellery, and copper statuettes (copper was rarely used for making implements). But everywhere soapstone (steatite) seals have been discovered. They often have holes in them, perhaps for a string, so that they could be carried round the neck. They were used to mark or sign the containers and packages of goods. The short inscriptions, so far undeciphered, could be names or slogans for certain products.

The majority of the objects from the Indus civilization were found in houses and other secular buildings. The few tombs (none of high-ranking people) have only modest contents. Were there no temples? Was there an organization that was not backed by religious power? It has been suggested that the religions of the Indus civilization were connected with the world of the open air and open spaces and that therefore real temples were not necessary. In the case of some statues and statuettes thought to be of local gods, experts have pointed out features that are similar to later Hindu gods, especially Shiva, sitting in meditation with his legs crossed under him.

Overland transport in the areas near the urban centres consisted of large carts with solid wheels pulled by buffaloes. We have interesting terracotta models of these (p 33). Long-distance trade used the caravan routes across Baluchistan. Sea-borne trade followed the Persian Gulf, using Bahrain as a port of call; the docks excavated on that island have features in common with docks at Harappa and also at Ur (p 91).

Towards 1700 BC the Indus centres were already in decline. Two centuries later, the valleys were invaded by a people from the north who were most probably Indo-Europeans. They could have been the Aryans who gave rise to the future civilization of India. At Mohenjo-daro remains have been found of many individuals who had fallen to the ground, some with head wounds. It is not a burial, but clear evidence of a massacre. The Indus civilization was destroyed. The cultivated areas, the soil of which was already suffering from an increase in salt content as a result of irrigation (and possibly from an excess of ash from brick production) were abandoned and became more arid. The region died.

The 'new' Indian civilization was to develop elsewhere, in the plain of the Ganges and its tributaries. The first signs of it emerged in 1500 BC. These included writing; the tradition of the Vedas, which were to become the sacred books of Hinduism and which had previously been handed down orally, became 'fixed' in an ancient form of Sanskrit. Indian civilization flourished greatly around the sixth and fifth centuries BC. Buddhism was founded by Gautama Siddhartha (about 563–483 BC), the prince turned preacher, who became the Buddha or 'Enlightened One'.

We know nothing about the Indus civilization except through archaeological excavations. Was it a true empire? Various things suggest that it was: the planned and monumental structure of the cities, the building works to control water, the organization of activities, the existence of writing and even of standard weights. The last word on this empire will only come from more research and excavation.

Opposite: Impression of the granaries at Harappa, a city of the Indus civilization that stood on the banks of the Ravi River in Pakistan 4,000 years ago. The Ravi is a tributary of the Indus, and today is 9 kilometres (5½ miles) from the site of Harappa as a result of a change in its course. In the lower part of the granary buildings there were ventilation ducts.

Ladders lead to the various levels and bridges connected the two blocks. The complex was more than 30 metres (100 feet) long, and was built near an area consisting of small dwellings, probably occupied by workers, and buildings that were certainly workshops.

5. Civilizations Without Empires in Europe

Ages and Dates

The introduction of certain technologies, for example the use of a particular metal or alloy (mixture of metals), is taken as a sign of a new age and the passing away of its predecessor. This happened at different times in different places. The dates of these changes

Below: Chart indicating the approximate dates of transition from one cultural period to another in various parts of the world.

The red line indicates the start of the Copper Age (or Chalcolithic). The transition from the Chalcolithic to the Bronze Age is shown by the green line. The brown line shows the transition from the Bronze Age to the Iron Age. The yellow line indicates the appearance of writing, and thus the end of the prehistoric period.
Opposite: Ploughs used in four different areas in ancient times: Europe, Egypt, Crete and Mesopotamia. For the latter three the pictographic sign used to represent a plough in written documents of those areas is also shown. Only in the case of Mesopotamia do we know exactly how the animals were yoked to the plough. All the ploughs were made of wood and sometimes the ploughshares were hardened by fire.

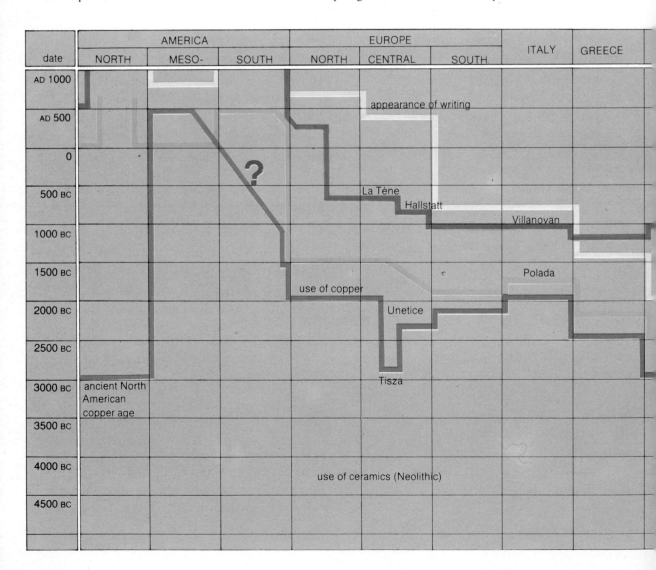

date	AMERICA			EUROPE			ITALY	GREECE
	NORTH	MESO-	SOUTH	NORTH	CENTRAL	SOUTH		
AD 1000								
AD 500					appearance of writing			
0			?					
500 BC					La Tène / Hallstatt			
1000 BC						Villanovan		
1500 BC				use of copper		Polada		
2000 BC					Unetice			
2500 BC								
3000 BC	ancient North American copper age				Tisza			
3500 BC								
4000 BC				use of ceramics (Neolithic)				
4500 BC								

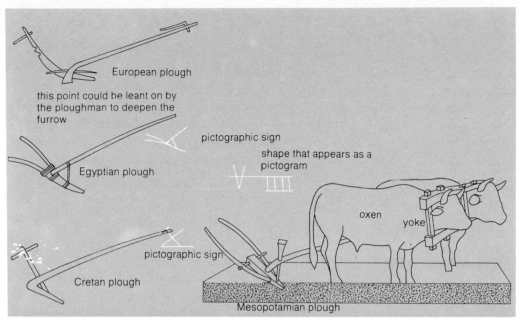

European plough

this point could be leant on by the ploughman to deepen the furrow

Egyptian plough

pictographic sign

shape that appears as a pictogram

oxen

yoke

Cretan plough

pictographic sign

Mesopotamian plough

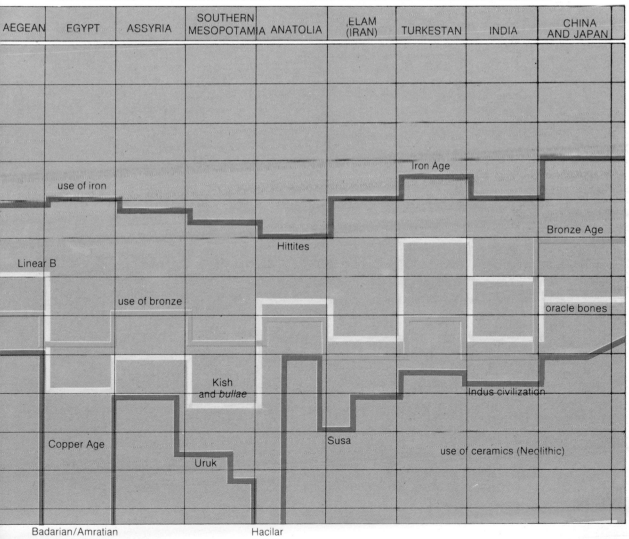

AEGEAN	EGYPT	ASSYRIA	SOUTHERN MESOPOTAMIA	ANATOLIA	ELAM (IRAN)	TURKESTAN	INDIA	CHINA AND JAPAN	
						Iron Age			
	use of iron								
								Bronze Age	
				Hittites					
Linear B									
		use of bronze						oracle bones	
			Kish and *bullae*				Indus civilization		
Copper Age					Susa		use of ceramics (Neolithic)		
			Uruk						
Badarian/Amratian				Hacilar					

151

depended on the environment, that is whether or not the raw materials could be found. They also depended on the mobility of the peoples concerned, that is, whether or not they could move about, make contact with others, and exchange raw materials and finished goods. The great empires tended not to be very forward-looking because of their vast and complex organization. They were rather slow to learn and adopt new techniques like the use of bronze and the plough.

Civilization without Writing

As we know, very many cultures have left no written evidence. The usual label given to these cultures is 'prehistoric'.

The diagram on the previous pages shows this. Over the great area of continental Europe, the various stages of metallurgy, that is, the various metal ages (see p 75), were reached before the appearance of writing. In other words, in Europe an important technological step forward in the history of human culture was made without one of the main things we have associated with our concept of civilization. In order to explain what seems to be a contradiction, let us look once more at certain points that we have been considering.

Writing appeared along with the great water-dependent civilizations. This most useful means of conveying information was originally an instrument of control, power, and discrimination between different classes of

people (see pp 95–6). The water-dependent civilizations were by nature 'fixed'; agriculture by irrigation tied the whole system to a limited territory.

Writing acted as a way of sending orders, of carrying out inspections and surveys in various places, and of sending the resulting information to the central power. The information was carried between the various fixed production areas in the form of a written message.

Let us now examine a different situation, one which comprised a collection of communities that were mobile, or only partly fixed in one spot; nomads that hunted and practised agriculture season by season, having some domestic animals and knowing how to make use of horses. This situation was

Opposite and below: Various objects from prehistoric Europe. 1. Bronze figurine with eyes of gold, from Bronze-Age Denmark (first–second millennium BC). Its clothing is interesting: the short skirt suggests that the climate was relatively mild. In more recent times an unfavourable climate, and perhaps floods, caused various peoples of Scandinavia to move south. These movements were the migrations of the German 'barbarians' towards the borders of the Roman Empire in the first and second centuries AD. 2. Vessels, found in various sites in north-west Switzerland, of the Horgen culture (late Neolithic and Chalcolithic about 2300 BC). The Horgen culture dominated and replaced that of the Neolithic Cortaillod culture in many areas of Europe (see p 104). 3. Stone (serpentine) axe of the Chalcolithic period, from Switzerland. It was perhaps a cult object. 4 and 5. Axes from prehistoric Danish sites. The one with geometrical designs on it is made of deer horn; the other, shaped like the head of a European elk, is of stone. The handles were of wood. 6. Ceramic figurine dating from 3000 BC. Found at the megalithic temple of Hal Saflieni in Malta, it is 11.6 centimetres (4½ inches) long. The subject is a mother-goddess known as the 'sleeping lady'.

Right: Artist's impression of a village built on a platform of wooden planks in the marshy area south of Lake Garda in northern Italy. At some sites in this area these platforms extended over hundreds of metres. The houses were roofed with thatch and held down with beams of timber. Life in this Bronze Age community must have been relatively simple: the economy was based on hunting, agriculture, and cattle raising. The range of manufactured objects, however, was wide, many being exceptionally refined. The materials used were bone, stone, ceramic, wood, and bronze. A typical culture associated with these settlements was that called Polada (a site near Lonato), and was characterized by pottery with coarse pastework.

Ledro, north-west of Lake Garda, is a site with many remains of the Polada culture and some splendid gilded bronze crowns have been found. *Below*: A typical cup or beaker of the Polada culture.

typical of late Neolithic Europe. These communities relied upon communication by word of mouth. The people themselves moved, and with them their own information, which could include technical skills or practical advice on new forms of farming. Since the people themselves travelled, there was no need to transfer information by using the written word. Inscriptions and dedications were not at all necessary in such a situation.

So, as we have nothing to read, let us concentrate on objects and their enormous variety of forms, decorations, styles, and motifs. From this 'dumb' evidence springs a great quantity of information, or news, rather as if instead of listening to a single official language, we were hearing many local dialects. A decoration, a technology, a way of building houses or huts, give us more information than an inscription; they tell us the tale of everyday life, its changes and challenges, with greater accuracy than any poem, chronicle or novel.

The Discovery of Metals

The mobility of the groups of people might explain the speed of the spread of the new technologies, and why there

154

were so many new discoveries. Above all it might explain the many cases in which the different processes were improved or perfected.

For example, copper in its natural state was found in two different types of deposit. It could appear as part of another mineral (for example the beautiful greenish malachite), or as natural copper. Certainly malachite was collected as a beautiful 'stone', and when accidentally burned must have revealed the copper that it contained. In areas in which this mineral was common, copper extraction by heating it (known as smelting) was discovered. Elsewhere, where natural copper was more common, it was discovered that impurities could be removed by hammering it. Fixed groups of people remained tied for a long time to one or the other of these two methods. Semi-fixed or mobile groups were able to discover, learn, or perfect the two methods, using them to suit whichever form of the metal was locally available.

The extraction of metals by smelting (also possible with gold and silver) made the production of alloys possible. The Copper Age is known as the Chalcolithic, meaning 'of copper and stone'. In many sites dating from this age, we find objects made of copper alloyed with antimony or arsenic.

Perhaps it was chance that led to the discovery of bronze, an alloy of copper and tin. This certainly took place in more than one place and at different times. The advantages of bronze are that it melts at a lower temperature than pure copper, and once it has cooled it is harder and lasts longer.

There was a difficulty, however. Copper was fairly widespread in a natural state. Tin, on the other hand, although easily found in the Near East, especially in the Armenian and Caucasus mountains, was only to be found in Europe in the Iberian Peninsula, Bohemia and the British Isles. In the Near East, the first bronzes appeared in Elam and lower Mesopotamia. The tin must have been transported there, whereas copper was sometimes collected from deposits formed by the rivers. The ancient name of the Euphrates, Urudu or Urutu, means 'river of copper'; this is almost certainly a reference to the presence of minerals in its water.

In Europe and perhaps in parts of central Asia, obtaining the two elements of the alloy must have depended on trade. Again, the mobility of the groups and the easy exchange of ideas brought about a remarkable leap forward in technology.

The 'Great Stones' of Europe

Like any other science, archaeology makes progress by correcting mistakes. In some cases, the discovery of a mistake leads to a complete change of theory or to a different way of looking at the past.

As a look at your parents' school books will tell you, the European cultures of prehistory used to be treated as the 'poor relations' of the great civilizations (Egypt, Mesopotamia, and so on), in spite of their achievements. Historians could not get away from the idea that such civilizations (the water-dependent empires) were in any case superior, that they were the 'mother' of all civilizations that came after them.

Today, prehistory, and particularly the Metal Ages, has made progress in the pages of text-books. Now, our illiterate but most civilized European ancestors are given equal treatment.

What has happened to change the historians' point of view? The answer is that by carefully using a method of dating more accurate than the counting of growth rings on trees (dendrochronology), it has been possible to correct the dates obtained. This method is called carbon dating and depends on finding the level of remaining radioactivity in carbon (called C^{14}). The dates of the monuments of prehistoric Europe obtained through the carbon method have been put right; it is almost certain that many of the megaliths (great stones) of Europe are more ancient than, for example, the pyramids of the first Egyptian dynasties. In the opinion of some historians, this greater age signifies greater importance; so it is worth the trouble to interest oneself in poor 'uncultured' Europe, and to include its cultures in the great picture of past civilizations.

But let us return to the monuments. Why were the megaliths built? Why did people undertake these works using great stones?

The answer is fairly simple: they wanted their work to last. The megaliths are tombs, temples and temple-

Opposite: Two men cut the outlines of daggers on one of the upright stones at Stonehenge, near Salisbury in England. These outlines are still visible today. Perhaps this activity had a magical or religious significance, a sign of a cult of weapons (axes, daggers etc) which was found in various European cultures. Weapons of this sort, clearly not used for any practical purpose, were put in tombs or offered to the gods. The last stage of the construction of Stonehenge took place in the middle of the Bronze Age (about 1400 BC).

observatories. The most ancient appeared in the late Neolithic period. People had already used stone for buildings when other construction materials such as wood were not available. An all-stone Neolithic village was built at Skara Brae in the Orkney Islands north of Scotland (photograph p 75); here tables, benches, and even buildings too small to do anything but lie down and sleep in, are made of stone.

The megaliths certainly were very different in size from those of the houses of Skara Brae. They were made to last, and were also large in order to be impressive, just like the pyramids. This is a fairly sensible explanation of the works of the Bronze Age. But the practical aspect of some of the structures should also be mentioned. They often turn out to have been aligned on certain astronomical features. The very fact that today the alignments seem a bit inaccurate to us makes it possible to calculate when these megaliths were constructed, as we know about the movements of the Earth's axis which have caused an apparent shifting of the pole stars. For example the temples on Malta (like Ggantija and Tarxien) are aligned, as is the passage grave at New Grange, in Ireland. The parallel rows of stones at Carnac in France (p 74) run for several kilometres. And even the

1

Opposite and below: Objects from Northern European cultures of the Bronze Age. 1. Figurine of an acrobat-dancer from the Danish Bronze Age. Note the skirt, head-dress and necklace, comparable to those of the statuette on p 152. 2. Tweezers for removing hair, and (3.) a razor with the outline of a boat engraved on it, both from the Scandinavian Bronze Age. 4. Bronze axe-head in the stone mould in which it was made. These objects were found in Denmark in two different places some 15 kilometres (9 miles) apart. 5. Hilts of bronze swords with elaborate inlays of bone, wood, and a substance obtained by dissolving amber in boiling oil or fat. They originated in the Danish Bronze Age.

pyramid of Cheops turns out to be orientated in a certain way.

Following the change of opinion about the age of the European monuments, there have been long arguments about the possibility that the Near Eastern monuments might be a development of them. In fact, such a view is not very realistic. The observation of the movements of the sun, moon and stars, and the alignment of monuments probably developed independently in the two areas.

The most famous European megalithic monument, Stonehenge, near Salisbury in England, was built at a place that was ideally suited for observing the sun and moon. This shows that the site was chosen on the basis of exact observations made by people who were dead before the work of building began. The stones were transported from quarries that were far away, perhaps by sea and along the River Avon.

The use of an observatory-monument like Stonehenge or the Carnac lines may well have provided valuable information for farmers. It is possible that the Mesopotamian ziggurats were used for astronomy. The Central American pyramids were certainly used for this.

What makes the European monuments different from the others is the comparative simplicity of their structure, and so they probably did not require back-breaking labour to build. They mostly consist of a series of two vertical stones (uprights) and a third stone (the lintel) placed horizontally on top of them. It is thought that the great

Opposite: In many prehistoric European sites there is evidence for cults relating to water. Wells and springs were surrounded by walls, and sometimes enclosed in buildings. Also, they were often full of objects such as weapons, statuettes and jewellery, offered to gods. This illustration of a sacred well is partly based on the structure of some of the 'well temples' of Metal Age Sardinia.

The World's Megaliths

The making of structures consisting of large stones had already begun in Europe by the late fifth millennium BC. The practice went on for centuries, in places scattered far and wide. Wherever prehistoric man wished to build for eternity, and also to impress other people, megaliths were the result.

Late fifth millennium BC: passage graves.

3500 BC: temple of Gigantija, Malta.

3000 BC: New Grange tomb, Ireland; possibly Gavr'inis (tomb on an island off Brittany, France); Los Millares tomb, Spain.

2500 BC: temples of Tarxien, Malta; Central European dolmens and menhirs.

Second millennium BC: building of stone towers (nuraghi) in Sardinia for defence and as dwellings. This type of structure was constructed and used until the beginning of Roman domination in the third century BC.

Late second millennium BC: 'Cyclopean' walls (made of large round stones) around the Mycenean cities of Tiryns and Mycenae.

1000 BC: colossal sculptured stone heads at La Venta, Mexico.

1000 AD: colossal statues on Easter Island, South Pacific.

The History of Stonehenge

2500–2200 BC, late Neolithic period: the circular ditch was dug, 108 metres (354 feet) in diameter, as were the 56 Aubrey holes within its circumference (named after their 17th century discoverer). In four of these holes, reference stones were placed to mark certain lines for observing heavenly bodies. A great stone called the Heel Stone had already been put up outside the circle. Near this was a simple lintel.

1800 BC, end of the Neolithic period: in the middle of the great circle, a double row of 'bluestones' were erected, and also the so-called altar stone. It is interesting to note that the bluestones (in fact bluish-grey) certainly came from Wales, 300 kilometres (185 miles) from the site of the monument.

1600 BC, Early Bronze Age: the inner ring of gigantic sandstone blocks (sarsens) with the five enormous trilithons in horseshoe formation inside them were built.

1500–1400 BC, Middle Bronze Age: re-use of the bluestones within the horseshoe, and between it and the ring of sarsens. Some holes outside this ring were made for stones that were never put up, or for movable wooden structures.

uprights (and also menhirs, colossal single blocks) were put up by digging a made-to-measure hole under one of the ends of the mass of stone, and then making it slide in by pulling it with ropes. Thus one end was fixed in the earth while the other was raised to the sky. Intelligent use of balance made this possible without needing thousands of people. To place the lintels in position on top of the uprights, they probably used tree-trunk scaffolding. By adding trunks firstly on one side and then on the other, and making the lintel rock to and fro, it could be raised without enormous efforts. Could it be that the European monuments are the expression of a common will, built by communities of people which were not directed by one powerful figure? If so, it

would be in contrast to such works as the pyramids of Egypt.

Life in Bronze-Age Europe (1800–500 BC)

Why did no empires arise in Europe (or, we must add, in central Asia) while the great complexes developed in the Near East? Probably because they were not necessary.

How did human communities live in the Europe of the Chalcolithic and Bronze Ages? We can see certain general characteristics, but the solutions worked out locally to important problems were many and various.

As far as food production was concerned, the Europeans of this period developed the agricultural techniques

Opposite above: Clay model of a cart found in Yugoslavia from the Bronze Age, second millennium BC.
Opposite below: Bronze ring decorated with gold from Serbia in south-east Yugoslavia. It is also from the Bronze Age, second millennium BC.
Above: The two sides of a small bell-shaped idol. It represents, in an extremely stylized manner, a human figure, possibly female, and was found in Serbia. Again, it dates from the Bronze Age, second millennium BC.

previously used by Neolithic peoples, taking advantage of the fertility of the soil where possible, and elsewhere using the 'cut and burn' method. There were no important works for irrigation, but they did build structures such as dykes and ditches for the protection of settlements. However, these were only on a small scale. Rain was relied upon to water crops. Interesting use was made of wood in the construction of layers of planks laid in such a way as to create an artificial platform above water, for example at the edges of lakes (see p 155). Sometimes these constructions covered an area some kilometres long. The houses were made of wood, but in some settlements the foundations or lower storeys were made of stone. Where the surface of the ground was soft, or where the level of the water changed a great deal, piles were used to give solidity to the structure. These were a series of large poles driven into the ground. They remained almost submerged or sunk in the mud, and on them was laid a platform of planks. The dwellings were built on this. At this point it is worth remembering that some of the modern reconstructions of such places, showing piles sticking out of the water like herons' legs and huts perched on top of them, are not correct. Pile dwellings of this type exist in some villages in Polynesia, but in a completely different environment, being by an ocean with strong tides.

Trade flourished. This is shown, as we have said, by the spread of the techniques of metal working and of the necessary raw materials. Even the ceramics indicate that there were frequent exchanges. The bell-shaped beaker (*glokkenbecher* in German) is found over a vast area in Bronze Age settlements. This type of ceramic container, shaped like an upturned bell and decorated with incisions (usually of a zig-zag pattern), has been called the Coca-Cola bottle of the age. They may have been made in several places but with similar techniques, as if following a standardized procedure; they are a most important guide for dating settlements. Since bell-shaped beakers are also found in various places in the western Mediterranean (in the islands, North Africa, and Spain), one of the ways in which they spread must have been by sea, probably as a result of voyages in search of tin. There was an active trade in amber, as in the Neolithic period.

164

The different communities lived by facing problems as they arose from day to day. It was never necessary to organize the work of everyone on a very large scale in order to cope with critical situations. To get out of a crisis, a group would often just move to another place. This was easily done, as the neighbouring area was not usually occupied by others. If it was, two groups might unite in a peaceful way, or else there would be battles and raids. So there were many dramatic events in different places, but never a single history or series of connected events arising from decisions taken in only one centre.

Bronze-Age Europe had no capital cities and no empires.

Burial Rites

Interesting information on the contacts between the various groups of people in Bronze-Age Europe can be found by looking at the way they treated their dead. A most ancient practice was burial, already found in the Mousterian period (pp 21 and 26). In the Neolithic period corpses were often placed in the ground under the foundations of huts. But at this time there were also places outside villages where the corpses were put in tombs that were sometimes similar in shape to the houses of the living. As we have already learnt, the name for such a place is a necropolis, or 'city of the dead'. Funeral ceremonies must have been very complex. In the great civilizations, a person's very high rank might even require the sacrifice of

Opposite: Impression of a Bronze Age settlement in Baden-Wurttemberg, West Germany.
Left above: Cross-section of a Bronze Age chamber tomb in East Germany.
Left centre: Bronze Age funeral monument in the form of a ship on the Swedish island of Gotland. It is 18 metres (60 feet) long.
Left below: Iron Age funeral urn (for ashes) from Scandinavia. It has a typical hut shape.

165

prehistoric
engraver

Camonica rose

reproducing an engraving

making a fake engraving

human beings at his funeral. These were perhaps supposed to serve the great personage in the afterlife. This was true in the case of the royal tombs of Ur. Burial was seen as a sign of total 'one-ness' or unity with the earth, which was a life-giving element.

Often weapons, jewellery, and even musical instruments were put in the tombs. Examples of the latter include the harps at Ur, and the Danish bronze horns called lur. Lurs have been found in a perfectly preserved state, and have actually been played and recorded by modern musicians.

Funeral rituals varied according to the ways of life of the different groups. For example, nomads, who were con-tinually on the move, found burial in the ground too great a separation from the dead person, and probably started the practice of cremation. The corpse was given over to another element, fire, and

the ashes were collected into jars, or funeral urns. These, like tombs, were shaped like miniature houses (p 165), and could easily be carried from place to place. People were probably very quick to think of the dead person as being united with the element air following the destruction of the body by fire. The smoke disappeared into the sky, so what remained of the dead person was mixed with the air, and went to some kind of 'heaven'. The ashes, collected in urns, could then be placed in the ground with offerings, of course, appropriate to the person's position in life. So we find urn burial grounds. This practice identified the urn-field culture, which was found over a very wide area of Late Bronze-Age and Iron-Age Europe. Some experts have con-nected the practice of cremation with increasing use of fire, which was looked on as a friend and a necessary tool for

Opposite: In Europe evidence reveals that Bronze-Age rock engravings were made for a period of over 1,000 years. Dating them is usually based on the different figures and objects (such as daggers, carts and ploughs) depicted in different periods, but it is always rather uncertain. The prehistoric people of the Camonica Valley which runs into Lake Garda in northern Italy are identified with the 'Camonica rose' shown here. It is thought that it may be a symbol of the sun. Engravings can be reproduced by laying a sheet of paper over them and rubbing with a crayon. However, it is often difficult to distinguish ancient rock engravings from more modern imitations.
Below: Scandinavian rock engraving from the Bronze Age depicting a sledge and animals.
Right: Bronze or Iron Age rock engraving of warriors from Italy.
Bottom Right: Another Bronze Age rock engraving from Scandinavia depicting the sun and its rays.

preparing metals. So it is possible that people who made their living by metalworking and using and dealing in metals, came to think of fire as the life-giving element instead of 'old mother earth'.

The idea that the elements were divine was also found in water cults. Everyone knew how life-giving this element was, and many peoples had sanctuaries (safe and holy places) by springs or natural wells. The ashes of the dead were sometimes scattered on water and urns thrown into it. Where water was used for travelling, for example near rivers and coasts, the stone tombs imitated the forms of ships. Ritual ships were also buried at the funerals of the god-kings of Egypt, and decorated

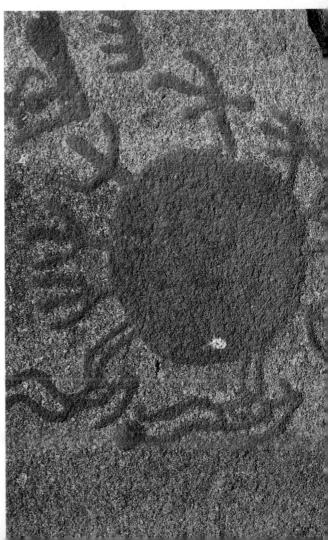

funeral ships were used much later by the Vikings.

On structures used for rituals (temples) or for the dead (tombs), decoration was scarce; often there was nothing more than simple abstract designs (photograph p 105) which were perhaps stylizations of natural shapes. But pictures from life were common: people at work and animals, often drawn on rock faces (p 167). These figures may have had a magical purpose, like the cave paintings of the Palaeolithic period. Certainly there were many pictures of wild animals. Perhaps they marked the point where a certain group had taken over an area. They also portrayed the results of people's skills and techniques: houses, chariots, ploughs, daggers, etc.

The Taste of Food

What did the food cooked and eaten in ancient times taste like? The question might not seem very serious or important, but it brings us to two interesting points, and also to a form of trade that certainly was important in Europe during the first and second millennia BC.

The first point has to do with the essential part played by plants in people's diet, even when this included a lot of meat. Long ago people discovered that certain plants added a good taste to meat, whether cooked with it or put on it afterwards. No cook can prepare a gravy or sauce without adding aromatic herbs or spices. Spices were collected and traded in ancient times. Another ingredient in the cooking of those times was oil. It was extracted from various seeds or vegetables, and from olives in the Mediterranean area.

A sweet taste was obtained from sugary fruit such as figs or dates, or from honey, particularly in Egypt where people kept bees. From fermented fruit and cereals moderately alcoholic drinks (like beer) were made. Although the Bible says that Noah was the first to make (and get drunk on) wine, it was probably first produced in the Mediterranean area.

What of a salty taste? This is our second point. As spices were easily obtained in ancient times, salt must have seemed less necessary, though nowadays, of course, we take its use for granted. The use of saltpans for extracting salt from sea water by leaving it in the sun to dry was only found much later. Even today in Near Eastern food there are plenty of spices but not much of a salty taste. If you were tempted to eat couscous, a North African dish made of semolina and various meats, you would find it both 'strong' and 'bland' at the same time.

Europe of the late Bronze and Early Iron Ages discovered salt. Those who could get it found that they could make a living out of it. Salt was not extracted from sea water but from the earth. Central Europe is very rich in deposits of rock salt (which is almost pure sodium chloride). The people of this part of Europe learnt how to extract the salt from mines, digging the crystals from the rich veins in which the salt lay. Or else they used an ingenious method of running water over the deposits to dissolve the salt and make the water salty. The salt was then separated from the water by boiling it in large open-air cauldrons over wood fires.

It is not surprising to find that the production and sale of salt was often associated with the production of

Opposite: Impression of the outside of a Bronze or early Iron Age salt mine in the region of present-day Salzburg, Austria. The salt was dissolved by water channelled along the underground veins: the salty water (brine) was then led into open-air cauldrons, where the salt was produced by boiling the water away. The wood for the fires came from the forests on the same mountains in which the mine shafts were cut. The salt was then distributed over a wide area.

entrance to
a shaft

entrance to
a shaft

channel for
brine

furnace

cauldrons containing brine

metals. The people who were 'the friends of fire' could use it as their instrument in many ways. Needless to say, the process of dissolving salt in water meant that the wood of many forests was used to extract the salt. The urn-field people grew rich on the salt trade. It is interesting to look in an atlas at the names of the cities, villages, and rivers of Central Europe: many are connected with salt, or *sal* in Latin. Examples include Saalfelden, Salzburg, Salzach, Saalach. Other names derive from the Greek word *hals*, also meaning 'salt', as well as 'sea' (for example, Hallein and Hallstatt). Clearly the salt trade was flourishing and spreading towards the south even before the spread of the Latin language (in Middle and High German, the word for 'salt-deposit' is *hal*).

The Production of Iron

Copper, gold, and silver are found in nature in a pure or almost pure state; each has its own recognizable characteristics. Iron, on the other hand, can only be extracted from ore. Tin is not found naturally in a pure state, either; the main ore from which it is extracted is cassiterite. We have seen that bronze was probably discovered by chance: perhaps a quantity of cassiterite, which may have been chosen for its shiny appearance, was added to a container of molten copper.

What about the discovery of iron? Did this come from a lucky chance as well? All we can do is make reasonable guesses. Someone may have seen a meteorite fall from the sky. Once people had overcome their fear of the

From Bronze to Iron

The transition from the use of bronze to the use of iron in prehistoric times was reflected in nearly all cultures by a change in the way of life. Very often the change came about through contact, or conflict, with other people. The Hittites are usually credited with the discovery of iron and its uses, but it is probable that even the Hittites owed this discovery to some previous culture.

In order to produce bronze, it was necessary to trade; ingredients for the alloy, copper and tin, often came from areas that were far apart. Thus trade was the key element in the spreading of this form of metalworking. In the case of iron, one of the greatest problems was the high temperatures necessary (at least 1,500°C (2,700°F)) for its production; of course, it was also necessary to find the mineral deposits and have mines to extract the ore. Once these problems had been solved, iron could be further treated by tempering it (heating it then cooling it suddenly in water) to make it suitable for the purposes of war; the wheels of light war chariots could be hooped with iron rims, and strong swords with double cutting edges could be produced. So it seems probable that the technique of iron working was spread by war and conquest. On the other hand, iron had more peaceful uses, as in the making of stronger and deeper-digging ploughs, and wheels for carts for transporting goods. All these innovations changed people's lives.

European Cultures of the Late Bronze and Iron Ages

Urn-field culture: occupied sites from the Caucasus to France over a period of several centuries. These people burned the bodies of their dead and put the ashes in ceramic vessels (urns) which were then buried in cemeteries. There is evidence for this practice in the late Bronze Age, for example in Hungary.

Villanovan culture (named after Villanova, outside Bologna in Italy): found on the plain of the River Po, as well as in other places in Italy. It had connections with cultures north of the Alps. The metal most used was bronze, but iron was used for weapons and objects showing rank and power. Burial usually consisted of the bones of the dead being burnt to ashes and placed in vessels (ossuaries).

Golasecca culture (named after a site on the Ticino River, near Lake Maggiore in Italy): urns typical of this culture have been found over a wide area of the regions of Piedmont and Lombardy in northern Italy and the canton of Ticino in southern Switzerland. Successive stages of this culture can be seen.

Hallstatt culture: the richest and most widely distributed of the cultures of the Iron Age. The extraction and sale of salt was very important in the areas of this culture, which also produced very elaborate swords.

La Tène culture: represents the final stage of the Iron Age. This is the culture of the Celts who spread over many parts of Western Europe. They produced splendid goldwork.

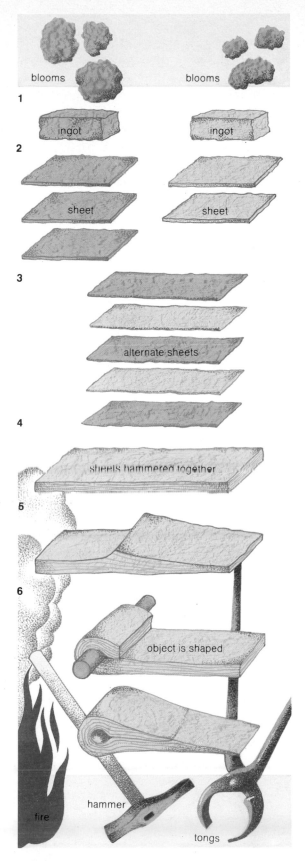

strange stone that had fallen white-hot from the sky, they might have broken it open and discovered a shiny and very hard metal. Iron is found in a pure state in meteorites, and often with a small quantity of nickel. Because such a happening is so exceptional, the metal may well have been considered divine, a 'child of heaven'. The heavenly origin of iron is recalled even today in the word siderite, which is the mineral iron carbonate. It comes from the Latin word *sidus*, meaning star.

And of course people began to look about on earth for the metal that fell

Left: Producing iron by lamination. 1. By melting the iron ore different blooms were obtained; these were spongy lumps full of impurities. 2. Several blooms were heated and forged with hammer blows into a single piece, forming a rough ingot. 3. Each ingot was beaten into a flat sheet. 4. A number of sheets were put on top of one another. 5. These were hammered together into one thick piece. 6. The laminated iron was kept hot and worked into the required shape.
Below: A very fine bronze axe dating from the seventh century BC. The decoration in the form of a horse and rider shows very skilful workmanship, even if the horse looks more like a dinosaur.

from the sky. They were perhaps attracted by the reddish haematite, or by the shiny pyrite, known to this day as 'fool's gold'. They tried smelting these minerals and ended up with a sort of spongy paste, full of dross (impurities), called the bloom. Someone then had the idea of hammering this mass of stuff; many hammer blows produced a compact material.

Heating and above all hammering is the technique that produces forged iron. Laminated iron is produced from putting together alternating layers from various blooms (see drawing on previous page). Other artisans relied on the power of fire and made the bloom red hot in stone containers.

How did they produce the temperature necessary for smelting? This must be at least 1,500°C (2,700°F). The answer is that they blew on the fire through a tube, perhaps a hollow reed.

The Uses of Iron

As we have discovered, either the Hittites or those before them in the Caucasus and Anatolia were the first to produce iron. The use of the new metal immediately had great strategic importance, that is, its use in war had a big impact. Swords that were both hard and could bend were a great improvement on breakable bronze daggers or weak copper blades. Iron hoops that could be fixed round the rims of wheels made it possible to build light battle-chariots.

When the power of the Hittites declined, their own speciality became everyone's property. Naturally the artisans who were already expert in handling bronze got the best results. For this reason, iron became a 'European' metal. But it was also widely used by the peoples of central Asia and by the Chinese (see p 226).

Left: Splendid fibula (a kind of clasp or brooch having a movable pin with a spring) from a Hallstatt tomb. It is made of bronze decorated with patterns punched into it. The Hallstatt culture was the most important of the European Iron Age. It extended over a wide area from the tenth to the eighth centuries BC. Its name comes from the village of Hallstatt, on a lake of that name, south-east of Salzburg in Austria. (Sites that give their names to cultures are called eponymous.)

Opposite: Diagram, made in the last century, of various tombs in the Hallstatt necropolis. The excavation was carried out by the Austrian archaeologist Georg Ramsauer. The numbers on the drawings show the order in which the tombs were excavated. The dead were buried with objects in everyday use: notice the many ceramic bowls and the bronze buckets (situlae). The tomb shown in the middle contained exceptional offerings of ornaments of bronze and gold.

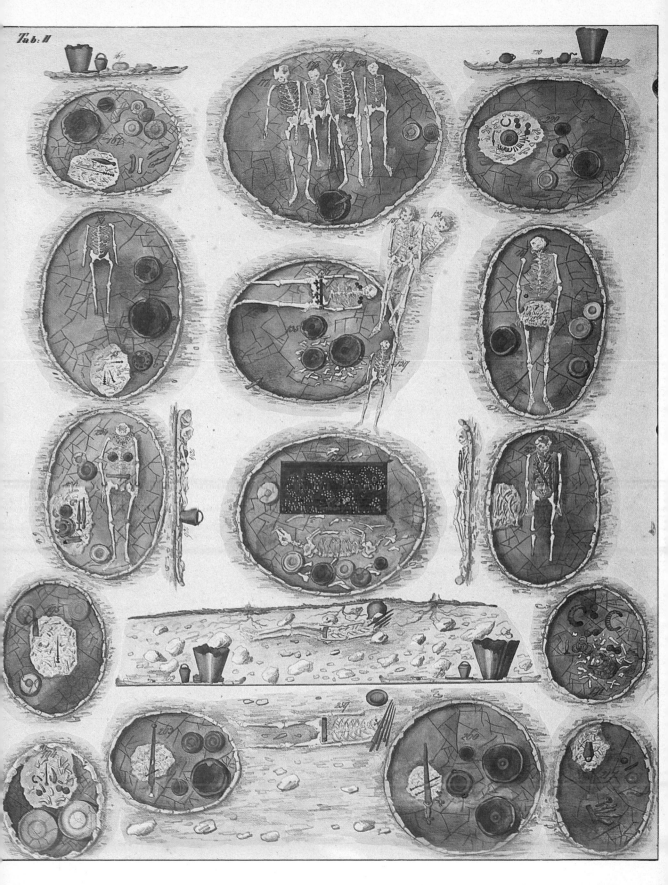

Often the reheating of the bloom and adding traces of carbon produced cast iron. Once the necessary ingredients had been worked out more exactly, the next step was to make steel.

The discovery of the technique of tempering followed fairly soon; iron swords became even harder if they were made red-hot, hammered, and then dipped in water. This is the process the legendary German hero Siegfried used when he forged the sword he called Nothung. In his opera of this legend, Wagner created a brilliant musical impression of the water sizzling on the red-hot steel.

The use of iron for the plough came relatively late (see p 151). In fact, the light type of plough that was used up to the first century AD did not need to be reinforced with metal. It was only in the days of the Roman Empire that the heavy plough with an iron ploughshare capable of making deep furrows first appeared.

In the European Iron Age we find very highly developed cultures which produced objects of great refinement, including splendid work in gold, the famous embossed bronze 'buckets' called *situlae*, and rich works of art made with hard stones. The great complex of urn-field cultures from the Bronze Age continued into the early Iron Age, which also gave rise to the cultures of Hallstatt in Austria and, later, La Tène in Switzerland. The peoples who developed from these cultures were the so-called barbarians, particularly the Celts, or Gauls, who were to be destroyed and taken over by the expansion of Rome. The Hallstatt civilization developed from the urn-field cultures in about the 10th to the 8th centuries BC. Some experts think that this was due to contacts with Asiatic peoples, particularly the Cimmerians, who were being pushed west by the advance of the Scythians (see pp 242–

7). The culture of La Tène, dating from the fifth century BC, was a development of that of Hallstatt.

There were also two fairly important cultures in Italy. The Golasecca culture was typified by urn burials in small structures with stone walls, called 'cists', which often contained other objects such as blades and pins. Then there was the Villanovan culture with its typical ossuary urns (which contained the bones of the dead) in the shape of a double cone. This culture was found in the Po Valley and stretched as far as the Apennines and Tuscany. It was one of the probable roots of the Etruscan civilization (pp 282–4).

Opposite and below: Iron Age bronze situla from Slovenia in Yugoslavia, dating from about the sixth century BC. The object was found in 1883. In the area of the discovery, a necropolis was later found. The decoration is in three bands: in the upper and central parts, animals and humans are depicted (the detail below shows a banquet with drinkers) and in the lower part is a procession of animals.

The situla is an object found throughout the late Iron Age. There are notable examples from sites in northern Italy (the Certosa situla, discovered near Bologna, dating from the fifth century BC), and in particular from the Este or Atestine culture named after the site at Este near Padua.

The refined metalwork of situlae was also used in the making of containers for the ashes or bones of the dead (cinerary urns and ossuaries), with interesting examples from the Etruscan area.

Europe Compared

Europe of the Bronze and Iron Ages has left great burial places with many small tombs, sometimes richly provided with offerings, but they are nothing to compare with the pyramids or with certain Mesopotamian royal tombs. The chiefs or kings of the European groups were not as powerful as those of the Near East. They were probably not treated as gods, and they were not despots.

Different environments, different densities of population, and different

CUT AND BURN

fire 'eats up' vegetation

hut

land cleared of trees is fertilized by ashes

RAISING SHEEP

rainwater can be better distributed by using catchment tanks and simple channels

milk-producing animals

cheeses

harvesting

hunting

hut

tent

fire

fire

stone for grinding cereals

herb-gathering

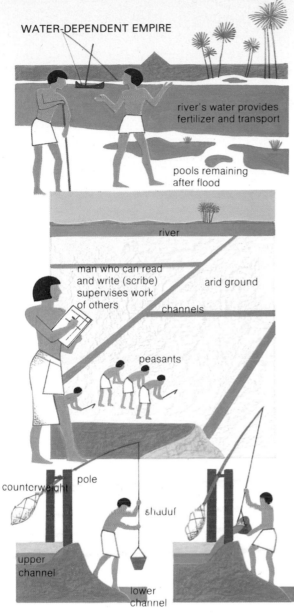

WATER-DEPENDENT EMPIRE

river's water provides fertilizer and transport

pools remaining after flood

river

man who can read and write (scribe) supervises work of others

arid ground

channels

peasants

counterweight

pole

shaduf

upper channel

lower channel

ways of using the world of nature all contributed to produce different civilizations and different types of society. There is no doubt that the Europeans of the Bronze and Iron Ages were oppressors; prisoners captured in the frequent fighting were turned into slaves. But their society was not divided into classes to the same extent as that of the water-dependent empires. For this reason, there was greater and more varied development in things that depended on the work of individuals, such as trade and technical skill. In history, there are no good or bad people, nor right or wrong solutions; there are only ways of dealing with what the environment offers. When these ways worked well, the civilization flourished, no matter whether it was great or small.

Some of the principal methods of producing food. In areas with steep and rocky ground where grass can grow, the most practical method of making use of the land is to graze animals. Grass, which mankind cannot use directly as food, feeds the animals, which in turn provide him with products of high food value, such as meat, wool and milk.

Where grazing animals are scarce, or do not exist, and where there are thick forests, people can use the vegetation by burning it: this provides open ground for cultivation and also fertilizes it with the ashes. This practice is called 'cut and burn'.

Where a great river flows through arid regions and floods regularly, a water-dependent empire may develop.

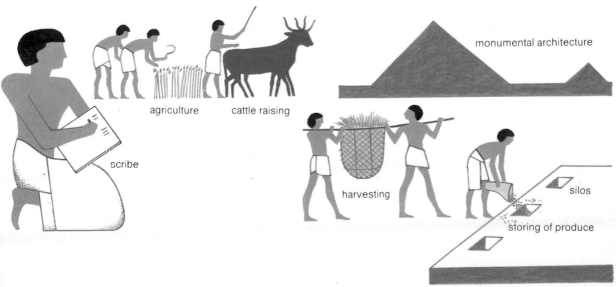

agriculture

cattle raising

scribe

monumental architecture

harvesting

silos

storing of produce

6. Other Environments, Other Empires

Mediterranean Civilization

Transport on rivers was usually easy when going downstream with the current. Going upstream against the current tends to be more difficult. In the case of the Tigris and the Euphrates, many stretches were dangerous, either because of strong currents or because the banks were swampy. Much of the work done in Mesopotamia was aimed at making the two waterways navigable by ships.

The elements were kinder in the Nile Valley. The wind generally blew to the south from the delta, making the voyage against the current easier. It was not necessary to rely totally on rowing as sails could be used. Also, the great African river is free of rapids and swamps for at least 1,000 kilometres (620 miles) northwards from Aswan where the first cataract is found. Works such as piers, mooring places and steps were still necessary, however, to make river shipping safe.

In any case, the movement of people and goods along the river was all part of the whole water-dependent system. The only alternative was the caravan travelling between the main centres of work and trade.

Other people had a waterway on which they could travel in all directions. Though it was more dangerous, it offered a much wider range of opportunities. This, of course, was the sea. Coastal shipping existed in Neolithic times, and short crossings between islands were undertaken even before that. Evidence for this is the obsidian trade in the Lipari Islands north of Sicily (see p 59).

At the beginning of the Bronze Age there were very long voyages in search of tin. Transporting heavy objects, like the stones of Stonehenge, must have been very difficult, but sea transport solved the problem. The first organized system of sea transport began in a large island, well placed in the eastern Mediterranean. This island was Crete. Other islands in the Aegean Sea soon became part of the system, both as 'stepping-stones' on the way to more distant destinations, and as producers of goods for trade.

Crete and the Minoans

There was certainly a local Neolithic population in Crete. There were a few smallish plains where cereals could be grown. Olives, figs and vines were also cultivated. It is thought that people from mainland Asia mixed with the local population. They probably came from western Anatolia, and were

Opposite: Ruins of the palace of Knossos on Crete.
Below: Artist's reconstruction of part of the great Knossos complex. The buildings often had several floors. The edges of the flat roofs, perhaps used for practical purposes, were decorated with 'battlements' shaped like pairs of horns which may originally have been gilded. The excavation of the palace of Knossos by Sir Arthur Evans (1900–1930) has been criticized because the archaeologists restored some of it, replacing perished timbers with concrete and setting modern reproductions in places originally occupied by fragments of paintings.

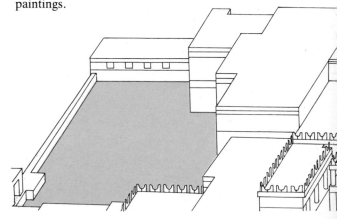

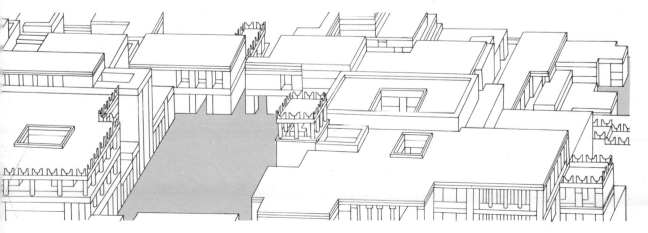

already skilled at bronze-working. Some experts do not agree with this theory, however, and think that the development in Crete was not aided by contact with other people. Whatever its origin, after 2500 BC a rich civilization flourished in Crete. It is called Minoan, taking its name from the mythical king and 'law-giver' Minos. Why a law-giver? It is now thought that the laws of Minos were in fact rules for managing trade by sea. Minos was perhaps a capable administrator of a great 'holding company' with many subsidiaries.

Why do we hesitate to use the term 'Minoan Empire' while many history books still do? Because we want to show the difference between the Minoan system and that of the water-dependent societies of the Near East, with which we have already dealt.

The evidence of archaeology reveals that around 2000 BC great buildings called 'palaces' sprang up in various Cretan centres like Knossos and Mallia. Knossos was discovered by the English archaeologist Sir Arthur Evans at the beginning of the 20th century. Evans was also responsible for the concrete restorations. These have perhaps made a more exact look at certain parts of the ruins impossible (see p 179). The traditional theory, that of Evans, sees these palaces as centres of rich royal courts, suitable for great kings if not semi-divine heroes.

The building could have been a sign of power and a place fit to be the centre of the bureaucratic organization of an empire. But we should notice that these palaces, not only those of Knossos and Mallia, but also those at Phaistos and Gournia, contain many rooms. Instead of a magnificent collection of royal halls, they consist of a complex chain of rather small rooms, often opening on to

corridors that link them all.

Were these palaces, or buildings, designed to impress? Perhaps they were great and organized workshops? Let us look at the evidence: there are signs of very practical organization. There is a network of drains constructed by tying terracotta (baked clay) pipes together. There are olive presses and large

Below and bottom: Two frescoes from Santorini, an island in the Cyclades in the Aegean Sea north of Crete. The excavations on Santorini were carried out in the 1950s and 60s and revealed palaces, painted halls and shops. Everything was buried, and thus protected, by many layers of volcanic material from an enormous volcanic explosion around 1500 BC. The frescoes show (below) a river with animals, and (bottom) a naval battle. Marshes and antelopes suggest that the scene is of part of the North African coast.

containers for collecting and pouring out the oil. At least 400 weights and spindles for looms for making textiles have been found at Knossos. There are cauldrons which were almost certainly used for dyes, probably made from vegetables and plants. There are plenty of kilns for making ceramics, and furnaces for metal working. The various rooms are arranged round great courtyards, along the sides of which there are often lines of enormous jars. These jars are larger than a man, and must have been containers for grain and perhaps liquids. There are also some fairly large rooms; one such room at Knossos was called the 'throne room' by Evans. Parts of the buildings have upper floors reached by means of staircases, some of which are in the form of columns. Perhaps these rooms were for relaxation, or work such as weaving.

The Minoan economy

So the 'palaces' of Crete may have been great centres of production which of course included showrooms and offices. These would have been necessary for the organization of production and distribution. Here we are not talking about royal palaces or complexes for bureaucrats. In other words, the Cretans did not have an empire. The laws of Minos were rules for sharing out tasks efficiently. Perhaps they included protectionist measures, meaning that only certain people had the right to

Opposite: The Minoan economy was linked to the sea. This scene of Minoan Crete shows the work of fishermen, who took food from the sea, and in the background some merchant ships. Sea-borne trade made possible the exchange of many kinds of goods. Many of the centres in Crete were organized in such a way as to suggest that workshops could produce textiles, ceramics, metal objects and oil in sufficient quantities to export them. Efficient production and distribution of these goods, secure harbours and trade routes, and the control of weights, measures, and coins were ensured by the central government.

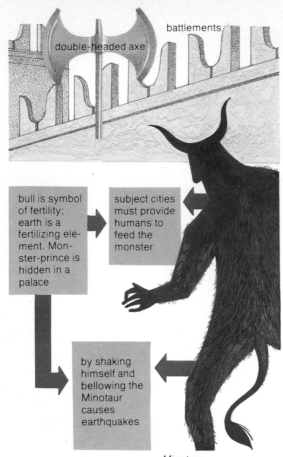

double-headed axe · battlements

bull is symbol of fertility; earth is a fertilizing element. Monster-prince is hidden in a palace → subject cities must provide humans to feed the monster

by shaking himself and bellowing the Minotaur causes earthquakes

Minotaur,
a monstrous bull-prince

light plough with a horizontal handle, which perhaps made fairly deep furrows possible; the user could press it deeper into the earth as well as steer it (see p 151). Ploughs, presses, jars, nets, hooks, and of course boats that handled well – the ancient Cretans showed a wide range of technical skills even in the things used for basic production.

Myths and the Minoan world

The Minoan production and trading system included, as well as Crete, various other Aegean islands, which were like so many branches of the 'company'. It is likely that there was also some foothold on the mainland. The Aegean islands, and Crete itself, are volcanic in origin, and some are real

produce certain things, and that certain people were better supplied. The aim of these measures was to ensure the best results from sea trade.

The sea was certainly the most important 'working part' in the Minoan machine. It provided food; fish was the main source of protein for the Cretans. If we consider the decorative motifs of different civilizations, it is unusual to find such a clear preference for a certain subject or theme as we do in Crete. The theme is the sea and its creatures; fishes, dolphins, shells, waves and squid are to be found on nearly every vase and every frieze (a strip of decoration on a wall).

A certain amount of food came from herding goats and sheep in the mountainous countryside. Food was also produced from orchards and the limited area of flat fields. The Cretans used a

volcanic cones or pieces of volcanic cones. In some places the land was fertile and very suitable for growing vines and olive-trees; in other places farming was hard, unsuitable for anything other than raising sheep and goats. The fertility of the earth has always concerned people in these parts. Their myths confirm this.

A very dramatic Cretan myth is the story of the Minotaur. The bull was a sacred animal, always connected with the idea of fertility. Examples include the bull Apis in Egypt, and perhaps the Palaeolithic cave paintings of bison. In Crete there was a connection between the sea and fears about the restlessness of the land (as manifested by volcanoes and earthquakes). The myth of the

Opposite: Legend of the Minotaur. The famous monster, half man and half bull, can certainly be explained as a symbol of fertility (which is probably true of all 'divine bulls'). What is more, Minoan stories about the Minotaur in the famous labyrinth of Crete provided an explanation for the cause of earthquakes. Young men and women took part in sports with bulls which may have had magical and religious significance; they would seize the bull's horns and somersault over its back.

Below: Golden cup found at Vaphio near Sparta in Greece. This splendid object reached the mainland of Greece through trade, probably having been made in Crete.

Bottom: Fresco from the palace of Knossos illustrating a man 'bull leaping'.

Minotaur tells how the god Poseidon sent a white bull from the sea for Minos to sacrifice. The king avoided this duty, so in revenge Poseidon caused Queen Pasiphae, wife of Minos, to fall madly in love with the bull. Daedalus, a skilled inventor and architect who symbolizes extreme technical skill, enabled them to mate by building a wooden cow in which the queen could hide herself. The child of Pasiphae and the white bull was the Minotaur, a prince who was half bull and half man. He was a shameful secret and was hidden in the maze of underground rooms built by Daedalus beneath the palace. The word labyrinth, the name given to this part of the palace, derives from *labrys*, the double-bladed axe used for sacrifice. The house of the bull-prince is also called the 'house of the axes' (which are 'two-horned'). The horn motif is found everywhere in Crete and the decoration of the palace battlements takes this form.

So the sea could be an enemy as well as a friend; it could take its revenge. The monster in the underground palace made itself heard, roaring and banging against the walls, shaking everything; in this way the myth explained the low rumbles and shocks of earthquakes, the terror of the islanders.

Another sea theme that found its way into mythology was that of the voyage of the Argonauts searching as far as distant Colchis (the northern shores of the Black Sea) for the Golden Fleece. It is highly probable that the myth was based on the true stories of the voyages of Aegean sailors, who may have passed through the straits of Gibraltar or up the great European rivers. The 'fleece' might be a memory of the ancient practice of filtering the sands of rivers containing gold or other minerals; sheepskins were used as they were greasy and trapped any valuable bits and pieces.

Finally there is the theme of contacts and conflicts with centres on the mainland, particularly with the people of western Anatolia from whom the first Minoans may have sprung. Crete was in a position to make heavy demands on the mainland populations, perhaps for essential raw materials. In the myth, Athens is forced to pay up in the form of young people sent every year to feed the Minotaur. The efforts of the Athenian Theseus to rescue his city from this heavy burden represent the efforts of the mainland centres to free themselves from the Cretan system, or to work within it more freely.

Mycenean civilization

The links between the Minoans and the mainland had another result, namely the continuation of the Cretan civilization in Greece itself. This was the Mycenean civilization which took its name from Mycenae, one of its most famous centres.

It is easy to get a wrong idea of historical reality by seeing the Myceneans as people who 'picked up the torch of progress' dropped by the Minoans. A linear view of historical development leads to mistaken pictures. In fact, there were several parallel histories, and the Mycenean centres were already flourishing in the 17th century BC, while the Minoan civilization was at its height.

Opposite: In the texts that tell of the mythical voyage of the Argonauts in search of the Golden Fleece of Colchis (a legendary country by the Black Sea), there are certain interesting details that suggest a real voyage. Some stories say that the sea around the ship became hard and broke into pieces. Could this refer to ice on the North Sea or glaciers near the source of the Rhône, Rhine or Elbe Rivers? The *Argo* (the Argonauts' boat) is said to have been carried over dry land. Could this have been from one river to another? This illustration shows imaginary Argonauts working hard to drag their ship across wooded country near the upper reaches of the River Danube.

Mycenean culture was no doubt greatly influenced by the Minoans, but it also developed locally and independently. There were various Neolithic cultures in Greece. The use of the megaron (a large hall with pillared porch) in the style of building and the types of fortification remind us of the solutions we have already seen at Dimini (see p 107). In the early stages the Cretans tried to make colonies out of mainland Greek centres, but later the situation was reversed and the Myceneans became masters of the islands.

These complex changes in the relations between the two peoples must have caused great changes to the economic system. The rise of the Myceneans started a process that ended with the decline of Cretan supremacy and their control of the seas. There are different types of evidence for what took place: archaeological evidence, geological evidence from studying the earth, rocks, etc, and linguistic evidence from studying languages.

Setting out from their solidly walled cities, the Myceneans tried more than once to conquer the Minoan centres.

Below: Head of a woman in a fresco from Tiryns about 1500 BC; Tiryns was one of the principal cities of the Mycenean civilization.
Opposite above: Head of a woman made of plaster and painted limestone from Mycenae and dated about 1500 BC. Note the hairstyle with curls over the forehead.
Opposite below: Head of a woman in a 1300 BC Mycenean fresco discovered in 1970.

The great so-called palaces had no walls or defensive moats, but were open to the outside world. Traces of destruction have been found dating from about 1600 BC onwards. It is possible, however, especially in Crete, that this destruction was caused by local revolts. Could it have been the peasants and fishermen, sick and tired of supporting the artisans and traders, who revolted? It is possible that the Myceneans approved of these revolts and even encouraged them. Whatever happened, the 'palaces' gradually became part of the Mycenean system.

The Minoan world suffered a severe blow as a result of a natural catastrophe. Around 1500 BC, the island of Thera literally exploded in a volcanic eruption of extraordinary violence. The gigantic wave thrown up by the undersea quake ruined all the coastal centres on the Aegean Sea. Many Cretan palaces were destroyed by the cataclysm. Some people believe that the memory of this exceptional event gave the Greek philosopher Plato the idea for his description of the sinking of Atlantis.

Atlantis was a land imagined by Plato, but with such a great many details that we are tempted to think that he used historical information about various ancient places which had splendid legends attached to them.

All that remains today of Thera is part of the crater left by the volcanic explosion. An archaeological project has removed part of the lava flow and has brought to light buildings, objects and frescoes (wall paintings) that are typical of a minor centre or 'branch' of the Cretan system. It is interesting that Thera seems to have produced more oil than would have been needed locally. It may have been a centre that produced oil to supply the rest of the system.

Very few human remains have been found. The inhabitants of Thera may have escaped by sea, having been

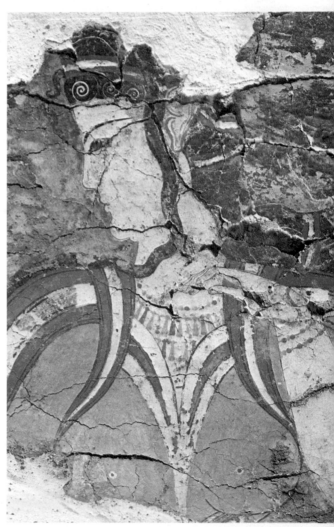

warned of the disaster by tremors and rumblings. Or they may have been killed when their ships were struck by the giant wave.

It seems likely that the Myceneans were responsible for the reconstruction of the island centres. Under them the great island chain was managed from the mainland. The operations of the Myceneans may have been partly caused by pressures from other peoples to the north. It is probable that these people, Indo-Europeans like the Myceneans, may have mixed with them and become part of their world.

At one time a pictographic (or pictorial) style of writing was used in Crete. This was replaced by a new form of writing, which Evans called Linear A, based on almost abstract signs. Later, from about 1500 BC, and certainly connected with the presence of Myceneans, a third form of writing appeared, which Evans called Linear B. This was deciphered by the Englishman Michael Ventris in the 1950s, and he proved beyond doubt that Linear B is an alphabetic form of writing of an Indo-European language, a very old dialect of Greek.

How did the basic economy change? The Mycenean world probably valued ships, but not fishing. It went in for trade in metals, and as metal working flourished so did the trade that went with it; Mycenean metal work is found as far away as the Danube region and Syria. War was almost a way of life, cities attacking other cities and taking revenge if attacked. Among the sea peoples who raided and sacked Egypt towards the end of the second millennium BC we must include the Myceneans. They also fought wars against nearer mainland peoples, especially in western Anatolia, and these were the basis of the legends of the Trojan War as recounted by the Greek poet Homer in *The Iliad* and *The Odys-*

Above: Ruins of Mycenae. The circle that encloses the royal tombs can be seen, marked by a double row of stone slabs.
Opposite above: One of the golden masks found by the German archaeologist Heinrich Schliemann in the tombs of Mycenae in 1874–76. Schliemann called it the Mask of Agamemnon. He was king of Mycenae and a hero of the Trojan War. Today we can date it to around 1600 BC, whereas the legendary war between Greece and Troy is most likely, from the historical evidence, to have taken place in 1300 BC.
Opposite below: Diagram of the Mycenean tomb known as the Treasury of Atreus, built about 1500 BC.

tomb is entirely covered by a mound; its
outer edge is marked by line of large stones

vault with false cupola

side
chambers

entry passage between two stone walls

sey. These sagas contain a great deal of history, even though the details relating to art, technology and ways of life reflect those of a later age. They appeared in the Greek world of about the eighth century BC.

The roots of modern Western civilization

Modern Western culture is very much the 'child' of Roman culture, and the 'grandchild' of Greek culture. There is no doubt that references to Zeus or Jupiter, Heracles or Hercules, Eros or Cupid, Aphrodite or Venus, or to Agamemnon are references which are familiar to many in the Western world today. It might even be true to say that many of us in the West know more about the adventures of Hercules or the Trojan War than about the lives of the Christian saints and martyrs. This is really not so surprising; the Greek myths and culture that greatly influenced the later and cruder Roman culture are extremely European.

In the Mycenean world, and thus in the beginnings of the Greek world and of modern Western civilization, the typically Indo-European tradition of the sea was important. In the Greek language, words relating to the sea and to coastal features such as points, capes and inlets, and certain terms to do with sailing are not Greek. They do not relate to Greek language structures and word roots. This suggests that they must have come from the most ancient languages of the peoples (Minoans and others) who lived on and from the sea. The same is true of the names of certain goddesses, especially that of the goddess of life and love, Aphrodite (which means 'born from the foam'). Aphrodite was certainly a mother-goddess not connected with the earth, but with the sea as the 'source of all life'. The Indo-European element is seen in the form of the male gods connected with the air, lightning, and fire

male gods of air and sky

bolts of lightning

mother goddesses associated with the earth, the 'mother of all'

sea goddesses symbolizing the wealth of food in the sea, a source of life

Opposite above: The three main types of god worshipped in the Minoan-Mycenean and Greek worlds.
Opposite below: Vessel from the Mycenean city of Tiryns, decorated with a horse, chariot, warriors, and dog and made about 1300 BC.
Right: Large vessel for mixing wine (*krater*) called 'the Warrior Vase'. It was found by Heinrich Schliemann at Mycenae. The painted decoration shows a line of armed men, with strangely large noses. It dates from about 1600 BC.
Below: Ivory carving from Mycenae, dating from 1300 BC. The large figures are two mothers with their arms round each other's shoulders, both leaning towards the child. They probably form a 'trinity' (three associated gods), but so far nothing else of the sort has been found. Note the hairstyles and the way the clothes are made.

such as Zeus and the war god Ares who was linked with a world in which the forging of swords was important. This divine domination by male figures (Zeus, Poseidon the sea-god, Hades the god of the underworld) perhaps reflects the domination of society by men and their roles as metal workers and warriors. In Minoan society women had played a greater part than in Indo-European societies. The queen may have managed textile production in the Cretan workshops.

Another great civilization whose economy was based on the Mediterranean Sea was that of the Phoenicians, an account of which is given on pp 272–81.

Prehistory of the New World

Tracing any real history of the American world before the arrival of the Spanish conquistadores is very difficult. The European explorers of the 16th century indulged in such widespread destruction and massacre that little was left of the world that used to exist there. Most importantly, they wiped out local traditions that could have given some

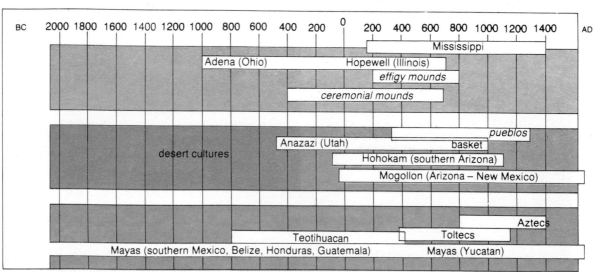

194

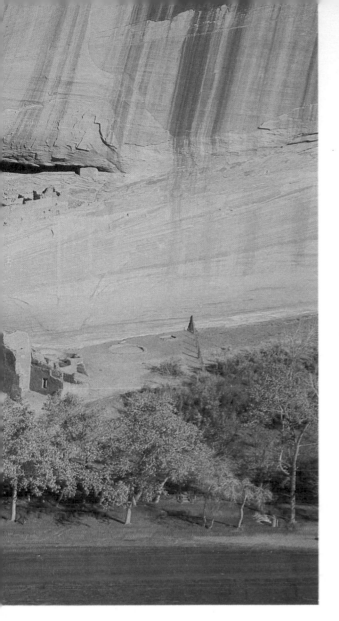

explanation of the previous history of the cultures. What happened later on the American continent has only added to the confusion.

In the areas colonized by the English and the French, later to become the United States and Canada, colonialism destroyed many of the traces of previous cultures. It is only fairly recently that a search for 'roots' has led to investigations into the past of the original inhabitants. The so-called Indians themselves were the inheritors of a very ancient culture.

Throughout the whole great region of Central and South America, the damage caused by the conquest was not the only difficulty. In addition to the perennial problem of poverty, Spanish and Portuguese colonialism showed no interest in the native cultures. More recently, the economy of the region has been affected by activities such as fruit growing and mining undertaken by multinational companies. The natural world has hidden many traces. In Central America the jungle has swallowed up whole Maya cities, while the peaks of the Andes mountains kept an Inca city hidden. The latter was Machu Picchu, which was totally forgotten by history and not discovered until 1912 by the American Hiram Bingham.

Above: View of Cliff Palace, an ancient settlement at Mesa Verde in Colorado, USA. The village consists of 200 dwellings, some with as many as four floors. The walls are made of mud bricks and stone. The buildings are positioned under an enormous rock face, which served to shelter the buildings from rain and to provide a 'heat regulator', shielding the place from the almost perpendicular rays of the summer sun, and catching the heat of the slanting rays of the winter sun.
Opposite: Principal cultures of North and Central America.
Right: Kivas at Pueblo Bonito in New Mexico, USA. The kivas were rooms, half underground, which were perhaps used for meetings or initiation ceremonies. The latest buildings of Pueblo Bonito date from AD 1130.

If we try to outline the development and spread of American civilizations and cultures in a logical order, we are likely to find ourselves missing the point. This is because we would have to keep examining different theories to explain it. So we have chosen to use a less ambitious method by looking at each of the regions of the continent individually from north to south. The diagram on p 194 and the box on p 212 show the parallel developments in the different areas.

North America

In the great stretch of North America that is now the United States, there were various Palaeolithic cultures, traces of which consist mostly of certain kinds of arrowhead. Development to the Neolithic period was very slow. The farming of animals was very rare. The great herds of bison were an ever-ready source of food. Sufficient numbers of bison could always be killed in organized hunting expeditions, which were not so different from the slaughter of domestic cattle in other parts of the

world. The existence of 'wild' food did not necessarily cause people to be nomads. Little villages sprang up and gradually organized themselves into groups. Agriculture was practised near such centres: beans, maize, and various kinds of pumpkin were grown. It is thought that these plants were introduced by people from the south (Mexico) who had domesticated them.

The two principal cultural areas were the woodlands, to the east of the Mississippi and in Ohio, and the desert or south-west cultural area, the arid region stretching towards the canyons of Arizona, Colorado and New Mexico. These cultures flourished over a very long period, from 1000 BC to the period of the European invasion.

Each culture had its own ceramics and manufactured objects, like the woven reeds of the 'basket' culture. Metals (gold, silver, and copper) were worked with hammers but were never smelted; thus alloys such as bronze were unknown. The native Americans' first experience of iron was when they came up against the swords and armour of the Spanish conquistadores.

In the desert region, the villages were sometimes complex structures, with houses (adobes) made of sun-dried mud bricks. Some of them were built up against cliff-faces or under large overhanging rocks. The shade of the rocks sheltered the buildings in the hottest part of the year, and acted as 'storage heaters' in winter by absorbing the warmth of the sun. The layout and height of the buildings took into account the angle of the sun's rays at different times

Left: Rock Eagle Effigy Mound, near Eatonton in Georgia, USA. The eagle has a wingspan of 36 metres (118 feet). The square in the lower part of the picture is the roof of a tower recently built to allow the monument to be seen from above.
Opposite: The Great Serpent Mound in Adams County, Ohio, USA. This impressive effigy mound, measuring 400 metres (1,312 feet) may date from as early as AD 400.

of the year, showing that accurate observations of the movements of the heavenly bodies were made.

The woodland regions have monuments of enormous size; these are mounds, artificial hills which in many cases cover tombs. Particularly remarkable are the so-called effigy mounds, where earth was built up into the shape of animals. It is thought that the eagles, bears and snakes were totemic animals, the magical and god-like protectors of human groups.

Mesoamerica and Maize

Archaeologists and anthropologists use the term 'Mesoamerica' for the area that includes Central America and Mexico. Important civilizations and cultures have sprung up here, and even some empires. It is likely that maize was grown for the first time in this area. We already know (see pp 42–3) how a great

Above left: Jar from Teotihuacan, dated about AD 400–600, and measuring 28 centimetres (11 inches) high. The decoration is the result of a complex and ingenious technique which is almost the same as that used for frescoes. A layer of damp plaster was spread over the jar and the design was traced on it with a pointed instrument. Colours were then applied while the plaster was still damp, and the outlines traced in black.
Above: View of Teotihuacan today. On the left in the middle distance is the Pyramid of the Sun, and in the centre is the long Avenue of the Dead lined with the bases of many minor temples.
Opposite below: Fresco in a building that perhaps belonged to the ruling house of Teotihuacan, built about AD 400–600. It shows an armed merchant. As with all frescoes, the drawing was made on fresh plaster.

increase in the population of an area is generally connected with the use of cereals. In America maize (*Zea mays*) was the only cereal.

We do not know what the wild form of maize was like. We can only suppose that the seeds had husks, that they were covered. Today maize seeds are 'naked'; this is a great advantage as the bran produced by grinding the husks

with the seeds of other cereals such as wheat, barley and rye has little nutritional value except as dietary roughage. Perhaps wild maize was related to a plant that is still common in Mexico today called teosinte (*Euchlena mexicana*). In any case, the plant known to us is very productive, and does not need special care when grown. In the words of Edward Hyams, the English historian of agriculture, it is an 'invitation to idleness'. But maize needs mankind. The unprotected seeds can easily be attacked by insects and other creatures, and may rot if exposed to humidity. Storage in dry man-made conditions is almost essential for modern maize. Also, the plants with the highest yield, producing the biggest and largest number of grains, are hybrids or cross-breeds. Thus, a well-ordered and well-farmed field will produce much better results from maize than a wild or semi-wild area. It could be said that in America mankind and maize have been undergoing a symbiosis since very ancient times. Symbiosis is a word used in biology to refer to the way two forms of life live in partnership, to each other's advantage.

The Mexican Region

Many of the Mesoamerican cultures were highly developed, some of them building large monuments, but extended over rather limited areas. Sometimes, however, a culture spread to several centres by conquering them. The Maya civilization had the longest history, and covered the widest area. This we shall deal with later. First, however, let us look at some of the other cultures.

There are important monumental remains at La Venta (in Tabasco state, Mexico, see map p 202). The site is an island surrounded by marshes. There

are man-made mounds of earth and a cut-off pyramid, suggesting that it was a cult or ceremonial centre. The paving stones came from quarries 160 kilometres (105 miles) away. Around the monuments there were certainly many houses or huts made from tree branches. The culture of La Venta is best known for various statuettes, and for the gigantic stone heads, three to four metres (9 to 12 feet) high and weighing several tons. They perhaps represented mythical ancestors. The culture of La Venta was called the Olmec culture, and it flourished from about 1500 BC.

Towards the Pacific coast of the state of Oaxaca in Mexico there is the ceremonial centre of Monte Alban, whose first structures go back to 2000 BC. The monumental buildings are later in origin. This culture was called Zapotec. The economy of Monte Alban settlement was based on the cultivation of maize and many small grindstones have been found.

The civilization of Teotihuacan arose in the Valley of Mexico around 600 BC, and lasted for more than a thousand

Below and opposite are various statuettes from Mesoamerican cultures.
Below left: Two statuettes from Tlatilco, west of Mexico City, dating from 1000–500 BC. The female figure on the left is six centimetres (2⅜ inches) high and is wearing a crown with a pendant. The figure with two heads is also female and is 11 centimetres (4⅓ inches) high.
Below: Figure with a large head-dress from Guerrero state in Mexico, an area that had links with the Olmec culture. It is 16.5 centimetres (6½ inches) high and dates from about 600 BC.
Opposite left: Painted ceramic statue from Nayarit state in Mexico. It is 71 centimetres (28 inches) high and dates from about AD 300–500.
Opposite right: Zapotec female figure with an elaborate hairstyle and wearing a necklace and poncho. Dating from about AD 600–1000, it is 34 centimetres (13⅓ inches) high.

years. The site of Teotihuacan city is 45 kilometres (27 miles) north-east of Mexico City, and the name means 'the place where men become gods'. The pyramid-temples are enormous and impressive. The great 'sacred city' was probably the centre of some kind of empire. Several other sites, from Monte Alban to Maya cities in Guatemala, were in contact with Teotihuacan.

Around the sacred centre, the city covered an area of about 20 square kilometres (7.75 square miles) and consisted of low buildings sometimes decorated with frescoes. In its most successful period, around AD 600, Teotihuacan may have had a population of 125,000 people. The economy was based on agriculture, with intensive fishing on Lake Texcoco. Arts and skills flourished, as did trade, particularly in obsidian from quarries near the city. This obsidian spread throughout Mesoamerica.

Teotihuacan was sacked and burnt around AD 700, perhaps as a result of an internal revolution against the class of priests who ruled the city. There followed a period of Toltec influence. The

Toltec people established themselves in the Valley of Mexico towards the middle of the first millennium AD. Their capital was Tula, which also had monumental architecture.

The Toltecs were the first Mesoamerican people to undertake a really planned conquest. An important example of their success was the way they mixed with and dominated the Mayan culture on the Yucatan Peninsula (see p 210). It appears that basic food production (maize) was not sufficient for their population and it became necessary to take over other productive areas. It could also have been useful for them to make a religious and commercial centre like Teotihuacan powerful again. The Toltec conquest foreshadowed some of the typical features of the rise of the Aztecs (see p 218).

The Long History of the Mayas

We shall devote more space to the history of the Mayas, as this can be reconstructed in a reliable way over a considerable period of time. This is particularly so in the light of recent archaeological discoveries, which seem to push back the origins of the civilization deeper into the past. Their story was typical of a certain way of life and its response, in a manner only found in Mesoamerica, to the problems and possibilities arising from the environment.

Today we know that the first Mayas already had flourishing agricultural centres more than 4,500 years ago. The fairly elaborate form of the ceramics found on these sites suggests an even more ancient cultural history. The most important of these sites are in Belize near the coast of the Caribbean Sea, like the one named Cuello after the owners of the site.

On the Pacific coast of Mexico a non-Mayan ceramic object has been dated to 5,000 years ago. Of course we may assume there was a pre-ceramic stage in the Neolithic period, but there is no evidence for it. What is important is the continuity of a tradition that links the very first Mayan settlements of the third millennium BC with the great monumental centres of the period called 'classic' (AD 300 to 900), and even with the cities of later periods.

The beginnings of the Mayan civilization

From what we know of the hut foundations discovered at Cuello, the huts were similar to those that must have surrounded the ceremonial centres of the classic period. These huts were

Opposite: The structure of a typical Mayan dwelling. The diagram at the top is based on what has been found of hut foundations, holes for supporting poles, and sometimes elevated platforms. The walls were made of wood, and the roof of thin rafters and layers of thatch. Of course, such structures have not survived, but the Mayan architects have shown us what they looked like by making some stone buildings which look just like huts and which have survived. For example, the stone structure of the House of the Tortoises (centre) at Uxmal is similar to that of a house with a raised floor of cane or wood. Another example is the so-called Nunnery, also at Uxmal, a detail of the facade of which is shown at the bottom.

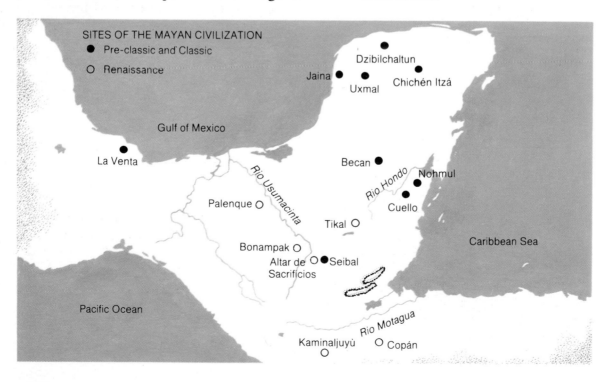

SITES OF THE MAYAN CIVILIZATION
● Pre-classic and Classic
O Renaissance

Dzibilchaltun
Jaina
Uxmal
Chichén Itzá
Gulf of Mexico
La Venta
Rio Usumacinta
Becan
Rio Hondo
Nohmul
Palenque O
Cuello
Tikal O
Caribbean Sea
Bonampak O
Altar de Sacrificios O ● Seibal
Pacific Ocean
Rio Motagua
Kaminaljuyù O O Copán

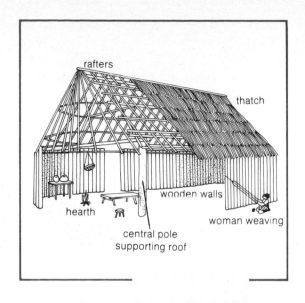

rafters

thatch

wooden walls

woman weaving

hearth

central pole
supporting roof

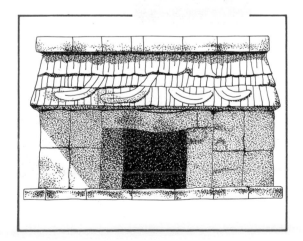

dated by the carbon-dating method (see glossary) from the remains of wood in the holes for the central columns. The appearance of such huts was repeated in stone buildings like the 'house of the turtles' in Uxmal, a Mayan city of the classic period.

The Belize excavations show us an important stage in the development of the basic Mayan economy. In areas of jungle cleared by the 'cut and burn' method (p 176) and rich in natural fertilizing substances, a certain kind of snail is found (called *Neocyclotus dysoni cookei*). The discovery of the shells of this snail in an ancient layer of earth is convincing proof that cut and burn agriculture was practised at the time that layer was formed. The Cuello excavations show that the first Mayas in this area did not use this method of agriculture. Not far away there is evidence of agriculture on fields made by draining marshy areas.

The staple diet of the first Mayas was a paste of maize flour. The teeth of some of the skeletons found in local tombs are very worn down. This is explained by the presence of grains of sand in the flour. This tooth-wearing sand came from the grindstones used to make the flour. The diet of the inhabitants of Cuello was enriched by wild game, such as deer and agouti (a rodent like a large guinea pig).

Were there many centres like this? Probably there were. Cuello must have had trade links with sites 350 kilometres (217 miles) away which supplied jade, found among some tomb offerings. The stones for grinding maize came from quarries at least 150 kilometres (93 miles) away.

Other buildings were built on the foundations of the Cuello huts at a later date. These were perhaps sacred and were destroyed around 600 BC. There was a tradition among the Mayas of building new temples on the sites of old

Left: Profile of a Mayan man. This large bas-relief, which is 215×85 centimetres (7×2⅔ feet), comes from Yaxchilan, a ceremonial centre in the Mexican state of Chiapas, which flourished in the sixth to eighth centuries AD. The bas-reliefs are dated 726. This date can be worked out exactly from the complex historical information left by the Mayas.
Below: Plate decorated with the figure of a man decked with feathers or perhaps dressed as a bird. Dated about AD 600–900, it comes from the Mayan site of Uaxactun in Guatemala.
Opposite left: This bas-relief of the profile of a Mayan woman comes from the same place and is the same size as that on the left. Interesting details of it are the tattoos near the mouth, the large necklace, the particularly receding forehead and the elongation of the skull; the Mayas artificially induced such deformities by binding the heads of new-born children. This may have been done to achieve their ideal of beauty, or to fulfil magical or religious rites.
Opposite right: Small painted and engraved ceramic vase, 16.5 centimetres (6½ inches) high, from Yucatan and dated about AD 600–900.

ones, as if they formed 'steps' to get nearer to the gods.

The city of Tikal had about three thousand buildings, ranging in size from colossal to small; they covered an area of 16 square kilometres (6 square miles). Who supported such a city, and how? We can answer these questions cautiously with the use of several 'maybes'. Maybe before many of the great monumental centres of the Mayan classic period were built, there were villages on the same sites. Before the inhabitants of these villages practised the forest-burning method of agriculture, there may have been a stage during which clear and reclaimed land was farmed.

The environment and economy of the Mayan centres

In order to explain the evidence that archaeology has given us about the Mayan settlements, and those of Mesoamerica in general, we should not

This is the story of how everything was still, calm, and silent; nothing moved, no sound was heard, and even the vault of the sky was empty.

This is the first story, the first word. There were still no humans, not a single animal, no birds, no fish, no crayfish, no trees, no stones, no caves, no crags, no plants, no forests: There was nothing but the sky.

From the beginning of the first chapter of *Popol Vuh* (a 16th-century book chronicling the legends and history of the Quiché-speaking Mayas of Guatemala).

lose sight of the environmental conditions of the area.

For example, the fact that the Mayan pyramids were built of solid limestone blocks held together with mortar and decorated with stucco (plaster) was a response to the fact that there is plenty of limestone in the soil. This provided material for blocks, cement for mortar, and stucco. To obtain the lime for cement, a simple but efficient system was used. Pyramids of stone and wood were built and then set on fire; the powder produced from the burnt stones was an excellent base for mortar and stucco.

Let us also look at another basic fact of American life: the lack of large grazing animals that could be domesticated (see p 78). The problem for the Americans was how to make use of plants that could not be consumed directly as food. There were no cows or similar animals to which they could be fed and which would then provide meat, milk, manure, and useful materials such as

skins and horns. Nor were there any animals like the donkey, horse or camel to provide power for work and transport. The Mayas used the cut and burn method of agriculture, so for them, fire was a kind of domestic animal. It 'ate up' the jungle, and with its ashes it provided manure; it supplied work of a sort, by destroying trees; it did not provide materials, but was useful in transforming raw materials, as in the production of cement.

The environment provided maize as a crop which was high-yielding and easy to grow (p 198). People made it the key to their entire economy. This brought many risks, but there was no other choice. The risks were those of all monocultures, that is, cultures which rely on the cultivation of only one type of crop. The ground became less fertile more quickly than if several different crops were grown on it in rotation. If the single crop was attacked by pests such as insects, or by disease, most of it could have been destroyed and thus produce famine. It was also true that an almost exclusive diet of maize could lead to vitamin deficiency (known as avitaminosis) and its serious consequences, namely illness from the lack of the body's essential needs, and lack of resistance to other illnesses.

The environment provided various kinds of food, and use was made of nearly all the possible choices. We know that as well as maize the Mayas ate beans, pumpkins, sweet potatoes, many spices such as peppers, and made a bitter cocoa drink from cacao seeds. Where possible, fish and shellfish were caught. Deer, tapirs, armadillos, peccaries, iguanas and snakes were all hunted. The honey of wild bees was collected, while the grubs of certain insects such as wasps were reared for food. Maize and honey were used to produce alcoholic drinks, and there was an interesting attempt to breed a type of hairless dog that could be roasted and eaten in the same way as a pig, without being skinned. Plants such as coca and tobacco were also used for their pleasurable effects (see p 214).

The jungle also provided materials that were considered desirable for religious purposes. For example, a whole range of resins (sap from plants) was used for incense. The heating of one of these resins led to the discovery of rubber. This was made from latex, the sap of a tree called *Hevea*, of the Euphorbia family. According to some experts, the Mayas chose to build their centres in the jungle so that they could easily obtain resinous plants.

Life in the Mayan cities

According to a rough calculation, the productive area necessary to maintain a city the size of Tikal must have been at least 500 square kilometres in area (195 square miles). However, there is no archaeological evidence to suggest that this was the case. Round the ruins that

can be seen emerging from the jungle today, there are no traces such as foundations, pole holes or hearths of great collections of houses or huts. The area that could have been used for small and temporary constructions is nothing but a narrow strip around the great monuments and other stone structures such as plazas and roads.

How can this contradiction be explained? What *were* these cities? What was life in them like?

As we have seen, the Mayas used fire

206

Above: View of Tikal, the Mayan ceremonial centre in Guatemala. An agricultural village existed on this site as early as the seventh century BC. The ceremonial centre itself developed from the first century AD. A date corresponding to AD 292 has been deciphered on a Tikal stele and is the most ancient date recorded on a Mayan monument. The group of monuments in the photograph date from the eighth century AD. Tikal was the largest Mayan centre; over the 16 square kilometres (6 square miles) so far examined, there are traces of 3,000 buildings.

Right: Head modelled in plaster, dating from AD 600–900. Plaster was one of the most widely used materials in Mayan decoration.

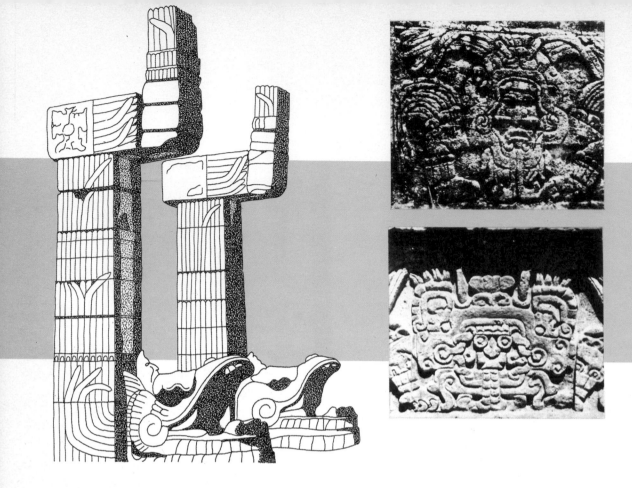

to work for them like a domestic animal. Part of the population was semi-nomadic. Having completed their cut and burn operations in one place after a year or two, they would move elsewhere with their 'beast', fire. Thus, the cities are not evidence of a fixed population. They are ceremonial centres used by a slow, but constant, flow of people.

The Plaza of a larger present-day Mexican or Guatemalan town gives us a picture something like this: a great crowd gathers there from hundreds of different villages for the fiesta of the patron saint; sacred ceremonies take place, and everywhere food, goods and news are exchanged; the inhabitants of the town itself are not very many, but on fiesta days the streets are packed. Centres like Tikal, Copan and Uaxactun were probably sacred cities, used in a similar way and thus often full of people who did not live there. All the visitors contributed to the economy of the cities, so their productive areas only needed to be big enough to support the residents, especially those in charge of the temples. Some buildings might have been storerooms or granaries.

The peasants and semi-nomads travelled on tracks through the jungle, or opened up new ones. They may have used canals for part of their journeys, travelling along them on rafts. A number of canals are thought to have been built, perhaps partly to channel rainwater for irrigation. However, there can never have been a great network of canals to compare with a network of roads, as some recent researchers have claimed. There were no true roads or people who lived by travelling and trading along them. The Mayas had no beasts that could pull or carry; they never made carts, though they had knowledge of the use of the wheel. Examples of the latter include many children's toys, and wheels for pottery. The fine roads that criss-cross the cities were used for processions, which must have been magnificent.

Just as the peoples of the Mesopotamian city-states identified themselves with a local god, the Mayas felt themselves to be united by similar cults in their chain of sacred cities. The power of the class of priests must have been very great. Was there a military or civil power as well? Were there local kings, heads of united groups, or generals? Maybe there were, but never with powers comparable to those of the rulers of water-dependent empires in the Near East. The network of sacred cities was not a true empire, even if there was some form of organization from the more important centres. This would have dealt with trade, the movement of groups of people, and when necessary, military operations. Such military operations would have been, above all, of a defensive nature; the Mayas of the pre-classic and classic periods were not great warriors.

Opposite: Two of the serpent-shaped columns which supported the roof of the Temple of the Warriors at Chichen Itza are illustrated on the left. Their heads, with gaping mouths, are on the ground and their tails are raised. The columns would have been topped by a lintel which supported another shorter column, giving a question-mark shape to the tails of the snakes. Chichen Itza was a Mayan centre in Yucatan that was given new life during the Toltec period. On the right are two bas-reliefs of the face of the god of wind and fertility, Quetzalcoatl-Kukulkan. The top one is from Tula, the Toltec capital, and the bottom one is at Chichen Itza. The similarity between them is clear. It is still difficult to say whether the Toltecs took over Mayan cities still in use, or whether they settled in centres that had already fallen into disuse.
Below left: Gate of the Governor's Palace at Uxmal, a Mayan centre in Yucatan.
Below right: Complex stone decoration in the Mixtec palace at Mitla in southern Mexico. The Mixtec people succeeded the Zapotecs in about the seventh century AD.

The final period of Mayan civilization

In the period known as the 'Renaissance', the majority of the classic Mayan centres such as Tikal, Palenque and Copan were abandoned. The jungle swallowed them up, and the sacred places were forgotten. New centres were born in the ninth and tenth centuries AD, though perhaps on or near old settlements. The majority of these new cities were in northern Yucatan, an arid region where rainwater was collected in natural underground cisterns called cenotes. These were formed when surface layers of earth and rock were worn away until limestone rock was exposed and could not be penetrated by water. Many of the cenotes of renaissance Mayan cities were man-made. Sometimes offerings to the gods were thrown into the cenotes. The victims were humans as well as animals.

The architecture, the ceramics, certain forms of ritual, and the presence of certain gods clearly show that the new centres developed under strong Toltec influence (see p 201). Today it is thought that cities like Chichen Itza and Uxmal were in fact Toltec-Maya cities, perhaps ceremonial centres, managed and occupied by a mixed population that was fairly war-like. The various centres worked together to a certain extent. For this period one could well speak of a type of organization typical of empires. It was an arid region needing works in connection with water (digging canals and cenotes) and a centralized government managing production; these are characteristics we know already from the Old World.

Another period of Mayan supremacy probably followed; various cities joined to form a league called Mayapan, after its capital. In the second half of the 15th century great disorder set in. If the league of Mayapan had imperial ambitions, these soon ended in ruin. It is clear that the cities declined, which perhaps means there was a decline in their productive areas. There is evidence of epidemics of various diseases (perhaps related to vitamin deficiency). Some say that the collapse of the cities of the league was caused by a series of sieges in which the peoples of the coast further to the north cut off the supply of salt. So maybe Mayapan collapsed not through hunger but lack of salt.

Left: A ring at the ball court of Chichen Itza.
Opposite: A building found in nearly all the Mayan centres is the ball court. The few descriptions by the first Spanish chroniclers leave a very uncertain picture of what the game played on these courts was really like. It must have been some kind of religious contest. Each team usually consisted of three men who wore knee pads, feathered head-dresses and some form of protection around the body. The ball could only be struck with the elbows and the thighs, and the players had to knock it through the stone rings at the top of the sloping walls on either side of the court. The way the ball bounced could mean the end of a team as its members were often sacrificed. The more the result of the game depended on chance, the more divine it appeared.

At the time of their conquest, the Europeans found only the tattered remains of a once-great civilization, and took practically no notice of it. The inhabited centres were widely scattered and there was no real resistance to the invaders, and thus no need for repression and massacre.

The situation was very different further north, in the central highlands of

Mexican and Mesoamerican Cultures

Mexico and various other regions of Central America as far as Colombia show traces of a large number of cultures that have often influenced each other's development. In many cases, however, similar developments were probably the result of similar environmental circumstances. Commercial exchanges certainly took place, especially in the case of materials such as jade, a stone that was supposed to have magical powers and thus was traded over the whiole area. The dates to which the cultures belong are uncertain. Even in the case of the Mayan civilization, it is difficult to be exact about dates in the early periods. Of course, it is easier in the period of Mayan history in which dated monuments were made. Many buildings and statues bear complex glyphs (pictographs or hieroglyphics) which relate to a calendar and can be deciphered and translated into dates. This shows that astronomical observation was fairly highly developed among the Mayans. Some of the architectural structures may have been used as observatories.

The La Venta culture produced ceremonial centres, enormous stone heads, and statuettes. Its people were called the Olmecs. The culture existed from the second millennium BC to about 600 BC.

The Monte Alban culture produced ceremonial centres and bas-reliefs. The people were called the Zapotecs and existed from the late second millennium BC to the early centuries AD.

In the Valley of Mexico the first monumental ceremonial structures were at Cuicuilco (600–700 BC). Then followed the great Teotihuacan culture. Teotihuacan was the largest sacred city in the Mexican area. The earliest buildings date from 600 BC, but its greatest splendour came in the first centuries AD. The city was then taken over by the Toltecs, and flourished again under their domination. The Toltec capital was Tula.

The history of the Aztecs is more recent. They may have originated from sites on the Pacific Coast near southern California, and then made themselves the masters of the Valley of Mexico. They carried out impressive land-reclamation schemes on the salt lakes of the high central plain of Mexico, and built large, splendid cities in the 14th century AD. The social structure was that of an empire, with much power in the hands of the priests and soldiers. The Aztec empire lasted about 150 years. In the first decades of the 16th century the Spanish conquistadores destroyed it.

Mexico, where the Aztec civilization had arisen and destroyed others; the conquistadores wiped it out.

South America

The most ancient American ceramic object dates from about 6,000 years ago. Palaeolithic sites exist on the edges of the pampas (grassy plains) of Argentina, at Ayampitim, and also in Tierra del Fuego, Ecuador, Bolivia and Colombia.

Many plants later cultivated by man may have originally come from the vast Amazon basin. It is certainly the home of some of them, for example, potatoes, coca, cacao, tobacco, tomatoes, pineapples, and peanuts.

Opposite left: Cylindrical container, 114 centimetres (3½ feet) high, representing a sun god. From Palenque, it dates from about AD 600–900.
Opposite right: Vase in the form of a shell, 18 centimetres (7 inches) high, with a god emerging from it. From Uaxactun, it dates from about AD 600–900.
Above centre and left: Female figure with long skirt, 13 centimetres (5 inches) high, and kneeling figure 15 centimetres (6 inches) high. Both are ceramics painted in the fresco technique dating from about AD 900–1250 and discovered at Ecatapec.
Right: Painted ceramic statuette, 19 centimetres (7½ inches) high, representing a priest with a mask and a chest ornament. It dates from AD 600–800 and is from Jaina, a Mayan centre in Yucatan.

South American Neolithic communities first flourished in the valleys that descend from the Andes to the Pacific. The west coast was rich in a most useful product from the sea called guano. This is a manure formed by the droppings of fish-eating birds.

How did the change from Palaeolithic to Neolithic cultures take place in South America? Here is a series of theories which seem to fit together in a convincing way.

Many different Palaeolithic groups had begun to 'domesticate' certain plants in the Amazon area. Naturally these people were hunters as well, but very few of the animals they hunted could be truly domesticated. Almost the only exception to this was the guinea pig. Both the pampas and the jungle were rich in game, however. Spreading westwards, the groups found themselves at the foot of the Andes mountain chain. They decided that certain plants could probably be grown at higher altitudes. This was particularly true of the potato; coca also turned out to be most useful, as its leaves contain the drug cocaine and when chewed caused the user to forget fatigue and stimulated breathing. At high altitudes it is easy to get short of breath because there is less oxygen in the air.

So did people cross the Andes with the help of potatoes and coca leaves? There is probably a grain of truth in this idea. They then found in the valleys an environment favourable for crop-growing, and on the coast they found guano, the 'marine manure'. This was carried back up the valleys and used in them. In a fairly short time, the valleys of Ecuador and Peru saw a remarkable development of the human community.

This leads us to a further theory, namely that an increase in population forced certain groups to move northwards up the Isthmus of Panama. So it could be possible that Mesoamerica was

Opposite above: Detail of one of the stones from the so-called castillo at Chavin de Huantar, a site 3,000 metres (9,850 feet) up in the Andes of Peru, and inhabited from the second millennium BC.
Opposite: Underneath the castillo is a complex of passages which meet and cross. In the middle of this cross is the so-called *lanzon*, a monolith 435 centimetres (14 feet) high and no doubt the object of fertility cults.
Above: View of part of the castillo at Chavin de Huantar. The castillo is thought to have been a place of worship.

partly populated, or repopulated, by people from the south. It is important to notice that these people already had a rich and varied type of agriculture. The environmental conditions in Meso-america gave rise to particular agricultural techniques, such as cut and burn or land reclamation. This theory would explain the mysterious appearance of certain plants in the Central American area. There are also certain cultural echoes that seem to link motifs, decorations, and ceramics of the north (for example at Monte Alban in Mexico) with others of the south (for example at Cerro Sechin, near Trujillo in Peru). The flow of people and ideas may well have gone both ways. Perhaps maize was carried south by people returning to the valleys of the Andes. This particular plant was so successful in the Andes that some researchers maintain that it originated there.

The high plains and valleys of Peru

The South American cultures present a rich and varied picture. There were important centres at different altitudes along the valleys, and also on the high plains. The very long Pacific coast afforded easy travel, and thus easy trade. It also made conflict and conquest easier.

A notable centre on the high plains is Chavin de Huantar in Peru, which is at an altitude of 3,177 metres (10,425 feet), and was first inhabited 7,000 years ago. The remains of domesticated guinea pigs were found here. Perhaps it was in this very area that the first attempts were made to domesticate the 'camels of America', the llama and the alpaca. The first traces of semi-domesticated creatures go back to 2500 BC. The llama was chosen as a beast of burden, while the alpaca was used mainly for its wool. Obviously both animals were used for their milk and meat. Both seem to have descended from the guanaco (*Lama guanicoe*). To this day the people of the Andes accompany these animals rather than actually own them; it is in fact very difficult to make them breed in captivity. At Chavin de Hauntar there are traces of canals and terraces, and there was intense cultivation of potatoes, pumpkins and maize.

The most important cultures of subsequent periods in Peru were the Mochica (from the basin of the River Moche), the Paracas and the Nazca. As well as practical structures such as canals and dams, the Moche civilization has left the remains of pyramids built of mud bricks. There were ceremonial centres and fairly extensive agriculture-based cities. Many splendid materials were used as rich burial offerings. In the valley of the Rio Ingenio, near Nazca, we find animal forms, traced on the ground, which were perhaps totemic symbols used in religious and magical ceremonies.

Empires great and small

The impressive ruins of Tiahuanaco consist of nothing but stone. They are near Lake Titicaca in Bolivia, at an altitude of 4,000 metres (13,000 feet). The site was inhabited from the third century BC, but its period of greatest flowering was between AD 600 and 1000. Since the Tiahuanaco ceramics are so widespread, we may consider this

Opposite: Fragment of woven material which was the border of a shroud wrapped around a corpse in the necropolis of Paracas in Peru. It dates from about 400–100 BC. The figures represent warriors carrying daggers and javelin throwers. The interesting head-dresses were made from the skins of seals or sea-lions.

Right: Outline of a humming bird, one of the figures in the valley of the Rio Ingenio, near Nazca in Peru, which were constructed in the last few centuries BC. The enormous designs, some more than 100 metres (330 feet) long, were made by removing stones from the arid ground to create lines of bare ground.

Below: The Gate of the Moon, a monolith at Tiahuanaco in Bolivia.

centre as a trading and administrative one as well as a sacred city. It could in fact have been the capital of an empire. In the Tiahuanaco region there are traces of canals, water catchment areas, and terracing. In the areas of moderate to high altitude, farming had to rely mainly on rainwater, despite the water works. However, the 'empire' was quick to try to conquer more productive areas such as valleys and a strip of coastline.

A more ambitious scheme of unification was achieved by the Chimu empire with its capital at Chan Chan, north of present-day Trujillo in Peru. The system included many valleys and the coast, and flourished from about AD 1300 to 1466. The ruins of Chan Chan are impressive and cover an area of about 28 square kilometres (11 square miles). Unfortunately the efforts of archaeologists have exposed the mud-brick structures to the rain, and they are now literally crumbling away before the eyes of those who visit the ancient capital.

Chan Chan was an enormous administrative centre. Within its wide limits there were palaces that were almost towns in themselves, each with a maze of rooms, open courtyards and sacred buildings. It is possible that each palace represented a certain area of the territory of the empire, or that it housed a particular governmental ministry in charge of certain economic activities. The Chimu empire had great fortresses like the southern one, Paramonga, a few kilometres north of Lima and built of mud bricks and small stones.

The Chimu area was to be entirely included in the Inca empire, which also included much of the former Tiahuanaco territory and extended as far as Quito in Ecuador.

The Destruction of the Inca and Aztec Empires

We shall look briefly at the empires of the Incas and the Aztecs. The Inca empire was the greatest single-state organization in America before the European conquest. Peoples of the high plains of Peru, perhaps because of population pressures, began to practise farming on terraces. These people succeeded in dominating the various groups that formed the Chimu empire.

The social structure of the Inca empire was an extension of that of the clan. As in a clan there was no true private property. A third of all the land belonged to the Sun, and the production from this could be stored and used for the good of one and all; another third was the king's, the divine Inca, and the rest was for the cultivators.

The Aztec empire lived off the success of its warriors; their world of conquests, prisoners, and victims for sacrifice was a striking and forbidding one. Perhaps the Aztecs were driven to this behaviour by heavy population pressures. Some anthropologists, Harris among them, think that the sacrifice of prisoners was nothing but a mask for cannibalism. In fact the diet of the Ancient Mexicans was always short of protein. Is it possible that this exceptional state of affairs led to the exceptional solution of eating other humans and explaining it as the will of the gods?

The development of the Inca and Aztec empires may remain a mystery; the conquistadores saw to that.

Opposite: Among the Incas, a great part of the harvest, especially maize, was stored in large granaries to be used in emergencies. In this reconstruction of a scene from Inca life, the man in the cloak is checking quantities of grain being put in the granary; he is using a quipu, a device consisting of strings which the Incas used for counting. Note the stonework of the granary and the way the irregularly shaped stones are perfectly fitted. Llamas (one is in the left foreground) were used as beasts of burden.

China from the Neolithic to the Bronze Age

Let us return to the Old World, to the vast territory of China, and examine economic and cultural developments there during the long period from the Neolithic world to the Age of Metals. In this period of Chinese history the structure of society was dependent upon water control – as in other countries – but with interesting local variations. The structured Asiatic production method (p 122) was evident with its many facets.

The relationship with rivers was always of utmost importance. In fact, in this vast complex the area of the Yellow River was joined to that of the Yangtze River. These watercourses were a source of life and sustenance, but there was always the constant threat of devastating floods. Other 'floods', equally terrible, were becoming more and more severe; these were the invasions of people from the north and the north-west, the Xiung-Nu, whom we know as the Huns, and the Mongolians, the ever-present close enemy. These invasions were probably a consequence of the movement of population from Central Asia, which also resulted in migrations towards Europe (p 104).

The development of China evolved, therefore, with continual expansion of water works for productive and protective purposes, and constant defensive and offensive activity against invaders. A military empire was the logical outcome of this state of affairs. It grew, broke up and rose again in a series of complex events. The splitting up of the central power into many small domains governed by local lords marked many episodes and affected many interesting economic developments.

The Shang period

Historical and archaeological data about the Shang dynasty allows us to form a fairly precise picture of this period (16th to 11th centuries BC). The capital city was often moved, undoubt-

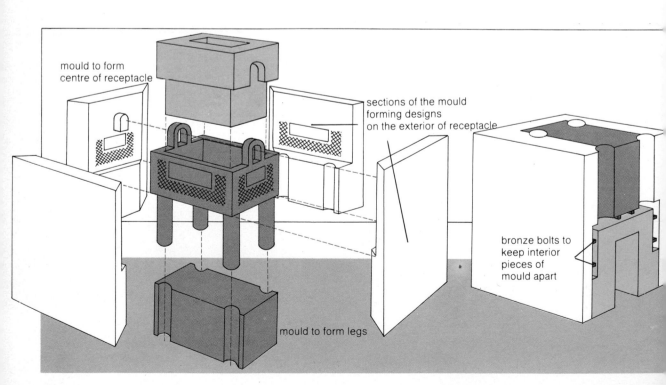

mould to form centre of receptacle

sections of the mould forming designs on the exterior of receptacle

bronze bolts to keep interior pieces of mould apart

mould to form legs

edly because of military action and floods (the two common enemies). We have obtained a great deal of information from excavations near An-yang in northern Honan, where the capital city of Great Shang flourished. We must remember that in the past, and until AD 1852, the Yellow River flowed to the south of the great Shantung peninsula. Today, it flows 200 kilometres (124 miles) to the south of Tientsin. The old course of the river was, for a stretch,

Below: Construction of an ancient Chinese bronze receptacle for incense. Bronze was already in use by Chinese craftsmen during the second millennium BC. The outer moulds were made of baked clay and their inner faces were the same shape as the object, but reversed. Other pieces of clay filled in the hollow part of the receptacle and the spaces between the legs. Molten bronze was poured into the mould (which was turned upside down) through the gap left for one of the feet, or from the bottom. The mould could then be taken apart and used again.

Right above and below: Two beautiful objects from the period of the Shang dynasty of China (1600–1120 BC). The owl (above) was probably used as a container for offerings. Food to be used during sacrificial ceremonies was probably cooked in the tripod or three-legged vessel (below).

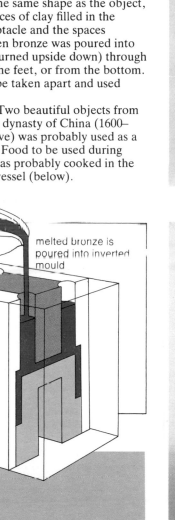

melted bronze is poured into inverted mould

parallel to the so-called Grand Canal which joins the Yellow River to the Yangtze River and other waterways.

At An-yang buildings from the Neolithic to the Bronze Age can be seen. However, a clear contrast does exist between examples of the Neolithic and those of the Bronze Age. Bronze Age metal work appears with designs which were already extremely refined and buildings were so arranged as to create a fortified city with defensive walls. The buildings were made of wood and stood on vast raised bases of packed earth. In this whole area, ruled by the Shang dynasty, there were important water works (canals and dykes), but in most cases these ancient constructions have been incorporated in other more recent ones and are thus difficult to spot.

However, the excavations at An-yang have provided full information on the economy of that great city and so, indirectly, on that of the Shang empire. The simple houses were modest, like the Neolithic huts. The palaces, however, were made up of buildings which were longer than 30 metres (100 feet), consisting of halls supported by columns which rested on flat, bronze bases fixed into plinths of packed earth and stones. The rooms were also important as they were used as stores for provisions. The most important features of these excavations are, however, the tombs. These revealed the great sacrifices, even of humans, that were carried out at the burial of people of high rank, such as kings. These are almost a replica, built 1,500 years afterwards, of the royal tombs at Ur. We thus know that the Shang social structure had at its head an absolute monarch, a divine person in homage of whom human sacrifices were made.

The Shang people cultivated grain and millet, but at this point rice was not yet extensively grown. Scythes were made of flint and grinders were used to mill the grain. Domestic animals included cattle, pigs, sheep, dogs, chickens and other poultry. The cultivation of the silkworm was widespread. Linen was also made. Silk cloth was used by the rich, and ordinary people used, then as now, linen, coarse woollen cloth, skins and leather.

Many war chariots with pairs of horses and charioteers were buried in the An-yang tombs. We can see therefore that although the horse was a domestic

Opposite above: Chinese oracle bones used to communicate with the gods. During the third millenium BC, questions to the gods were carved on these bones (animal shoulder bones and tortoise shells). When the bones were heated on a sacred fire, various cracks appeared in them which crossed the written characters and gave the gods' answers. It is thought that Chinese pictograms and characters originated from these marks on the sacred bones.
Below and opposite below: Development of some Chinese characters. There are many characters depicting actual objects (which are often symbolic of other things). These characters have never been simplified and the signs have never been used to represent sounds. However, many characters have been interpreted in different ways in different regions. Thus an old Chinese saying, 'The Chinese are a race divided by their single method of writing', reflects the confusion which arises from the variety of meanings that can be given to a single character.

subject	pictogram	ancient characters	modern characters
man			
hill or mountain			
tree			
dog			
moon			
water			
bird			

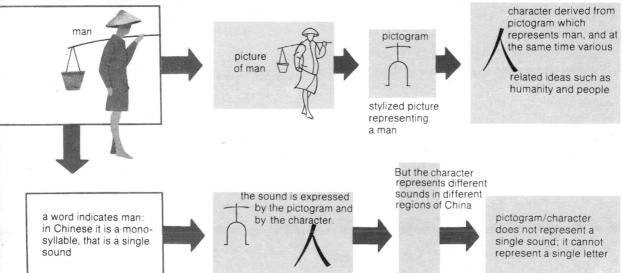

man

picture of man

pictogram

stylized picture representing a man

character derived from pictogram which represents man, and at the same time various related ideas such as humanity and people

a word indicates man: in Chinese it is a mono-syllable, that is a single sound

the sound is expressed by the pictogram and by the character.

But the character represents different sounds in different regions of China

pictogram/character does not represent a single sound; it cannot represent a single letter

animal, it was probably not very common and was only used by the king and high ranking men. The chariots were made of wood, rushes or bamboo and had reinforcements and ornaments.

Very few products made of metal were used for practical purposes. Parts of bows and lance heads were used more for show than for actual military use. Instead, many bronze objects were destined for ritualistic functions.

Some of the human skeletons from the An-yang tombs are headless; the bodies seem to have been piled up, while the heads were laid in a separate place. Perhaps these sacrificed individuals were prisoners of war or slaves. From these and other signs we may conclude that the Shang waged both defensive and offensive wars in order to capture men who could be used for agricultural work. To increase basic production it was necessary to increase, at all costs, the number of hands. Obviously this had its dangers, as a slave needed food and might also rebel.

The evolution of Chinese writing

The main similarity between the Neolithic period and the Shang period was the ritual practice of divination which was carried out by burning bones. People believed that the cracks which appeared in bones (shoulder blades from sheep and cattle or tortoise shells) that were placed on a sacred fire could be interpreted as messages from the gods. To be able to interpret these messages clearly it was necessary to ask the questions in a very precise way. Figures, which represented the subject of the question, were therefore carved on to the bones. Chinese characters evolved from these figures and it is interesting how they have been retained in written Chinese.

In many written languages the sign which represented the subject was called a pictogram. This changed so that it

also represented actions and words. As the characters developed they were simplified and eventually they came to represent a sound. For example, in Egyptian writing the sign for bread, a small loaf called *ta*, was also used for the letter t. In Chinese, the sign which is similar to the figure of a man walking means 'man' and we read it as *ren*, but it has never evolved to reflect an actual sound. Thus, there are thousands and thousands of Chinese pictograms. These to all intents and purposes become characters, and by giving a meaning to the figures they ultimately become words. Of course, many characters are created to convey ideas and concepts, but not sounds. For example, when the sign for the moon (p 222), read as *Yuen* and also indicating month, is combined with the sign for sun, which also indicates day and is read as *rir*, it gives a double sign which is read as *ming* and means light or splendid; it even becomes the name of a dynasty, the Ming or 'brilliant' dynasty which ruled from AD 1368 to 1644. We see the character for sun-moon, we understand light, and we read *ming*.

Above: Detail of a horse's head from a Shang statue. The horse has been an important animal in China for a long time, as can be seen from the presence of chariots with sacrificial horses in the tombs of An-yang, dating from the 11th century BC. *Opposite and below*: The technique of working with lacquers (protective coatings of varnish) probably has ancient origins in China. This material is rather fragile and is easily broken. The statue and the ornament shown here are made of lacquered wood and date from the third or fourth century AD.

If the signs are drawn one below the other, they are read one after the other and the compound word is formed. The written characters meant different things in the various parts of the Shang empire. They were never applied in commerce, but instead became a form of communication used by the central administrative system. They also formed the basis of one of the richest and most varied literatures in the world. But writing remained the exclusive possession of the elite class. An unquestionable achievement of the Chinese Cultural Revolution in the 1960s was the establishment of a basic alphabetic language common to all the areas in the vast Chinese territory. This happened with the universal reading of Mao Tse-tung's famous Red Book.

The Chou, Ch'in and Han dynasties

About 1000 BC the Chou people succeeded in defeating the most important Shang strongholds. They were nomadic tribespeople from the west of China. Their new empire joined together most of the vast Chinese river basins. The Chou kings governed the area using the system known as Ching-t'ien – the name comes from the fact that the fields were divided up according to a pattern similar to the design of the character for *ching*. Many village communities were formed and every family in the community could cultivate its own field, but also had to help the other families cultivate a large portion of land belonging to the king. The families took turns periodically on different pieces of land, a type of peasant rotation instead of crop rotation.

The great mastery that the Chinese had of bronze metal work and, in particular, the high temperatures used to produce it (as recently discovered remains of pots and furnaces have revealed) overshadowed the fact that they had also been working with iron for some time, both forging and casting it. This new metal, however, was first used for practical purposes only around the year 700 BC, and the results were remarkable. The manufacture and extensive use of iron hoes and ploughs made farming much more profitable and favoured the emergence of a feudal system.

The central power of the Chou (from 770 BC the capital city was Lo-yang) was first weakened and then collapsed completely in about 475 BC. In the meantime, commerce, which made merchants ever richer, developed as a great unifying element. Money was invested in constructions connected with water. Many canals were dug with iron spades. One, 150 kilometres (90 miles) in length, brought water for the irrigation of the western lands of Ch'in and was also used for communication purposes. Another connected the Yangtze River

Opposite: Clay warrior. This and similar statues were life size and they guarded the entrance to the tomb of Shih Huang Ti, who was the first emperor of the Ch'in dynasty (221–207 BC). This 'clay army' was made up of 8,000 statues, or at least that is the number of pieces which have so far been discovered in an archaeological excavation which was started in 1974. These statues, buried next to the dead, suggest that a substitute sacrifice might have been made; in other words, the statues took the place of human sacrifices for the tomb. In the earlier Shang tombs, skeletons of men have been found, human sacrifices who were often beheaded prisoners. *Below*: Everyday Chinese objects dating from the first centuries AD, and a section of the famous jade suit (made from strips of jade joined together by threads of gold) which covered the body of Prince Liu Sheng of the Han dynasty (second century BC). The body of his wife, Tou Wan, had a similar suit. These were found in Liu Shang's tomb.

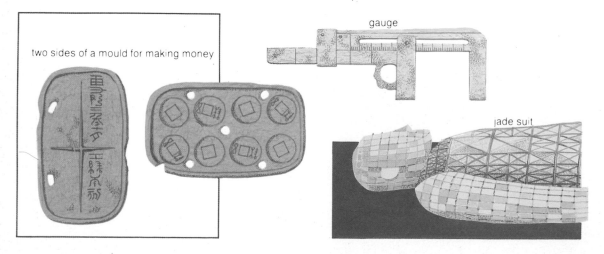

two sides of a mould for making money

gauge

jade suit

with various watercourses, creating a vast navigable network.

In 221 BC a Ch'in king, Shih Huang Ti, imposed his rule on the existing states and provinces and founded a new dynasty. Iron weapons and, in particular, a new harness for horses to pull chariots were quickly adopted by the various states. The harness consisted of a large, rigid and padded breast-plate which allowed the animal to pull a heavy weight by pushing with its shoulders but without being strangled by the soft collar. Such a technical innovation was unknown to the rest of the ancient world and was only rediscovered in Europe around the year AD 1000.

Under the rule of the Ch'in, money, weights and measures were also introduced. These encouraged commerce which was controlled by the central government. Writing was formally adopted and was used in all states for official and administrative correspondence. The power of individual lords was weakened, and to the north and west the country was enclosed by the Great Wall. This famous construction did not, however, discourage invaders; attacks from the north and from the southern regions destroyed the Ch'in state.

With the new Han dynasty, which began in 206 BC, the old boundaries of the lands belonging to individual lords were accepted. In fact, through efficient bureaucracy, the co-ordination of all these units in to one whole was achieved. The government assumed the responsibility of protecting these areas against predators, the Huns and others, and commerce really flourished. The Han exported, as far as Rome and sometimes even further, bronzes, silks, jade, lacquer ware and pottery. They imported purple cloth, carpets, coral, plants, rare birds and also horses.

This was the golden age of China.

Above: Japanese Emperor Nintoku's tomb in Sakai near Osaka, dating from the fifth century AD. The mound which covers the tomb has the characteristic shape of a keyhole and is surrounded by a moat full of water. Similar and equally imposing tombs of other royal people have been discovered, as well as many smaller tombs belonging to people of lower rank. They all date from the fourth to the sixth or seventh centuries AD.

Above right: Typical examples of Japanese *haniwa* clay statues which were placed inside the tombs of clan leaders and royal people. *Haniwa* means 'tubes of clay', and they were so named because they were hollow pottery. These examples are 58 centimetres (23 inches) and 65 centimetres (26 inches) in height and date from the fifth to the sixth centuries AD.

Opposite: Mural on the interior of a tomb on the Japanese island of Kyushu, from about the sixth century AD. The scene is framed by two objects which look like decorated fans. At the bottom there is a boat tossing on the waves, on the left a groom with his horse, and at the top another horse.

The Isolation of Japan

In Japan, cultural development has always been rather slow in comparison to similar progress in civilization in the rest of the world. Let us look at a map of the Far East. The Sea of Japan, more than 1,000 kilometres (600 miles) wide at its widest point and 200 kilometres (120 miles) at its narrowest, separates the Japanese archipelago from the Asian continent. It is easy to give isolation as the reason for this cultural backwardness, one instance of which was the slow rate of progress from the Neolithic period to the Metal Age.

However, it is necessary to point out that in this case isolation was not only a characteristic of the Japanese people, but was also an essential factor in their cultural development, their economy and their whole way of life. A certain degree of isolation had to exist if complete independence was to be achieved.

The Yayoi people

People can live in total isolation provided they have adequate resources. In a group of islands, food comes from the sea, at least for those people who live along the coast. The Japanese have always been fishermen and remain so to

this day. Of course, fishing may not be able to satisfy the total demand for food. Neolithic man in Japan supplemented fishing with the cultivation of grains (at some stage rice predominated, p 103) and there was an increase in animal farming. Many domestic animals were kept, for example poultry, pigs, sheep and goats, although at first there were not very many horses and cattle.

In order to fish it was necessary to have good boats and good boats could also be used to travel; for example, to reach the continent by crossing a strip of

sea. The geographic location of these islands allowed the inhabitants to travel to other places if they so wished, and so to break their isolation if they felt this was in their best interest. Of course, the opposite was also true; the sea could bring invaders. Both these things happened frequently throughout ancient Japanese history. Raw materials and technical information on metal work were imported from the continent. Thus we can understand why bronze and iron appeared on these islands almost simultaneously. A complete technical process, developed elsewhere, was brought to Japan.

During the first century BC the Yayoi culture arose, taking its name from a district of Tokyo. The first discoveries

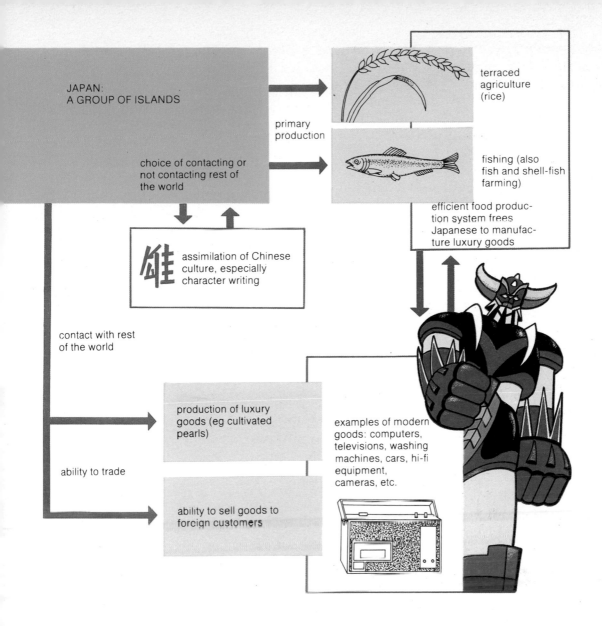

JAPAN:
A GROUP OF ISLANDS

choice of contacting or
not contacting rest of
the world

primary
production

terraced
agriculture
(rice)

fishing (also
fish and shell-fish
farming)

efficient food produc-
tion system frees
Japanese to manufac-
ture luxury goods

assimilation of Chinese
culture, especially
character writing

contact with rest
of the world

production of luxury
goods (eg cultivated
pearls)

examples of modern
goods: computers,
televisions, washing
machines, cars, hi-fi
equipment,
cameras, etc.

ability to trade

ability to sell goods to
foreign customers

concerning this period have shown us the emergence of fisherman-farmers who were already using bronze and iron to make objects of value (decorated bells for example), but who still used stone knives and very simple wooden containers. These people created remarkable terraces for rice cultivation and were skilled at using potters' wheels (Jomon pottery, p 103, was made without a wheel; the vases never had a regular circular section, but often had square sections).

Above: The Japanese method of production and the way in which they tried to create a commercial empire. As the Japanese were islanders, they were able to isolate themselves from the rest of the world if they so wished. They were, however, excellent sailors and could make contact with others, copying their customs but always ensuring that a certain amount of their own tradition remained.
Opposite left: Vase in the shape of a man with a beard, perhaps representing a dead ancestor whose spirit was thought to be powerful. This example is from the Yayoi period.
Opposite right: Bronze bell from the Yayoi period. It is thought that it may have been used in some sort of ritual.

The people of the Jomon culture are generally called Ainu. The spread of metal work, the use of the potters' wheel and the cultivation of rice seem to have coincided with a withdrawal of the Ainu people to the northern regions and to Hokkaido Island in particular. This probably happened because a group of people from the south began to take over and established Yayoi culture – it was an invasion which was probably set off from Korea.

Physically these new inhabitants resembled Mongolians with their almond-shaped eyes and lack of body hair. The traditional people of Japan descended from them. They were organized into clans or family groups. Food production and works of construction connected with water (such as terracing and canal making) were very soon co-ordinated by a central authority. Even here the individual who was 'above all others' was looked upon as a god, a celestial king (tenno) to whom the name 'exalted gate' (mikado) was given. He was the emperor. The first man to receive this title was the legendary Jimmū Tennō (who reigned in the 7th and 6th centuries BC).

The organization of the Japanese Empire

What kind of an empire was this pre-historic Japan? It was a union of territories which were governed according to their rank; this was an extension, in fact, of the clan system. The work of the farmer-fishermen ensured that a social ladder was maintained. It is, however, important to point out the ability of these ancient Japanese to absorb anything from abroad that might be useful, either to everyone or only to those of high rank. Because they had ships they were able to distribute merchandise, that is, to trade. So this commercial characteristic of the Japanese has very ancient roots indeed. The co-ordination of these activities by means of a complicated bureaucratic network occurred much later, during the first half of the first millennium AD. A suitable control method, character writing, was imported from China, as was the Budd-

Opposite: Gables in the Izumo Sanctuary at Taisha-machi in the province of Shimane in Japan. These buildings were regularly restored and added to (the last work was carried out in 1744), but the original shape can still be seen and dates from the first centuries AD.
Below left: The simple structure of the Izumo Sanctuary. The roof overhangs the walls forming large eaves. The roof of the porch is supported by columns. A characteristic of these buildings is the crossed roof beams at the top of the roof.
Below: Reconstruction of a typical Yayoi house.

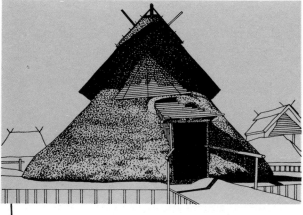

hist religion. The emperors thought that this religion would further unite the people, who had until then adhered to cults which had descended from the traditions of the clans.

The remains of houses from the prehistoric period are of particular interest. Among them we must draw attention to the very rich excavations at Toro, near Shizuoka, 150 kilometres (90 miles) south-west of Tokyo. The enormous difference between the ordinary people and the tenno is shown by the tombs,

Opposite: The palace at Pasargadae in Iran which belonged to the Persian king Cyrus The Great. The name Pasargadae comes from the name of a famous Persian tribe to whom the king belonged. The palace was 12 metres (39 feet) high and was surrounded by magnificent gardens. The latter were called *pairidaeza*, from which we get our word paradise.
Below: Procession of Persian and Median dignitaries in a bas-relief from the Apadana Hall (audience chamber) in the palace at Persepolis in Iran. The Persians are wearing ribbed, cylindrically shaped hats; the Medes have smooth, rounded ones. The men walk alternately to show that the two races, once enemies, are now friends.
Bottom: The expansion of the Persian Empire.

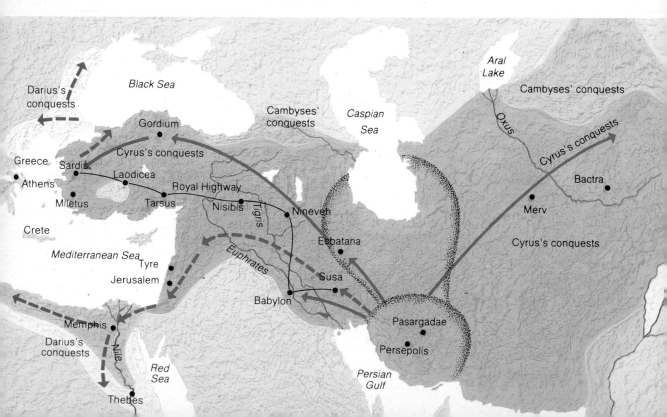

described as 'key-hole' because of the curious shape of the mound. The biggest, that of Emperor Nintoku (313–399 AD) near Osaka, has a mound which is 480 metres (1,575 feet) in length and is surrounded by a moat full of water. The emperors' tombs contain great wealth, but there is no trace of any sacrifices.

The Lands of the Persians

When we consider the civilization and history of the Persians, we come across two outstanding facts. Firstly, there is a central point in their history, an event which undoubtedly completely influenced everything that happened later. We are referring to the conflict with the Greeks. The other important fact is the conflicting information obtained from the written word. Writing was by now widespread. Persian history is for the most part distorted because we have learnt about it from Greek, Hebrew (mostly from the Biblical book of Esther) and Roman sources. These accounts were used for publicity purposes. An example of historical propaganda is the different accounts of the battle at Kadesh between Egypt and the Hittite Empire (pp 261–2).

The true history of the Persians can be reconstructed by careful reading of ancient texts of other civilizations, in particular the last five books of the *History* by the Greek Herodotus, and by comparing them with the texts written by the Persians themselves. The latter took the form of diplomatic correspondence between various kings written in Aramaic script, which was considered 'international', and also inscriptions in cuneiform characters. Information can also be obtained from archaeological evidence.

Persian history and the actual details of that civilization are a fairly recent discovery. The first systematic excavations were carried out by Ernst Herzfeld at Persepolis in Iran in 1931.

Between the 16th and 12th centuries BC successive groups of Indo-Europeans known as Aryans reached the vast Iranian plateau. The name Iran comes from the ancient Persian *Aryânâm*, which means the lands of the Aryans. This area faced the Elam region to the west which had sustained various cultures from the Neolithic period and had always been crossed by trade routes between Mesopotamia and the valley of the River Indus. Elam was a region which could adapt itself to an agricultural way of life, but also to the rearing of livestock. The mountainous regions and the plains contained many fertile areas but, above all, they were enormously rich in mineral deposits.

Together these two regions were a really successful combination.

The Aryan nomads, who were excellent horsemen, gave rise to two separate groups: the Medes, who settled in the north and east, and the Persians, who occupied the area to the south-west.

Creation of the Persian Empire

The Medes became part of classical history with their written tributes to the kings of Assyria (p 267). Their attempts to expand towards the west caused a conflict with the Assyrian Empire in Mesopotamia. Revenge against the Assyrians was carried out by the Mede Cyaxares (625–585 BC), who also ruled the Persians. The Persians, led by Cyrus, then rebelled against the Medes. Cyrus was Cambyses' son and Achaemene's nephew. The Achaemenid dynasty founded by Cyrus was named after him. From this time the conquered Medes were known as Persians.

In traditional history books the Medes appear as the people whose submission indicated the emergence of the Persians. Excavations carried out in the 1970s at Hamadan, the site of Ecbatana, the ancient capital of the Medes, have revealed imposing buildings, a fortress containing large administrative buildings, store-houses and dwellings. The arrangement of rooms and structural features of the famous Persian palaces at Pasargadae and Persepolis are similar to the buildings at Godin.

Under Cyrus, known as 'the Great', the Persian Empire expanded from what is now Pakistan and Afghanistan to the whole of Mesopotamia, Anatolia and the Eastern Mediterranean coast. All this happened within a period of 30 years. Cambyses II and Darius extended this vast empire even further to include the lands up to the River Indus, Egypt and Macedonia in north-

236

I, Darius, the Great King, the King of Kings, King of Persia, King of the other lands, son of Itaspe, grandson of Arsame, an Achaemenid. King Darius says: 'My father is Itaspe; Itaspe's father is Arsame; Arsame's father is Ariaramne; Ariaramne's father is Teispe; Teispe's father is an Achaemenid.

King Darius says: 'Because of this we are called the Achaemenid people. We originally had a dynasty; originally our clan was royal'.

From an inscription at Behistūn

Opposite: Inscription found at Behistūn in Iran in which Darius lists his victories and his ancestors. The first attempts at deciphering cuneiform writings were made using this inscription by listing the signs which were repeated often and corresponded to the names of the Persian kings which were known in Greek. The Persians used two languages: one was similar to Indo-European and called Ancient Persian; the other was Aramaic, from a Semitic group of languages, and was used in diplomatic correspondence.

Right: Darius the 'King of Kings'. A bas-relief found on the wall of a rock at Behistūn.

Below: Darius's palace at Persepolis, built in the fifth century BC.

ern Greece. In the reign of Xerxes I (486–465 BC) rebellions occurred in Babylonia and Egypt, but were suppressed. Xerxes also waged an unsuccessful war with Greece, which witnessed the battles at Marathon in September 490 BC, Salamis in September 480 BC (see illustration on pp 240–41), Plataea and Mycale both in 479 BC.

The empire of the 'King of Kings'

In common with other people who lived on the plains, and with the Indo-Europeans we have already come across, the Persians were very active. They were excellent horsemen; in particular they perfected the skill of charging, and were able to shoot with a bow and arrow while on horseback. Military combat was swift and deadly. The object of their attacks was to conquer fertile and well-run lands. The Persians neither killed the people they conquered nor sacked their cities, but simply absorbed them and their countries. A notable exception to this rule was the sacking of the Greek city Athens in 480 BC, which Xerxes hoped would be an example to others.

The Persians extended the cultivation of crops from one region to another; for example, they transplanted to the east of the River Euphrates various types of

trees which had previously been found only on the opposite bank. Their main crops were wheat, barley, olive trees and (in Mesopotamia) rice. Fruit trees were also important; many strawberries and plums were grown (the name peach comes from *persica* meaning Persian). Flowers too were cultivated, especially roses. Horses, donkeys, cattle, dogs and bees were kept. Fishing was common on the lakes, the sea and along the rivers.

In order to grow crops successfully it was necessary to have plenty of water and so many canals were built (existing structures were often rebuilt, as in Mesopotamia, for example). These canals were often navigable. In particularly dry areas, special underground aqueducts called *ghanats* were constructed. These consisted of clay pipes with ventilation shafts and collection wells placed in them at regular intervals.

This enormous area was divided into 23, and later 31, administrative regions called satrapies. The rulers of these regions, or satraps (our word comes from the Greek which was similar to the Persian word *Khshathrapavan* meaning 'protector of the kingdom'), behaved like local kings. They were efficient and very autocratic; for example, they required that their subjects lie down and kiss the ground in front of them

Left: Gold Persian coin depicting an Achaemenid king dressed as a warrior (notice the bow and arrow). The coin is smaller than three centimetres ($1\frac{1}{6}$ inches) in diameter and dates from about 330 BC, the time of Alexander the Great's conquest of the Persians.

Opposite: Artist's impression of a stage post along the Persian Royal Highway where fresh horses were kept for the Empire's messengers. This famous road joined Susa in Iran with Sardi in Turkey (see map on p 234) and was undoubtedly an efficient system of communication between the capital and the other cities of the Persian Empire. It is probable that this road was also used for trading. It would have been a caravan route along which merchants could safely travel because of the military garrisons which would have been stationed at regular intervals along it. Thus it would have contributed to the Persian Empire's wealth and power.

before speaking to them. They were, however, under the control of the central government's emissaries and they had to make gifts, such as cereals and other produce, to this central body. The satraps therefore imposed taxes of their own, so that, although they kept the Persian 'King of Kings', they in turn were kept by the local population. Each satrap had his own army and took charge of all public works.

Commerce flourished. In particular there was a constant exchange of raw materials, manufactured goods (cloth and carpets) and spices (incense). The Royal Highway constructed by Darius, which was used by the messengers of the various satraps, was undoubtedly also used as a trade route.

We notice, once again, the Indo-European character of the Persian gods. Mithras, the most popular god, was worshipped mainly by the lower classes for many centuries. The cult of this god competed against Christianity for a long time. Ahura Mazda, 'the Wise Lord', was also worshipped. These were typical sun, air and fire gods, masculine but benevolent. The teachings of Zoroaster, the Persian sage, date from the 6th century BC.

The only weakness of the Persian Empire was its great size. In such a large organization, many areas tended to be autonomous. This independence caused problems to the central government, and others were able to take advantage of this weakness.

The Persian Empire was finally conquered by Alexander the Great of Macedonia (Greece) in 331 BC.

Right: Artist's impression of the battle of Salamis. Salamis is an island off the south-east coast of Greece near where the Greeks defeated the Persians in a naval battle in 480 BC. It is thought that the battle became a kind of land conflict because the boats were so close together. Arrows and burning torches were fired from a distance, then when the boats were close enough an infantry attack followed with man-to-man combat.

7. The Fall of Mesopotamian and Nile Civilizations — the Phoenicians and the Etruscans

The People of the Plains

Many of the civilizations we have looked at were indeed monumental. Their lands bear witness to massive buildings (temples, palaces and fortresses), dykes, aqueducts, wharfs, observation posts, drains and even gardens and parks. The lasting remains of these great civilizations have often revealed enormous stone blocks, impressive brick mounds, colossal statues (like the Great Sphinx at Giza in Egypt), figures in bas-relief on walls made of rock, and tombs cut into the stone of mountains.

In most cases this monumental evidence has always been visible, time has never completely obscured it. Obviously, archaeological excavations have greatly increased our access to these great monuments. Everything that was large, solid and lasting has been brought to the surface, even if it has meant moving earth, sand or volcanic ash, or diving beneath the sea.

In the past we knew about other

Right: Scythian gold buckle about 12 centimetres (4¾ inches) in length. It is in the form of a lion attacking a horse. According to some experts this choice of subject represents a desire for 'spilling blood', and is not a simple representation of an event in nature; the scene is symbolic of a people dedicated to raiding and fighting. Information obtained from ancient descriptions portray the Scythians as savage murderers.
Below: Gold deer from the Scythian tomb of Kul Oba in Crimea. It is 20 centimetres (8 inches) in length and must have been used to decorate a shield or the harness for a horse. In Scythian art the representation of animals was common.

civilizations and other people mainly by reading ancient texts. Names could be given to certain people who did indeed live, work, attack others or become the victims of an attack. All this information was, however, rather imprecise and unsubstantiated. Recently, there have been great archaeological moments when an entire civilization, a way of life, has suddenly been removed from the realms of legend and has actually been revealed before our very eyes. Real objects are much more fascinating than interesting but seemingly unreal stories.

We know that shifts in population and consequent historic events can be connected to an almost continual restlessness on the part of people of the central Asian plains. We have already seen that the movements of these people not only resulted in the development of the Hittite Empire, and the establishment of the European Iron Age (evidenced by the cemeteries at Hallstatt), but also in the emergence of the Indian civilization, and the battles between the Chinese, the Huns and the Mongolians.

Today, we do not have to rely on conjectured descriptions of the people of the central Asian plains because, thanks to archaeological discoveries, we can find out who they were and how they lived, and we can see that they were highly civilized.

When we speak about an empire, we

usually refer to a particular land or country. With nomads it is impossible to do this and so we must think in terms of migrations, different races and a way of life based on improvisation. The nomads of the plains of central Asia considered the rearing of horses to be their most important activity and grazing lands were therefore of paramount importance. Organizing the herd, deciding on movement, and delegating the various associated jobs were their main tasks. In this way the land could be efficiently used. Canals, dykes, reclamation and administration were the essential tasks in the running of an empire. The so-called Regal Hordes (this name was for a long time used to describe these nomads of the plains who were able to work so efficiently) were, in fact, a productive unit who achieved excellent results.

The Cimmerians

The economy of these nomads (or hordes) was based on hunting, but it also relied on the use of land which could be cultivated. However, they did not always cultivate land themselves. For example, nomads would sometimes demand to be kept by the inhabitants of the areas they invaded; or they would exchange useful products such as manufactured goods brought from afar; or they would simply demand payment from the locals to protect them against another advancing group of nomads who would be even more ferocious.

The Cimmerians reached Anatolia in Turkey. There they built large fortresses and co-ordinated troop movements from them. Fortified villages, perhaps built on ancient foundations, have been found in the valley of the River Kuban which flows from the Caucasus Mountains to the Black Sea. Their metal work was particularly advanced and we know that there were travelling blacksmiths who peddled their products and services. The latter collected old pieces of metal, melted them down and made new objects.

The Scythians

The Cimmerians were probably expelled by another nomadic tribe, the Scythians. The discovery of various tombs in the region of the Altai Mountains in central Asia has shown that these people were exceptionally skilled at metal work. The contents of the tombs have been particularly well preserved because of the extremely low temperatures of the area. The objects have been preserved in a kind of natural freezer for over two thousand years. Archaeological findings have confirmed and added to existing historical information so that we have been able to piece together a fairly accurate picture of Scythian civilization.

Greek art, descriptions by Herodotus, Assyrian and Persian accounts all agree. The reason for the success of these nomadic groups was that they attacked very swiftly with well-trained horses. The horsemen carried light weapons. Their bows were made of two pieces of horn fixed together with

Above left: Silver and gold vase, dating from the fourth century BC, found in a tomb in Crimea on the Black Sea. Two Scythian warriors with long hair and beards, wearing typical Scythian clothes and carrying arms can be seen on it. The fine engraving is particularly remarkable, especially in the bearded faces.

Opposite: Detail of the top of a gold comb. The group, resting on a base of five crouching lions, consists of a horseman, two foot soldiers and a wounded horse. Their clothes (note the wide trousers) are Scythian. The horseman's helmet and shield seem to be Greek or Macedonian. It is thought that this ancient masterpiece was created by a Greek craftsman who used some of the characteristics of his own culture in a typically Scythian composition (fighting men). But it is also possible that this group depicts an actual conflict between the Scythians and the Greeks or Macedonians. The comb dates from the fourth century BC.

Left: The most important sites where Scythian tombs have been discovered are indicated by the red triangles.

bronze or iron. Their withdrawal tactics were just as efficient as the attack itself. The Scythian ranks disappeared and regrouped on high, dry ground. They did not need to have camps near the scene of the attack because their soldiers could remain on horseback for a long time, probably as a result of their light weapons. Their equipment and their families were transported in covered carts; pottery models of these have been found and were perhaps used as gifts.

This way of life would have created fairly stable settlements. The Scythians kept cattle and sheep (milk, cheese and meat were important in their daily diet). They made leather goods and actively traded them. Actual cultivation of crops was rare, but wheat would have been locally bought. An important part of Scythian commerce was the slave trade, in which they took prisoners and sold them as slaves. Some semi-permanent camps were used as markets for this activity.

Obviously tombs were permanent fixtures. To construct them, cavities in the ground were often lined with tree trunks and then hidden by artificial hills. The funeral ceremony itself reveals the power which the head of the group could command. The ceremonial procession consisted of men and animals, some of whom were sacrificed and buried in chambers next to the actual tombs. Warriors wounded themselves in honour of the dead king; they also sat inside special leather tents and inhaled the smoke from hashish (a substance extracted from the hemp plant) which was burned in small bronze braziers. Herodotus described these rituals, and in modern terms they seem like a sauna, intended to cleanse the body after the ceremonies. We now know that these tents were not Turkish Baths, but places where, under the influence of drugs, the warriors could

246

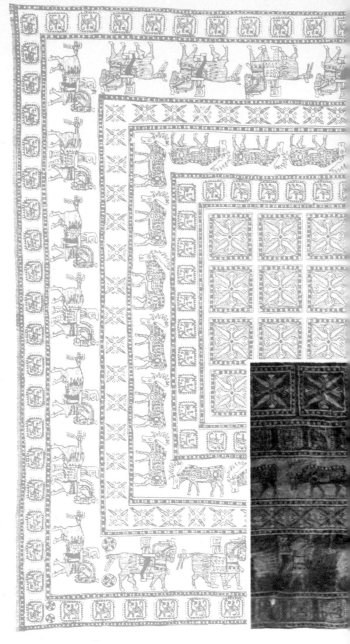

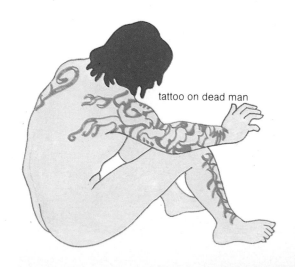

tattoo on dead man

commune with their ancestors and their gods.

The contents of the tombs included panels of embroidered silks which undoubtedly came from China, and carpets which had probably been made by Persian craftsmen. However, the gold objects stand out among the rest. Their decorations show a great interest in animal life and a pride in their own customs, depicting hairstyles and personal effects.

Some information on Scythian myths can be obtained from much later legends belonging to the people who lived in Ossetia in the Caucasus region. The practice of divination (foretelling the future) was of particular importance to the Scythians as they relied totally on their success in wars and in commerce. Because of their mobility and the 'portable' nature of their gods, these groups did not build temples.

Left: Impression of the Carpet of Pazirik created from the small piece (bottom right hand corner) recovered from the frozen tomb of Pazirik in the Altai Mountains of central Asia.
Below: The Pazirik tomb, showing the section which has been excavated. The tomb contained a man's body which was extensively tattooed (opposite bottom), and that of a woman. Among items found in the tomb was a felt-and-leather harness for a horse (below right).

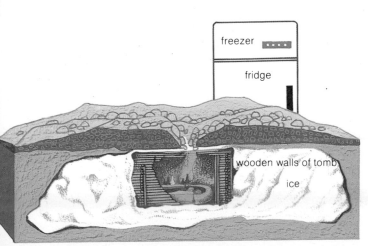

freezer

fridge

wooden walls of tomb

ice

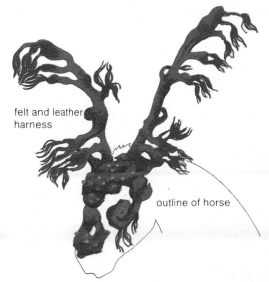

felt and leather harness

outline of horse

The New Kingdom of Egypt

We now continue with an examination of Egyptian events, which we interrupted on p 120 after having studied the Middle Kingdom. Internal rebellions, which had already been apparent during the rule of Sesostris III's successors, allowed groups of Asians first to

Above: Funeral temple of the Ancient Egyptian 'woman-king' Hatshepsut, at Deirel Bahri in the Nile Valley. This imposing building consists of two terraces supported by columns.
Above left: Piece of limestone which formed part of the decoration of an inner room of Hatshepsut's temple. The short lady with large buttocks is the Queen of Punt.
Left: Statue of Hatshepsut wearing a king's head-dress. The statue was found in her funeral temple and is made of white limestone; traces of paint can be seen on the head-dress, her eyebrows and eyes.

infiltrate the Nile delta and then to penetrate further south. These invaders must have had other nomadic tribes following them. In the general confusion the Egyptian way of life was threatened, and famines and uprisings took place. The Asians were able to impose their authority by implementing emergency measures. They settled on an eastern branch of the delta and held court at Avaris as though they were pharoahs of Egypt. These princes, known as the Hyksos, had excellent military equipment including an army of light war chariots. Nowadays it is thought that the Hyksos were a mixture of peoples: Semites from the east Mediterranean, and Hurrians, mostly Indo-Europeans, from east of the Euphrates.

During the period of Hyksos domination (called the second intermediary period), there were also a number of attacks from the south. The people of Nubia (a region of the Nile between Aswan and Khartoum) advanced agressively along the valley. Officially the rule of the King of Avaris was accepted, but the Theban princes maintained a dignified independence, particularly in economic affairs as the organization of industries in this area had been quite efficient.

However, the situation remained permanently dangerous. The risk of Thebes becoming isolated was added to the fact that natural disasters such as floods could cause a collapse of Egyptian civilization. The Theban lords decided, therefore, that they would become the 'heroic saviours of Egypt': they would liberate this 'black' land (so called because of the colour of the Nile mud) from the 'yoke' of the foreigner (propaganda slogans have remained the same over thousands of years). Kamose (17th dynasty, about 1680–1580 BC) began this military operation and Ahmose, founder of the 18th dynasty (about 1580 BC) completed the operation. The New Kingdom of Egypt had begun.

Thebes became the capital of the whole of Egypt and within a couple of centuries was probably the largest and most magnificent city in the ancient world. Thebes covered on extremely large area and was known as the 'city of one hundred gates'; (according to ancient tradition, this distinguished the city from a Greek city of the same name and which was modestly called 'the city of seven gates'.

The Egyptian Empire became highly efficient with a comprehensive and competent bureaucracy employing many clerks. Having expelled the Hyksos, why didn't the Thebans use their capital city, Avaris? We can only

Opposite: Diagram of an Ancient Egyptian farm. There were poultry pens (for geese, chickens and guinea fowl) and the cattle had well-ventilated stalls. The dwellings were in the centre. Depending on the size of the complex there were a number of storage bins for cereals, areas where fruit trees were grown (date palms did not need to be cultivated) and beehives. Each farm had its own temple with images of the local gods and those of the state religion.

Below: Fresco (wall painting made while the plaster was still damp) from an Egyptian tomb at Thebes of the eighth dynasty. Here a farmer is seen leading his herd. Notice the tufts of hair on the bulls' heads and the shape of their horns.

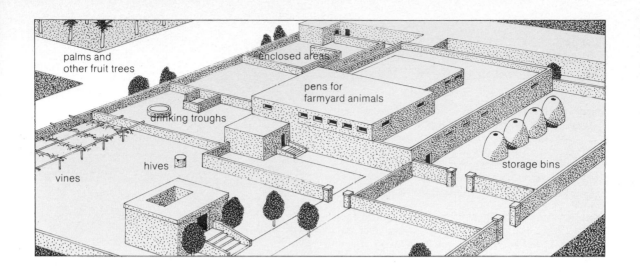

palms and other fruit trees

enclosed areas

pens for farmyard animals

drinking troughs

storage bins

hives

vines

answer this question hypothetically. Perhaps Thebes, lying about 600 kilometres (360 miles) south of Lisht (the capital founded by the 12th

Right: Detail of a fresco from an Egyptian tomb at Thebes which shows a party. A rich array of fruit and vases (which may be offerings), two dancers, two double-flute players and two other figures, possibly watching the show, can be seen.
Opposite bottom: Fish-shaped container, made from a multi-coloured paste, found in Tell el Amarna in Egypt.
Below: Example of Ancient Egyptian art. The pool in the centre of the garden is full of ducks, fish and water lilies and is shown viewed from above. The side sections have been painted as though seen from the pool. This is a mixture of separate but realistic images, put together in a planned way.

dynasty), was well placed for both the northern and southern frontiers, which were equally at risk. Also, it is possible that great importance was given to Thebes' local god, Amon, god of sun and air, depicted as a man with symbols of the sun on his head. This religious unity, in which one God was more important than others, increased the power of the priests and undoubtedly gave great prestige to the rulers. The kings of this period were said to be the sons of Amon.

With victory over the Hyksos and the Nubians, the Thebans found that creating an empire was a difficult task which kept them fully occupied. Frontier clashes were impossible to avoid and it became necessary to change military activity, with occasional defensive raids evolving into a sustained policy of conquest. It was necessary to have a permanent, well-armed and highly trained army. In this 'military' Egypt young men wanted to become soldiers, especially in the cavalry section. The infantry, however, did the hardest work and their complaints have been handed down to us in various texts.

Frontier battles and family quarrels

Egypt reached its peak in territorial terms during the years of the 18th dynasty. Lands as far as the upper reaches of the River Euphrates to the north, and to the fourth cataract of the River Nile, near Marawi in Sudan, approximately 300 kilometres (180 miles) north of Khartoum, to the south were conquered.

Nubia became a sort of colony, while the wide strip of land along the eastern Mediterranean was a protectorate. Egypt's major disasters and her principal glories occurred in this region. Amenhotep I, Thutmose I and Thutmose II finished conquering this area; inscriptions describe their exploits. In Queen Hatshepsut's reign trade routes

became particularly important. The exploitation of the Nubian regions and expeditions into the kingdom of Punt (unidentified, but possibly could have been in the region of Eritrea and Somalia) provided Egypt with raw materials. The country lacked timber and minerals, as well as gems, spices and other luxury goods.

Hatshepsut was without doubt an exceptional leader in Egyptian history. Many books give intriguing descriptions of the private life of this woman who made herself 'king'. Documents and building inscriptions tell us that Hatshepsut was not only a queen consort

but that she herself ruled from 1490 to 1468 BC. In order to strengthen her claim to power, she claimed to be Amon's daughter (many pictures show her pregnant mother next to the Sun God), and also Thutmose I's daughter, which she was in actual fact. This female 'king', who is portrayed in statues as having a regal head-dress and often a false beard, married her half-brother, Thutmose II. On his death she married her stepson Thutmose III, and, in fact, reigned for many years in his place. It is certain that upon Hatshepsut's death, perhaps not a natural one, Thutmose III had her name removed from every-

Opposite above: Colonnade of Amon's Temple at Karnak in the Nile Valley.
Above: Statue of Amenhotep, son of Hapu; it is one metre (3 feet) high. Amenhotep was the architect who built magnificent buildings for the Egyptian king Amenhotep III (1417–1397 BC). Many were subsequently incorporated in new structures or damaged by time. The most important remains of this period are the so-called Colossi of Memnone which had decorated Amenhotep III's temple. Today they stand alone. Amenhotep was not only a brilliant architect, but he later became a sort of 'healer' and had a sanatorium near Deir el Bahri. He was extremely popular and was deified after his death.
Opposite: Statue in grey basalt (volcanic rock) of the Egyptian king Thutmose III of the 18th dynasty. It is 90 centimetres (35½ inches) high and was discovered at Karnak. Notice his heavy false beard and his elegant features.

255

thing. The habit of removing certain references from monuments and inscriptions was quite usual. However, Thutmose III's rage was so great that we are led to believe that he really wanted to erase this female 'king' from history.

These family incidents indicate that there was a weakness in the power structure. They tarnished the divine image of the rulers, especially as far as the bureaucrats were concerned. The bureaucrats were among the people who would gain most from the sheer size of the Empire, and they can be considered almost as a 'middle class' of that time. The rise of this group of people, who certainly worked for their own ends in trade and as craftsmen, is reflected by an increase in the number of non-regal tombs. The rulers concentrated on the search for glory and prestige by military conquests. After Hatshepsut's death, Thutmose III waged annual campaigns in Syria.

Throughout the country, and in the capital city in particular, the power of the priests increased, and so did that of the middle class. The priests were the representatives of the cult of Amon who had by now become a national god. They were in the service of the state and were well paid; in Thebes Amon 'owned' large pieces of land. The military class was also becoming stronger.

Amenhotep III (1405–1367 BC) combined his military actions with clever diplomacy. He was in contact with all the major powers of the age, from Babylonia to Assyria, Crete and the Hittite Empire, the most dangerous of all his neighbours.

Akhenaton and his new religion

Amenhotep IV, or Akhenaton as he was later known, was a fascinating figure. The fame he had as a fanatic and heretic, his battle against the priests, the new style of art which flourished under his rule, and his beautiful wife Nefertiti (said to have been 'the most beautiful woman in the ancient world', a reputation which was never surpassed if her portraits are to be believed), were all factors which made Akhenaton a popular figure.

What was so new about the worship of the sun as initiated by Akhenaton? The oldest Egyptian Sun God was R', pronounced Re or Ra. This god *was* the sun, but at quite an early stage the cult had to be translated into actual experience and religious practice. Thus sunlight, and with it the symbolic circle, became associated with various other gods, almost all of them depicted as part human and part animal. This also happened with the god of life after death, Osiris. We have already mentioned Amon, an ancient local god of Thebes

Opposite: Aton shines his rays on the Ancient Egyptian King Akhenaton and his queen Nefertiti; the cult of the sun is born.

You rise, O beautiful Sun, from the horizon of
  the sky,
O living Aton, you who begins life when you rise
  in the east;
You fill the whole earth with your beauty,
You are beautiful, great, magnificent, high over
  the land.
Your rays encircle the earth to the limit of your
  creation . . .
When you set in the west, the earth is dark, as
  though dead.
Men are sleeping in their rooms with covered
  heads,

and they cannot see each other . . .
The earth is silent,
while its creator rests beyond his horizon . . .
The earth exists because of your hand,
it remains as you have created it . . .
You are life,
because we live in you . . .
You rise for your son, Akhenaton, who has
  come out of your body.

[The king's royal titles and the name
of his wife, Nefertiti, follow]

From the *Hymn in Praise of Aton*, probably written
by Akhenaton

and we can picture him as a divine sun having human form with the head of an animal. Aton, the new god, was the sun's disc; he was that life-giving force which reaches down to everyone from the great star, and he did not have a human form. The gods of the sun and air of the Indo-Europeans (which were similar to the Hebrews' Yahweh in that He could not be represented as a human figure) can be compared with this new god.

Akhenaton's choice of this particular god (Aton) has been explained in various ways. He wanted to liberate his people from the belief in dozens of different part-man, part-animal gods, which derived from ancient gods worshipped by the Neolithic ancestors. He proposed to overcome superstitious fears with the idea of a good and only god who was the source of life. Certain parts of the *Hymn in Praise of Aton* (p 256) can be accepted by anyone, regardless of their own religious belief.

On the other hand, and here we begin to study the final phase of this period of Egypt's history, any suggestion of a new and abstract god of the sun brought in its wake an open quarrel with the priests of Amon, the most powerful people in Thebes. Akhenaton wanted to remove power from the priests, whom he probably feared. He destroyed ancient temples and ancient images of the gods.

By eliminating the old gods he risked upsetting the people. Here, however, it is important to consider the evidence which is often neglected. The king ran a 'publicity campaign' to convince his subjects of the benefits of the new religion. He wanted everyone to understand him. The *Hymn* was written in a new, modern language, rich in shades of meaning, but which was simple and probably very close to the spoken language. Of course the *Hymn*'s message, that the sun is universal life and the king is the son of the sun, could be

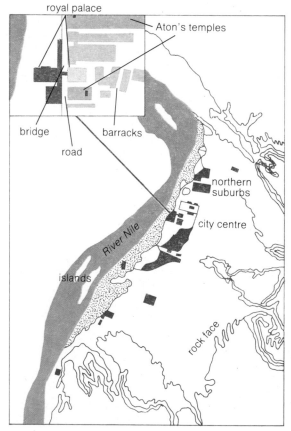

Opposite top: Ancient stone engraving of Akhenaton and his family worshipping Aton. The divine sun's rays are depicted reaching towards the figures and ending in the shape of a ring and a cross, symbols of life.

Opposite bottom: Map of the Tell el Amarna area of Egypt showing the buildings in Akhetaten (Aton's horizon), the capital city founded by Akhenaton. The inset shows the buildings in the royal palace. The long road was used for processions and was crossed by a bridge linking two wings of the palace. The royal family and the king in particular (one of his titles was Son of Aton) would stand on this bridge in order to see and be seen by the people. This capital city was abandoned after the death of the 'heretic' king and was forgotten. Archaeologists, therefore, found a complete picture of an Egyptian centre at the height of the New Kingdom.

Right: Akhenaton attempted to get rid of Amon's priests. The worship of the sun also eliminated all the old gods represented by animal heads (which had first been worshipped by the Neolithic and pre-Neolithic people of the Nile Valley).

Below: Flying ducks in a cane field painted in tempera (colours mixed with glue or egg yolk to produce a matt finish). This painting was found in Akhenaton's royal palace.

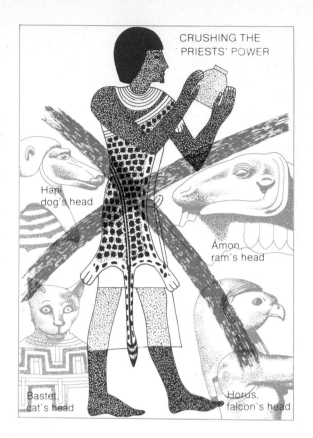

CRUSHING THE PRIESTS' POWER

Hapi, dog's head

Amon, ram's head

Bastet, cat's head

Horus, falcon's head

259

understood by everybody and so was, in this sense, democratic. It confirmed the power of the sovereign and this power was strengthened by the god.

It is quite obvious to us that Akhenaton, not wanting to search for glory in war and unsure of his power over the rising middle class, tried to obtain support from, and gain popularity with, the people by championing a good and more truthful religion. He also moved his capital to Akhetaten (meaning Aton's horizon), a new city founded 370 kilometres (230 miles) north of Thebes (near the modern village of Tell El Amarna).

Akhetaten contained a palace with a bridge which crossed the main road so that the ruler and his wife and family could appear before the people to receive their homage. Was Akhenaton being democratic or was he simply ahead of his time? Or, conversely, was he being realistic, seeking to gain the approval of the people in a subtle way? It is difficult to say. Akhetaten had well-organized factories, a state archive which has provided us with an exceptional collection of diplomatic documents, many temples, a working-class district, and various craft shops.

Queen Nefertiti must have had a principal role in this reform. She appears at Akhenaton's side in many official pictures. On her death the king joined with Smenkhkare, the husband of one of his daughters, and they probably ruled together.

The priests of the god Amon became powerful once more under Akhenaton's successor, the young King Tutankhamun. The discovery in 1922 of his tomb, intact and full of treasures, has lent him an importance in history which he did not deserve according to the actual events in Egypt. The capital city returned to Thebes, but the years that followed were very unstable ones, both internally and on the frontiers.

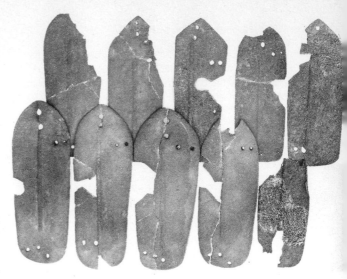

Above: Pieces of armour used by the Hittite and Egyptian armies at the battle of Kadesh on the River Orontes in Syria (1286 BC).
Opposite top left: Presenting propaganda as factual news is an ancient practice. Even today it is often difficult to find out the truth because news reports are often presented from a particular point of view.
Opposite top right: Maps showing Kadesh in Syria.
Opposite bottom: Part of a chest, from Egypt's 18th dynasty, painted with battle scenes. The pictures are very similar to those on the walls of Ramses II's temple which depict the battle at Kadesh, although the latter are much larger. The paintings are not historically accurate, nor was the Egyptian report of the battle, in which Ramses stated that he defeated the Hittites by himself. The Hittite version of this famous battle contradicted the Egyptian texts. The most important evidence was obtained from diplomatic documents which confirm that neither the Egyptians nor the Hittites achieved a victory at Kadesh. However, the Hittite advance was stopped and they never again ventured towards the southern regions of Palestine or Egypt.

Order was restored once again by Horemheb, 'the strong man', a general who made himself king and with military help gave the Theban priests new prestige.

Akhenaton's heresy had, however, left its mark. The army and the priests emerged much stronger and with greater authority. An agreement of mutual support was established between these two groups and in future only a limited number of exceptional men were allowed to emerge as rulers. They had to rely on their military victories in order to reign.

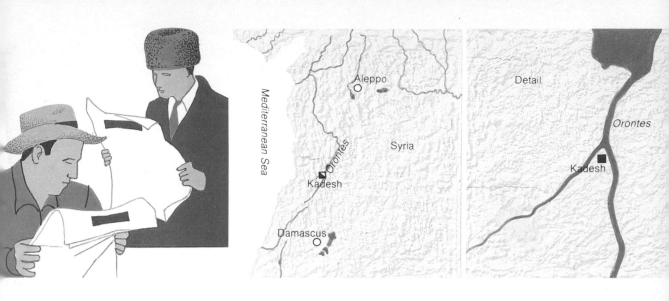

inal frontiers, they exchanged gifts and arranged marriages between their royal houses. So their conflict was resolved by diplomatic means.

However, Kadesh still remains one of history's most significant events. Had things gone differently and Egypt been

Left: Obelisk, part of Ramses II's temple to the god Amon at Karnak in Egypt. Many obelisks were built during the New Kingdom. They had their origins in the ancient temples to the sun (see p 121). Obelisks were often covered in gold (like the tips of the great pyramids).
Below: Part of a statue in grey granite of Ramses II, discovered at Tanis in the Nile Delta.
Opposite right: Vase in gold and silver, an example of the extraordinary ability of the craftsmen during Ramses II's reign.

Ramses II – an important period

Ramses II is undoubtedly one of ancient Egypt's most important historic figures. But his great fame was also due to the intense publicity which he was able to orchestrate, and to the imposing monuments which he built all over Thebes, the delta region and Nubia. This constant glorification of the royal person perhaps succeeded in curbing the power of Amon's priests.

Ramses II excelled as a great warrior. However, today we are in a position to reconsider the importance of his alleged victory at Kadesh on the Orontes River in Syria (p 137), over the Hittite army led by King Muwatallis and one of his brothers. Archaeology has also given us the Hittite side of the story. The date was probably 1286 BC. During the battle the Egyptians risked defeat and Ramses only just managed to avoid being overwhelmed during a retreat. The Hittites, however, could not strike the final blow, or perhaps did not want to, so the famous battle, which has been reconstructed in detail, was in fact inconclusive. After Kadesh, Egypt and the Hittite Empire agreed on their orig-

totally defeated, the splendour of Ramses II's period would not have existed and the whole of Egyptian history would have taken another course. Perhaps Egypt would have been ruined and the centuries of Egyptian Empire which followed would not have existed. We must remember that the Hittite civilization disappeared without trace despite its importance at the time, although it has been rediscovered by modern archaeologists. Egypt survived to enjoy some glorious eras as well as some dark ages.

The survival of Egyptian civilization

Ramses II and his successors continued to wage wars against the sea peoples – the Sicilians, the Sardinians, the Tyrrhenian people (perhaps the ancestors of the Etruscans), and the Achaeans and Myceneans from Greece. The priest-kings moved their capital city to Tanis in the delta in the 10th century BC. In 1940 the perfectly preserved graves of King Psusennes and three dignitaries were found on the site of Tanis.

In the 8th century BC Nubian kings conquered Egypt and managed to drive back an Assyrian invasion (see p 270). A new Assyrian invasion in 662 BC was, however, successful.

Independence from the Assyrians was soon established. A renewed period of wealth began later that century and witnessed intensive trading with Mediterranean people. The sea peoples were both suppliers to and customers of the Egyptians. In 525 BC Egypt became part of the Persian Empire (p 236) and remained so until 332 BC when Alexander the Great established a period of domination by Greek princes.

Under the Greeks Egypt flourished once more. Alexandria was unequalled in art and culture. In the year 30 BC Egypt was conquered by Octavius's Roman legions and the region became Rome's main granary, but it managed to retain some of its original character. This 'black' land continued to live on through successive events. Egyptian civilization passed on many of its most important features to the Greeks. To Rome it presented the concept of an empire in the style of an oriental state led by an absolute ruler.

The Babylonians

Around the year 2000 BC, the increase in power of the various city-states in central and southern Mesopotamia weakened the authority of the third dynasty of Ur. The building of walls and fortifications to the west, along the River Euphrates, was a defensive measure rather than a means of ensuring water supplies. They did protect, but ultimately did not stop an infiltration of a Semitic people from the north-west, the Amorites. Quarrels with the king of Mari, the flourishing city of Larsa (near Ur), and the cities of Elam in the south-east of Mesopotamia had a further weakening effect.

The Amorites took over the area where the two rivers, the Tigris and the Euphrates, converged and this became the site of Babylon (from *Babilu* meaning 'the name of God'), which was probably built on a more ancient centre.

The sixth king of the Amorite dynasty of Babylonia was Hammurabi (1728–1686 BC). This sovereign asserted his authority over the kings of Larsa and Mari. The lands of city-states further north, where Assyrian rule already flourished (see p 267), were also added to Hammurabi's empire, as was Elam up to the slopes of the Zagros Mountains. There was no destruction. In fact, the palace in Mari (with its excellent archives of tablets which have told us so much of this period) was actually completed under Hammurabi's rule.

The unification of these regions meant that Babylonia had excellent commercial routes from Mari to the Syrian coast, and to the Persian Gulf, at Larsa. It also controlled areas producing raw materials, such as those between the two rivers, mines in Elam and land where horses could be bred in the Zagros Mountains.

Hammurabi's fame as an able leader and politician is based on a book of ancient law called the *Code*. This is a collection of laws which Hammurabi said he had received from Shamash, the god of justice. However, the *Code of Hammurabi* put together laws and rules which had certainly been in use in Mesopotamia for some time. Today, we have found other sets of laws which are even more ancient.

Among the 282 laws in the *Code of Hammurabi* the most common were those concerning the rigid penal code; punishments included cutting off hands, executions, blindings and other mutilations. These were in some ways similar to the laws of the Bible. However, from the *Code* we can obtain important information on Babylonian social orders, and a picture of a truly democratic system of justice emerges. The law does not seem to have been the same for everybody. Punishments differed depending on whether crimes were committed by free people (bureaucrats,

Opposite: Head of King Hammurabi, the 18th-century BC king of Babylon, one of the Amorite dynasty.
Below: Stele (upright stone slab) in black basalt (volcanic rock), 2.25 metres (7⅓ feet) high. On it is inscribed the laws known as the *Code of Hammurabi*. At the top Hammurabi is being given the task of writing the laws by Shamash, god of justice.

Hammurabi, King of righteousness. 'Shamash gave me these laws. My words have been carefully chosen, my task has been unique; it only seems useless to the foolish, the wise realize it will bring us fame.'

If a man has a debt and does not have the money to repay it but has barley, the merchant must take the barley as interest, according to the law. But, if the merchant has charged an interest which is more than 100 sila [measure for barley] for one gur [another measure] of barley, or more than ⅙ of a siclo [silver coin, 14 grams (½ ounce) in weight] and 6 grains for 1 siclo of silver, he will lose everything that he has given [lent] . . .

If an inn-keeper has lent [given credit] a jug of beer, he must receive 50 sila of barley when the harvest has been brought in . . .

If someone has a debt and his field is flooded by a storm or the earth is carried away by a flood, or if he has lost his barley crop because of drought, he need not pay back the barley to his creditor, he 'dampens his ledger' [that is, he cancels the terms] and will not have to pay the interest for that year . . .

If a merchant has made a loan [of barley or silver] without witnesses [or without a contract], he will lose everything that he has handed over . . .

From the *Code of Hammurabi*

priests, landowners, artisans and merchants), partially free people (soldiers, fishermen and others involved in essential production), or by people who were not free (slaves, prisoners and insolvent debtors). Women usually had the same rights as men.

The rules governing credit (loans, securities and guarantees) were of particular importance. They controlled the sale of property and also gave protection against private speculation; maximum interest rates were set. The facilities given to credit houses, which were official organizations controlled by the central power, were listed. The *Code* ensured a minimum amount of justice for everybody; even the person who was not free was protected. It supported banks and temples under the control of the palace. It protected economic activity, favouring the middle classes. However, the state's power was great and reinforced, above all, the authority of the sovereign, who was further strengthened by his claim to be divinely appointed.

Babylon prospered for more than one and a half centuries, but there were many disputes within this vast territory. In 1595 BC the Hittites, under King Mursilis I (p 137), conquered the region, but they were soon forced to withdraw. 'Babylon of the Amorites' was, however, a thing of the past. Subsequently the Kassites, a mixed people of Indo-European origins from southern Iran, gained power in the region. Four more or less splendid centuries followed under Kassite rule. The people of Elam then invaded the area (about 1150 BC), but their influence was soon ended by the princes of Isin, a city near Babylon. King Nebuchadnezzar I, who unified the kingdom, was particularly important, but on his death, Babylonia came under the influence of the Assyrians (about 1100 BC).

Below: Bronze statue with gold face and hands of a man kneeling or praying. It is 19.5 centimetres (7⅝ inches) high, dates from the second millenium BC, and was discovered at the Babylonian city of Larsa. The inscription on the base states that the statue was an offering to a god from Hammurabi, King of Babylonia.
Bottom: Ruins of the ziggurat of Aqarquf in Mesopotamia, dating from the 14th century BC. The lines of canes which were placed between every eight or nine courses of bricks are clearly visible. The canes strengthened the structure. The left-hand side has recently been restored. Even today the top of the ziggurat is 57 metres (187 feet) high.

The Assyrians

The story of the Assyrians has a rather uncertain beginning. Towards the end of the third millennium BC, a mixed population of local people, unconnected with the Sumerian or Semite races, settled in northern Mesopotamia along the River Tigris and its tributaries, the Great and Lesser Zab Rivers. These people worshipped one god, Assur or Ashur, and they named their capital city Assur in his honour. Indeed the name of their country comes from this god's name. The Assyrians were very soon influential in various city-states as far away as southern Mesopotamia and the eastern Mediterranean coast. There were skirmishes with the Hittites but the Assyrians consolidated their position by annexing the lands of Mari under King Shamshi-Adad I (1813–1781 BC), who assumed the title 'King of Everything'.

Centuries of battles with the various centres in the area (in particular Babylonia) followed until the Assyrians fell under the rule of the Hurrians in Mitanni. A well-timed alliance with the Hittites enabled Ashur-uballit (1390–1364 BC) to liberate the area. The Assyrian Middle Rule began in this

way. It was characterized by a relentless policy of conquest.

Maximum power was achieved when the Hittite Empire fell in the 13th century BC. The Assyrians, who were already able horsemen, brought in blacksmiths and increased the number of iron weapons. The Assyrian army became the most perfect war machine of the period.

Under Tiglath-Pileser I (1115–1077 BC) Assyrian authority was extended along the whole of the eastern Mediterranean coast, except for Anatolia. The Assyrians expelled the people of these lands, killed many of their prisoners and destroyed their cities. Their cruelty (punishments were very severe even for their own people) has become legendary. Obviously, their aim was to crush any national identity felt by the people they conquered. Even cultural characteristics were absorbed.

This completely different pattern from the one we have seen was adopted by other empires; the relative tolerance of the Sumerians, or the Persians' respect for traditional local customs (p 238) had no place here. The Assyrians openly favoured usurpers and strong-arm men in the centres they wished to control. The uncertainty of life in the urban centres they annexed meant that many people returned to a nomadic way of life, trading from desert caravans and tending sheep. The Assyrians were, however, interested in horticulture on small areas near the cities, and in breeding animals, particularly horses. Religious leaders were rich and powerful. The land belonged to the god and to the temple, although the king and his nobles also owned land. The land in the upper Tigris valley was fairly fertile and farmers used ploughs which worked extremely well, although they were not yet very heavy (p 151).

The Neo-Assyrians

A kind of Dark Age lasting about 150 years followed during which the territory of the empire became smaller. However, it was once again extended by Assurnasirpal II between 883 and 859 BC. Assyria became a great power with a new and magnificent capital city, Calah (Nimrud, today). This city was built by exiled slaves and many craftsmen from the conquered lands worked there. Control of the trade routes between the east and the Mediterranean brought great prosperity. Diplomats were very active indeed, making treaties and agreements. Disputes over new territories took place.

Assurnasirpal II's son Shalmaneser III, who reigned between 858 and 824 BC, helped the Babylonian king quell a rebellion in his land. This was typical of the close links between Assyria and Babylon. Queen Sammuramat ruled Assyria as regent for her young son between 810 and 806 BC. Known as Semiramis by the Greeks (she has been featured in European literature and music) she is reputed to have created the famous and beautiful Hanging Gardens of Babylon. They were one of the so-called Seven Wonders of the World and show that much importance was given to cultivation.

The severity of the despotic Assyrian monarchs was often repaid in kind and some were themselves murdered, like Tiglath-Pileser III (745–727 BC) and Sennacherib (704–681 BC). There were many disputes with the priests but there was a period of truce between them and the royal court under King Sharrukin,

Opposite: Fertility goddess holding a vase. It is made in limestone and was found at the Mesopotamian city of Mari. It dates from 1792–1750 BC.
Above left: Part of a fresco from the palace in Mari, dating from the end of the 20th century BC.
Left: Stone statue of a queen of Mari on her throne. Her head-dress and gown are particularly ornate.

269

often called Sargon II (not to be confused with the ruler of the Akkadians [pp 131–2]). Sargon, who reigned between 722 and 705 BC, advanced as far as Egypt and founded a new large city with its own castle, Dur Sharrukin (Sharrukin's fortress), today known as Khorsabad, in northern Iraq.

The use of prisoners and exiles for construction work was typical of the military nature of the Assyrian state. The ordinary people and the peasants were not asked if these large buildings should be built, they were simply expected to make sacrifices to keep the prisoners and slaves so that they could work. The buildings were not usually as useful as the dykes and canals normally built in an empire which depended on the use and development of water resources. But they improved the conditions in which the people lived. Sennacherib moved the Assyrian capital to Nineveh and started many public works such as the aqueduct at Nineveh, which was over 50 kilometres (30 miles) in length. These works also served to occupy a potentially rebellious mass of people – the prisoners.

Essarhaddon (who reigned from 681 to 669 BC) conquered, and for a short time governed, Egypt as far as Thebes. Assurbanipal's rule (668–627 BC) was

marked by splendour, intrigue and crime. He was described by the Greeks as a pleasure-loving tyrant, a cruel and corrupt man. But during his reign he founded the Library of Nineveh. Here, thousands and thousands of tablets were collected together, forming a complete record of the different cultures in Mesopotamia, from Sumer to Babylonia and Assyria. The scientific writings (geometry, astronomy, mathematics and medicine) are of particular importance; there are also many trade and diplomatic documents.

The Medes conquered Assyria and brought about its downfall. Cities were razed to the ground and the people virtually exterminated. Nineveh itself was destroyed in 612 BC. Much later, when the Persians dominated this area, more tolerance was shown towards those who survived.

Neo-Babylonians – the Chaldean Dynasty

As Assyrian power diminished the Chaldeans took over Babylon. The Chaldeans were a Semitic people who lived on the edge of the Assyrian Empire and settled throughout the area, as the spread of their language into the whole of the ancient Near East shows. The most famous Babylonian kings of this dynasty were Nabopolassar (a Chaldean chief) and Nebuchadnezzar II. Nebuchadnezzar was an able politican who made peace with many countries, but he also waged annual military campaigns, especially in Syria and in Palestine. He conquered Jerusalem in 598 BC, then destroyed it in 587 BC, deporting its people to Babylon.

Left: Part of the outbuildings of the royal palace in Babylon.
Opposite: Remains of Babylon seen from the air. The buildings which can be seen today are those built by Nebuchadnezzar II.

The differences between Nebuchadnezzar and the Babylonian priests were very severe. This tension was to continue indefinitely. In 539 BC King Belshazzar was ruling Babylon on behalf of his father Nabonidus when Cyrus the Persian conquered the city. And so Babylon passed into history.

Below: Bronze bas-relief (about 830 BC) depicting the tribute paid to the Assyrian King Shalmaneser III by the Phoenicians.

The Phoenicians – People of the Purple Cloth

Phoenician civilization developed along the eastern shore of the Mediterranean. It occupied a strip of land between the sea and the Lebanese mountains which was bordered to the north by the land of the Hittites (Anatolia and Syria) and to the south by Palestine. Today, this area is fairly fertile, with rain during the

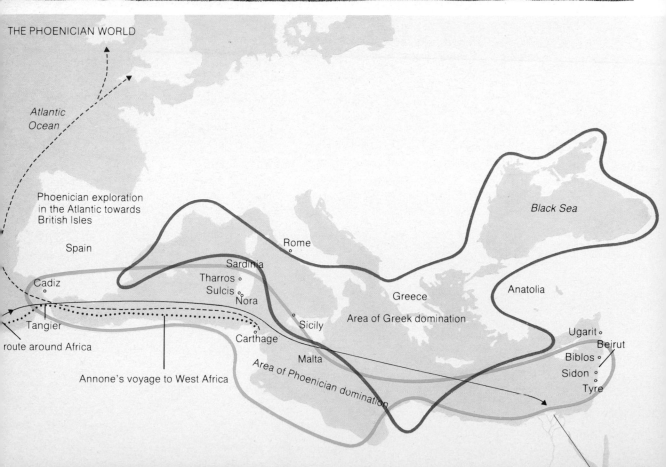

THE PHOENICIAN WORLD

Atlantic Ocean

Phoenician exploration in the Atlantic towards British Isles

Spain

Rome

Sardinia

Tharros
Sulcis
Nora

Cadiz

Black Sea

Anatolia

Greece

Area of Greek domination

Sicily

Tangier

route around Africa

Carthage

Malta

Area of Phoenician domination

Annone's voyage to West Africa

Ugarit
Beirut
Biblos
Sidon
Tyre

winter months. Perhaps conditions were much the same during the two thousand years before Christ. The trees which grew on the slopes of the Lebanese mountains were a great natural resource. These included pines, cypresses and, in particular, the famous conifer the Cedar of Lebanon (*Cedrus libani*). Minerals were found in the mountains and the sea enabled the people to fish and to travel. The Phoeni-

Briefly then, we do not know if the region gave its name to the product or vice-versa, but the Phoenicians were called 'the people of the purple cloth' as today we might call the Japanese 'the transistor people', referring to a product which was exported world-wide.

Origins and development

The Phoenicians' ancestors were probably the Semite people who, in the third

cians were able to make use of some of these natural resources in a special way.

The name Phoenicia comes from the Greek *phoinos* meaning purple, which describes the colour of the cloth they produced. In Mycenean texts we find the adjective *po-ni-ki-ja* (a feminine word) which means purple. The local name for this country was Canaan and the Phoenicians probably absorbed the Canaanites about 1200 BC. In texts from Akkad we see the word *kinakhkhu* which means purple and the similarity with the word Canaan is noticeable.

Opposite: Map showing the region (enclosed by the blue line) dominated by the Phoenicians, and some of their trade routes. One of these shows the journey around Africa. As a comparison the area dominated by the Greeks (enclosed by the red line) is also shown. It can be seen that the two areas almost met in Sicily where, in fact, there were conflicts and battles between the two peoples.

Above: Bronze weight having the shape of a man's head with a net covering his hair. It was found on the eastern Mediterranean coast at Ugarit, a flourishing Phoenician centre which traded with Crete and Greece. Probably owned by a blacksmith or someone dealing in weights and measures.

millennium BC, spread out from the northern regions of Arabia (p 130). It is certain, though, that in 1200 BC the people who settled along the Lebanese and Syrian coasts already had strong individual cultural characteristics. Perhaps the real formation of the Phoenician character occurred during an intermediary period of semi-nomadic life when there was a strong interest in commercial activity along the caravan routes. The oldest centres were similar to city-states, loosely linked by a common interest, namely trade. These cities included Byblos, Beirut, Sidon and Tyre, which soon became more important than the others.

In this region, which was protected and also isolated by the mountains of Lebanon, the obvious route to the east was to go north first. This route led to the upper valley of the River Euphrates and on it the towns of Alalakh, Ebla and Mari had flourished or were flourishing. Ugarit, today called Ras Shamra, near Latakia in Syria, was a particularly rich coastal town. We think that various cultural characteristics, such as the language of the growing Phoenician civilization, came from the area of Ugarit, which reached its height before 1000 BC. Perhaps the Phoenicians found it difficult to penetrate the great caravan routes which led to Mesopotamia. In the coastal towns, however, the people had for some time been familiar with the sea. Timber from the mountain forests was used to build ships. So, the Phoenicians chose to use the sea routes rather than travel by land. The Minoans before them had also adopted this form of trade.

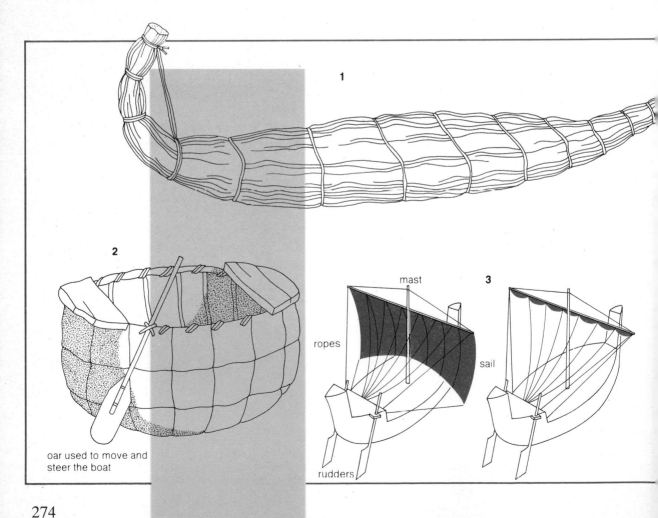

1

2

oar used to move and steer the boat

mast

3

ropes

sail

rudders

Their economy

The Phoenicians cultivated corn, barley, olives, vines, figs and sycamores. Dates were picked from the palm trees. Irrigation was rare but streams provided a certain amount of water naturally. Donkeys, cattle, sheep and goats were reared, but the most important source of protein was fish.

The beaches and the sea provided two sources of wealth for the Phoenicians. The fine sands were used to produce high-quality glass. Here we must point out that the Phoenicians did not invent glass, as is widely believed. It was already being produced and sold in many parts of the ancient world, at least in the form of a glass paste which was opaque and used for making various objects. The Phoenicians, however, were the first to make almost

Opposite: Boats of the ancient world. 1. Boat made from papyrus reeds used by the Ancient Egyptians on the River Nile and on sea voyages.
2. Mesopotamian boat (still used today in certain areas) made by sowing together pieces of leather and fixing them on to a wooden or wicker frame. The boat was made waterproof by covering it with tar. 3. Phoenician boat. It was steered by one man using two oars fixed together by a pole. The sail was raised and lowered from the deck by using ropes.
Below: Assyrian engraving from about 700 BC depicting a Phoenician bireme (a galley with two banks of oars). There is little detailed information on Phoenician boats, this engraving being one of the few contemporary illustrations.

transparent glass on a large scale, and they also introduced the technique of glass-blowing, producing light, hollow objects.

From the sea close to the shore the Phoenicians collected shellfish of the *Murex brandaris* and *Murex trunculus* species. A special gland in these creatures produces a substance which turns purple on exposure to light. The Phoenicians discovered that, with treatment, this could be used to dye material permanently, especially woollen cloth. We think that more than 100,000 fish would have been needed to produce 1 kilogram (2.2 pounds) of dye. Large piles of shells from the fish have been discovered near the ancient Phoenician cities, similar to the shell dumps of the Mesolithic Age known as 'kitchen refuse'. These, however, consisted of many different types of shells, whereas those of the Phoenicians contain only one type of shell. We have said that these mounds have been found 'near' the cities, but in fact the production of the dye was done some distance away because it produced an unpleasant smell.

The creation of demand for purple cloth

The Phoenicians were able to sell this purple cloth all over the ancient world thanks to an extremely efficient distribution network, similar to the system we today call 'door to door selling'. Whereas food, timber and metal were all produced in basic shapes and sizes, a beautiful piece of purple cloth was not. Almost all of the civilizations we have studied produced linen, wool and cotton cloth, and we also know that various dyes were used, as in Crete. The Phoenicians, though, were able to make a quality product and give it a mark of distinction; their purple cloth was therefore extremely expensive. It became a symbol of authority in the Roman Empire, and emperors and princes dressed in purple.

In a relatively short time the reputation of this purple cloth spread, and, in order to satisfy the demand, the Phoenician merchants enlarged their distribution network. There were a few difficulties in the east, but as the product was of such a high standard, many doors were opened. It made more sense for them to expand towards the west and so the Mediterranean was

Left: The legendary meeting between Polyphemus the Cyclops, who was rough and ugly, and Ulysses and his companions, who were clever and resourceful men, may have had an historical basis. Probably the Phoenicians and the Greeks sacked the coast of Sicily (where the Cyclops were believed to live) and tried to cheat the natives. Here, a Sicilian native watches helplessly as he is robbed by Phoenician raiders. The Phoenicians, however, soon realized that they could not base their economy on raiding. They therefore created a network of trading ports which gradually increased in importance and, in many cases, became flourishing cities.
Below: Silver coin discovered in Sidon (in Lebanon) and used by the Phoenicians about 400 BC. The coin was made by the Persian government and had been received by Phoenician merchants as payment. It shows a fortified city and a war ship. On the back there is the head of a Persian king.

systematically covered. Various ports of call were established along the coast. Sometimes the initial contacts with these coastal people were difficult, and the Phoenicians behaved like raiders; the same thing happened in the first Greek colonies and the Cretans themselves had perhaps used the very same tactics. However, an acceptable working arrangement was established at these ports. The Phoenicians would arrive on their customers' shores, and would only offer their product for sale to the people of high rank. When they left, they would be rich men. They had many suitable ports of call so that they could shelter during storms or during attack by dissatisfied customers.

The Phoenicians were able to sell many products by visiting different people and countries. They also bought goods and sold them again at a profit. However, they were well known for their luxury product, a useless but 'indispensable' item – purple cloth.

Phoenician colonies

The Phoenicians were certainly excellent boat builders and they were also very good at building harbours. Their choice of sites for ports and colonies was particularly remarkable. The Phoenician cities were rarely grouped together; obviously it was more useful to have ports which were some distance from each other so that fairly large areas could be covered with just a few settlements. The ports were nearly always built on headlands or on small islands near the coast. These natural features gave protection against the wind. A headland often has two bays, one on either side of it, and so giving a choice of two harbours. A small island is a sort of natural breakwater. The elongated islands which formed lagoons or enclosed areas of sea were particularly useful. The Phoenicians, therefore, built ports and cities along the African

coast and perhaps even in Sardinia and Sicily. Other ports of call have been found in Spain.

Why was it necessary to create cities? Did the Phoenicians want to colonize the whole of the Mediterranean? This Phoenician colonizing operation has been explained in many ways. It is possible that an increase in population in the restricted area of their homeland encouraged them to look for new areas in which to live. Other non-seafaring people would have tried to move into nearby lands and annex areas which were quite close. But the Phoenicians, who were so at home on the sea, considered the lands on the other side of the

I am Psr [only the consonants are written], son of Baalyaton, the kettledrum player.

Inscription found in an Egyptian temple but written by a Phoenician musician.

After having passed the Columns of Hercules, we sailed on for two days and founded our first city, Timiaterio. There is a large plain near this city . . . Inland we found an island . . . with a lake, and on this lake there was another island inhabited by savages. The women had hairy bodies and our interpreters called them gorillas . . . We captured three of these women, but they bit and scratched and did not want to follow their captors . . .

From the tale of the journey of Annon, the Carthaginian

Opposite: Phoenician inscription on a stone found on Sardinia. The inscription, which is rather disjointed, lists the crimes for which a man could be expelled from the island for a period of one year.
Left: Most of the Phoenician texts to have survived to the present are very short inscriptions. The short dedication here is followed by a piece from a famous passage of Phoenician origin but written in Greek. It is an account written by Annon of his travels. Annon was a Carthaginian commander (Carthage in North Africa was a Phoenician colony) who sailed along the western coast of Africa, probably as far as the mouth of the River Niger.
Below: Ivory box for cosmetics from about 1350 BC. It was discovered in Ugarit in Syria.
Bottom left: 'Woman at the window' – a recurring subject in Phoenician art. Here it is in the form of an ivory box. It is not known whether she is a goddess, a priestess or an ordinary woman.

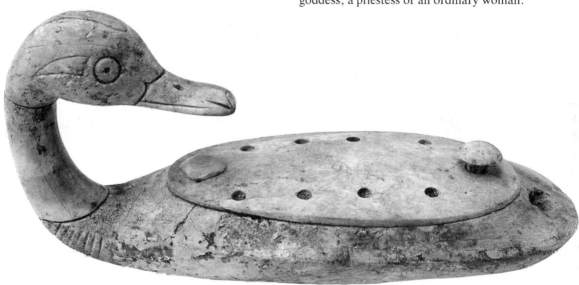

Mediterranean to be near. The Phoenician occupation and creation of individual ports and colonies, however, shows that a central power structure, which would have organized and commanded a systematic occupation of other lands, did not exist. The Phoenicians did not have the organization of an empire.

It has been suggested that the enormous demand for purple cloth caused the almost total extinction of, or at least an enormous reduction in, the shellfish population. The Phoenicians would therefore have had to travel westwards looking for other fish along the coast. In fact, in the cities of north Africa the

279

Phoenicians started a different business, almost an industry, connected with the sea: the preparation of salted fish. They obtained the salt from the sea by leaving basins of water out in the sun. The waters around these new settlements were so full of fish that this new activity seemed obvious.

We must remember that the Phoenicians also used the metals available in the western regions, in Spain in particular. They were able to buy tin and silver very cheaply, offering in exchange their precious purple cloth. They then sold the same metals in the east at much higher prices.

In the west the Phoenicians increased the numbers and types of domestic animals, mainly by exchanging various species with the local nomadic and semi-nomadic tribes. Horses, cattle, goats, sheep, pigs, poultry and bees (wax from the colony at Carthage was used in the preparation of medicines) were reared in the African cities. Elephants were also kept and proved to be the great strength of the Carthaginian army of Hannibal. Camel rearing was not, however, mentioned.

The end of Phoenician power

The Phoenicians could be useful trading partners. King Solomon of Israel became one of their allies and together they traded in the Mediterranean and the Red Sea. The Assyrians preferred to maintain their independence, and their King Sennacherib ruled the Phoenician cities along the Lebanese coast (p 268). However, Tyre remained independent and was only conquered in 573 BC, after a siege of 13 years, by the Babylonians under Nebuchadnezzar II (p 270). The eastern cities were subsequently captured by the Persians and then by Alexander the Great. In 332 BC Tyre was placed under siege once more, but this time it was only seven months

Above and opposite: Three laughing masks, discovered in three different Phoenician centres, which are typical examples of Phoenician art. They are made of clay and date from the late Phoenician period (700–500 BC), which is called Carthaginian, from the North African city of Carthage which was so important at that time. These masks, too small to be worn, were placed in tombs to keep away evil spirits; notice their expressions.

before the city fell, to Alexander.

The African cities and the colonies in the west remained prosperous for some time. There were serious battles in these regions against the Greeks, mostly in Sicily, and later war with Rome. Phoenician power was finally brought to an end with the defeat of Hannibal and the Carthaginians by the Romans in 202 BC. The Romans destroyed Carthage in 146 BC.

Rome expanded into the Mediterranean lands, but their advance into the continent of Europe was halted for another century. The Romans did not, at this stage, come into contact with European Iron Age civilizations which were technically quite advanced.

The Etruscans

The origins of Etruscan civilization present quite a few problems, and we are only able to give a very general explanation. It is in some respects a similar explanation to that given for the emergence of Phoenician civilization. This explanation contradicts the old assumptions, which were often based on legends and stated that the early Etruscans arrived from a distant country. These legends told of the Trojans' escape from their city after their war with the Greeks and their eventual arrival in Italy. Ancient historical sources do not give precise facts. The Roman historians, for example, were influenced by feelings of inferiority which they had towards the Etruscan civilization. Archaeology has provided us with more accurate information.

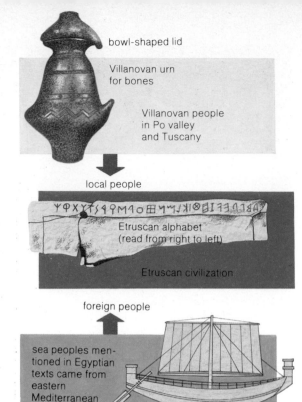

bowl-shaped lid

Villanovan urn for bones

Villanovan people in Po valley and Tuscany

local people

Etruscan alphabet (read from right to left)

Etruscan civilization

foreign people

sea peoples mentioned in Egyptian texts came from eastern Mediterranean

We can thus conclude that the Etruscans originated in the region of Italy where we now find their remains; they did not arrive from distant lands. These facts have been quite difficult to prove. The extraordinary splendour of the objects which were excavated gave rise to speculation. On the one hand, these remains strengthened the theory that there was a great Italian civilization, the forerunner of Rome; but on the other hand, Etruscan jewels, paintings and statues were so very beautiful that it was possible to think that they could only be explained by imagining that an already highly civilized group of people had arrived on uncultured Italian soil, such a civilized people that they became the ancestors of Rome.

Fortunately the archaeologists not only uncovered Etruscan buildings, but also proof of earlier Italian populations. As we have said (pp 153–75) the European Bronze and Iron Ages dis-

played a very high level of culture, good organization, a solid economy, excellent craftsmanship and a fairly high standard of living. Italy was also part of this cultural picture. In particular, the Villanovan culture (11th to 9th centuries BC), which was similar to other European Iron Age cultures, had many settlements that flourished in various parts of the Italian peninsula. The cemeteries are particularly well known because they were nearly always incorporated into cities belonging to later civilizations.

1

The Etruscan civilization developed during the 10th and 9th centuries BC in an area of Villanovan culture which today corresponds to Tuscany, part of Umbria and northern Latium in central Italy. It is probable that their cultural development was spurred by the arrival of groups of people from the east, perhaps those described as 'sea peoples' in Egyptian texts (p 263). These groups did not bring with them a culture which was already perfect.

2

Etruscan civilization was formed by two cultures merging together: one European, from the land, and perhaps having Indo-European roots; the other Eastern, from the sea and perhaps having links with Semitic cultures. Greek mythological subjects were common in Etruscan art and also in manufactured goods such as vases. These were made in Greece and sold as far as the Italian coast of the Tyrrhenian Sea. Also, Greek artists worked in many Etruscan cities for a period of time.

The Etruscan environment

Now that we have some understanding of how Etruscan civilization developed, let us try to understand why it developed in the Tuscany and Latium regions of Italy. Why did the groups of people who came from the east settle in this particular area? What did the land offer? It had minerals (mainly iron),

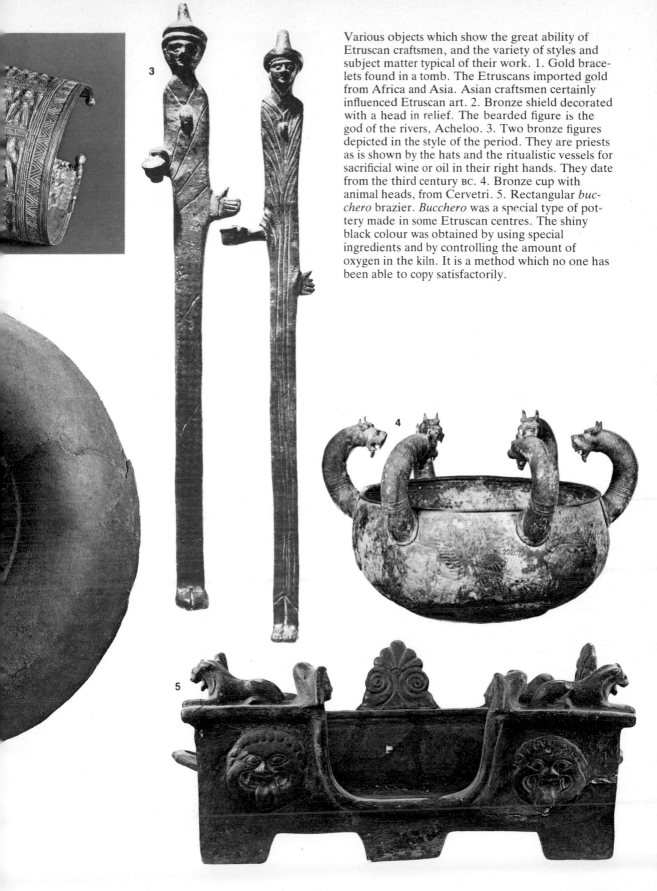

Various objects which show the great ability of Etruscan craftsmen, and the variety of styles and subject matter typical of their work. 1. Gold bracelets found in a tomb. The Etruscans imported gold from Africa and Asia. Asian craftsmen certainly influenced Etruscan art. 2. Bronze shield decorated with a head in relief. The bearded figure is the god of the rivers, Acheloo. 3. Two bronze figures depicted in the style of the period. They are priests as is shown by the hats and the ritualistic vessels for sacrificial wine or oil in their right hands. They date from the third century BC. 4. Bronze cup with animal heads, from Cervetri. 5. Rectangular *bucchero* brazier. *Bucchero* was a special type of pottery made in some Etruscan centres. The shiny black colour was obtained by using special ingredients and by controlling the amount of oxygen in the kiln. It is a method which no one has been able to copy satisfactorily.

many forests for timber and hunting, large areas which could be cultivated, many hills and areas of high land where settlements could be built and easily defended, good rainfall, hot springs, and rivers. The most important characteristic was probably the first. It is probable, in fact, that the people of the Villanovan culture had built settlements in this area because of the minerals.

The value of this resource was increased by the great ability of the Etruscan craftsmen. They were masters in the use of iron, but were also successful with bronze, silver and gold. As proof of their great technical ability, and the way in which they obtained the very best from the various metals, many of the skulls excavated from Etruscan tombs had false teeth made of gold; as well as teeth which had been carefully looked after and filled with precious metals.

Exploiting the environment

The Etruscans were able to build good boats using local timber, and they used them with skill. Their ports were well equipped. Certain stretches of the Rivers Tiber and Arno were used for communication purposes. A remarkable road network was built, with roads often running parallel to water courses. Transportation on land was by carts, and special lightweight pleasure carts were also built.

There are few examples of canals, but the underground tunnels, which carried sewage away from hill-top cities, are of particular interest. In some of the tunnels of the drainage system at Tarquinia, the marks of the pick-axes used by the Etruscans can still be seen. Aqueducts were used, and the hill-top cities usually had a number of wells or reservoirs.

Etruscan cities were nearly always

surrounded by walls. In some cases, Alatri and Amelia for example, their structure can still be seen under the Roman or medieval constructions. It is easy to distinguish the work of the Etruscan architects from later additions. They used enormous irregular polygonal (many-sided) slabs which were very carefully put together. Mortar was not used, the slabs being kept together simply by force of gravity. Similar styles of construction are found in the fortified Mycenean cities.

Etruscan city-states – small empires

Etruscan cities were enormously varied, as they always adapted themselves to their surroundings. The cities on the hilltops, therefore, looked like medieval castles, with walls and roads which were not always straight. The settlements on the plains consisted of many houses forming a single block, built according to a pattern which reminds us of the layout of Greek cities; an example was the city probably called Misa, near Marzabotto. Of particular interest are the towns which resembled large farmhouses, from which agri-

Opposite: Painted wall in the Etruscan tomb known as the Tomb of Hunting and Fishing, in the cemetery at Tarquinia. From the sixth century BC, it illustrates the natural surroundings of Tarquinia, a city only a few kilometres from the sea. The birds and animals are particularly beautiful.
Below: The two sheets of gold leaf on the left are inscribed in the Etruscan language, and the one on the right is in Phoenician. They were found in Pyrgi and are similar dedications to a goddess. However, the three texts are not the same, so it is not possible to translate the Etruscan text with the help of the Phoenician one, which we can read. The Etruscan inscription on the left is shorter than the one in the middle. The goddess is referred to as Astarte (a Phoenician goddess of fertility) in the Phoenician text, and as Uni-Astarte or Juno (later a Roman goddess) in the Etruscan ones. Pyrgi was situated on the coast north of Rome.

cultural work and the rearing of animals was carried out. The Holy Palace of Murlo, near Sienna, is particularly impressive. Remains have shown us how the inside walls of a house were built: a layer of plaster was put over a framework of poles and rushes. This same method was used until the mid 20th century in the building of attics in Italian country cottages.

Other information on Etruscan cities may be obtained from the cemeteries, the 'settlements' built as cities of the dead; these were exact copies of the cities of the living. In the cemetery of Crocefisso del Tufo in Orvieto, the tombs are positioned as though they were blocks of houses, with doors leading on to the roads, which cross at right angles. In many other cases the similarity between the cemetery and the city is not so obvious; the tombs are scattered here and there, but they are always next to a road, or roads, along which the people walked during the burial ceremonies. Cemeteries of underground tombs have also been found. Access to these was by means of a staircase or steep road.

One fact seems to have been a characteristic of Etruscan cemeteries: the city of the dead was always completely separated from the city of the living. Often this separation was made by a stretch of water. This was somehow connected with magical and religious beliefs.

The tombs were like 'houses for the dead' and they are our main source of information on the way Etruscans lived. The walls of the burial rooms were nearly always painted and the stone coffins, or sarcophagi (this comes from the Greek words literally meaning 'flesh devouring', and refers to the limestone coffins in which the bodies were placed; the limestone decomposed the bodies), are also painted or decorated in bas-relief. In many cases vases, common utensils, jewels and weapons were also found in the tombs.

Etruscan temples only had columns

at the front and were richly decorated with clay statues (see photograph on pp 294 and 295).

The Etruscans traded with many of the nations in the ancient world. An Egyptian vase of the late period was discovered at Tarquinia and there are many Greek objects there. It is probable that the Etruscans were also in contact with people in the west. It is certain that there were Etruscan cities further north in Italy, in the Po valley like Misa and Felina (which we now call Bologna).

Etruria was never organized as a united nation. The cities were small, independent units or empires. It was necessary to organize carefully all the activities of the cities; to control the craftsmen and merchants; to co-ordinate the work in the city with that in the surrounding agricultural areas, such as land reclamation, canal cutting, digging for drains and wells; and to provide an adequate defence system by building city walls, making weapons and creating

Main events in Etruscan history

About tenth century BC: group of sea people arrive in the area now called Tuscany in central Italy. They mix with the people already living in the area.

Eighth to seventh centuries BC: creation of cities. Main centres join and form the League of Twelve Cities.

Sixth century BC: expansion towards the River Po area of northern Italy, and to southern Lazio and Campania (area around Naples).

535 BC: alliance with the Carthaginian Phoenicians and expulsion of the Greeks from Corsica. The Etruscans control the commercial routes in the north-west Mediterranean.

Fifth century BC: the Etruscans rule Rome and commence civic building, reclamation of lands and create a constitution for the workers. Tarquinius Superbus expelled from Rome, ending Etruscan rule. The Greeks of Syracuse in Sicily defeat the Etruscans in 474 BC.

396 BC: Veii captured by the Romans.

Opposite: Detail of a section of the Tomb of Hunting and Fishing in Tarquinia (sixth century BC). The figures are taking part in a festivity (possibly a funeral banquet in honour of the dead).
Bottom: Interior of the Tomb of the Leopards in Tarquinia (late fifth century BC). At the top the two animals which have given the tomb its name can be seen. At the bottom there is a banqueting table with the guests lying on couches. The ceiling is decorated with geometric shapes.

military units. The people who were given these organizational tasks formed themselves, together with the priests, into a kind of upper class. We do not believe there was an actual military class, nor was there a permanent army. Etruscan cities were linked together by rather flexible agreements. Every so often two or three cities would group together against another. Only occasionally did one city rule over a large area consisting of many other cities.

The search for land

Etruscan expansion in the 6th century BC can be explained in terms of an expansion in the trading network. Cities in Latium (the region around Rome) and along the coast of Campania (the area around Naples) were used as ports of call, or as other less important areas of production.

Many history books tell us that the Etruscans did not go past the River Tiber (which runs through Rome), that they remained on the right bank of the river. Archaeological excavations have, however, contradicted this assumption. For example, there is a town near Orvieto in Umbria on the east bank of the Tiber where a few years ago a large Etruscan cemetery was discovered. This means that there was an Etruscan

Etruscan Cities

Etruscan name	Latin name	Modern name of the Etruscan site or of the nearest town
	Arretium	Arezzo
		Bagnolo San Vito
Felsina	Bononia	Bologna
Velsna	Volsinii	Bolsena
Capena	Capua	Capua
	Castellum Axium	Castel d'Asso
Cisra	Caere	Cerveteri
Ceisna (?)	Caesena	Cesena
Clevsin	Clusium	Chiusi
	Falerii Veteres	Civita Castellana
	Spina	Comacchio
Curtun-	Cortona	Cortona
	Cumae	Cuma
Vi(p)sul-	Faesulae	Fiesole
	Florentia	Florence
	Pithecusae	Ischia
Manuva	Mantua	Mantua
Misa (?)	Misa (?)	Marzabotto
Mutina	Mutina	Modena
Cusa	Cosa	Orbetello
	Urbs Vetus	Orvieto
Per(u)sna	Perusia	Perugia
	Placentia	Piacenza
	Pompeii	Pompei
Fufluna	Populonia	Populonia
	Graviscae	Porto Clementino
Rav(e)na	Ravenna	Ravenna
Arimna (?)	Ariminium	Rimini
Rumon (?)		
Ruma	Roma	Rome
	Rusellae	Roselle
	Punicum	Santa Marinella
	Pyrgi	Santa Severa
Saena (?)	Saena	Siena
Svеama	Suana	Sovana
Sudri, Suthri	Sutrium	Sutri
Tarchna	Tarquinii	Tarquinia
Veia	Veii	Veio
Vatluna, Vatlna	Vetulonia	Vetulonia
Surina (?)	Sorrina	Viterbo
Velauri	Volaterrae	Volterra
Velc, Velcha (?)	Vulci	Vulci

Right: Position of the roads and tombs in an Etruscan necropolis built into cliffs (cg at San Giuliano, Castel d'Asso, San Giovenale and Norchia, all sites near Viterbo). These structures (even the facades and the columns) were created by digging into the rock.

Opposite: Underground tomb at San Manno, Perugia. This one is of particular architectural interest. Usually these tombs were similar in shape to the inside of houses, with sloping roofs supported by beams. Here, instead, the vault is built in the shape of an arch. This was rare in Etruscan architecture. Another example of this is at Bettona, near Perugia, and arches were used in the building of some city gates.

city in the area near Orvieto. The Etruscans, therefore, also went eastwards. In many places along the Tiber and Arno Rivers there are shallow fords and deep gorges which were used to control the movement of boats.

As regards Orvieto itself, it is worthwhile mentioning the old belief that the present-day name of the town gives information on the history of the settlement. In Latin, Orvieto was *Urbs Vetus* meaning 'the ancient city'. Why did the Romans use this particular name? Probably because the city was ancient in comparison to a nearby city which had been founded at a later date by the same people who occupied Orvieto. This second city has been identified as Bolsena, situated on the lake of the same name and some distance from the

Etruscan names

Male Christian names

Ancient form	Modern form	Abbreviation	Latin equivalent
ara(n) th	arnth	a. ar. ath.	Aruns
avile (?)	avle o aule	av. au.	Aulus
	cae (kae)	c. ca.	Caius
cnaive	cneve		Gnaeus
vel	vel	v. ve.	Vel
velthur	velthur	vth.	
thefarie	thefri(e)	thi.	Tiberius
larece	larce	lc.	Larcius
larth	larth	l. la. lth.	
laris	laris	l. li. lr.	Laris
	luvcie (s)		Lucius
ma(ma)rce	marce	m.	Marcius
	sethre	s. sth.	Setrius
spurie	spurie	sp.	Spurius
	tite	ti.	Titus

Female Christian names

Ancient form	Modern form	Abbreviation	Latin equivalent
	velia		Velia
	hasti(a)	h. ha.	Fausta
	fasti(a)	f. fa.	Fausta
	than(i)a	th. tha.	Thania
	thanchvil	tha. thch.	Tanaquilla
	larthi	la. lth.	Lartia
ramutha, ramatha	ramtha, ra(v)nthu	r. ra.	Ramta

In transcription the letters th and ch correspond to Etruscan letters which had a similar sound to the Greek letters theta (θ) and chi (χ).

1

2

Opposite and below: Various types of Etruscan container used for keeping the ashes of the dead. All these objects date from the sixth century BC. The different designs result not only from the different ideas of the craftsmen, but also from the social and economic situation of the customer. 1. Typical example of a canopic vase (from Canopus, an ancient Egyptian city). The head forms the lid and, as is often the case, the handles look like large arms. The vase was usually placed on a throne. 2. Vase with a lid in the shape of a woman's head. Note the hands and breasts. 3. Urn known as Paolazzi from Chiusi. The figure is wearing what seems to be a checked suit. Notice the four vultures and the small human figures. 4. Urn in the shape of a man sitting on a throne.

Tiber. Today, having discovered the 'city of the dead' on the left bank of the river, opposite Orvieto, a new and exciting assumption may be made. Did the inhabitants of *Urbs Vetus* found a third city? Only a systematic dig will be able to give us an answer.

Etruscan presence to the north of the Apennine Mountains in the Po valley is very well documented. Another Etruscan city is being excavated at Castelnuovo, near Mantua, in the north of Italy.

Writing

It is necessary to look at the Etruscan language, as it has been the source of conflicting opinions. The Etruscans wrote using characters which were very similar to those used by the ancient Greeks. Thus these characters can be

Right: Etruscan decorative objects in clay, dating from the fifth century BC. Usually Etruscan temples were decorated with painted clay objects. The structure of the temples themselves were fairly simple. The slanting roof created a triangular section on the facade above the columns known as the tympanum. This was decorated with groups of figures mounted against a background. Obviously, when figures like this are discovered, it is very difficult to piece them together again, the fragments often being very tiny. The task of putting together the fragments from the tympanum of the Temple of Talamone is particularly interesting. The restorers began by studying the mythical stories of these figures, and then reconstructed the scene, not only by using the actual pieces, but also by creating a picture from the stories.

Below: Reconstructed tympanum (triangular gable above columns) and a detail of it from the facade of the Etruscan Temple of Talamone, north of Rome. It consists of a bas-relief depicting the Greek myth 'The Seven Against Thebes'.

Oedipus with his dying sons. Eteocles is on the left and is being supported by his mother, Jocasta. Polynices is on the right, held up by a friend

Amphiaraus enters hell on his chariot preceded by a winged demon

The Seven Against Thebes

After the exile of King Oedipus from Thebes and the death of Queen Jocasta, their two sons, Polynices and Eteocles, were to take turns on the throne, each ruling for one year. However, Eteocles refused to make way for his brother. Polynices then took refuge with Adrastus, King of Argos, and received his help. With Adrastus and five other leaders (Tydeus, Capaneus, Hippomedon, Parthenopaeus and Amphiaraus) he declared war on his own city. Each man in the group of seven attacked one of Thebes's seven gates. The attack ended in disaster – all the leaders were killed (Eteocles and Polynices speared each other to death). Of the seven, only Adrastus escaped and he eventually lead another attack against Thebes, destroying the city. Amphiaraus, fleeing on his chariot, was taken by the god Zeus to reign among the dead. According to an Etruscan version of this story, Oedipus and Jocasta, still alive, watched their sons duelling.

294

read today without much difficulty. We have thousands of examples of Etruscan writings, but usually these are in the form of dedications, people's names and memorial inscriptions. The longer texts are, however, very difficult to understand. Why? Because the Etruscan language does not belong to any group of languages known today. It is possible to trace the occasional word back to Indo-European expressions, but they are few and far between. The Etruscan language probably came from a basic Mediterranean tongue which almost totally disappeared with the arrival of the 'sea peoples'.

In summary then, we are able to read the Etruscan language and to understand words like, 'That person; so-and-so's son, he is offering something to a particular god'. We understand the names of certain objects and the names of the six numbers which are found on the sides of dice. We do not, however, actually understand the language; we do not know the grammar nor do we know how the sentences were put together.

History

The box on p 289 gives the main historical facts. We know very little apart from the details of the battles with the Greeks and the Phoenicians, and we know virtually nothing about the internal conflicts between the various Etruscan cities. We do know, however, that the Etruscans were annoyed by the exploits of a group of shepherd-bandits who had settled in the hills above one of the fords of the Tiber. In Etruscan, this place was called Rumon, meaning the ford. For a time the lords of Tarquinia, and perhaps also of Veii, were able to control this town, but eventually the people of Rumon, who were by now calling their city Rome and themselves Romans, expelled the Etruscans. However, Etruscan civilization was a great influence in the development of Rome, and many aspects of its culture were adopted by the Romans. This was unusual for the Romans as they usually destroyed the cultures with which they came into contact.

295

The Foundation of Rome

During their period of expansion the Etruscans had avoided the area near their southern cities, and Veii in particular; they had simply gone around it to enter southern Latium and Campania. This area was very marshy and malaria was rife. There were, however, a few huts on the hills overlooking the Tiber ford, near an island in the Tiber. Their remains have been found on the Palatine Hill in Rome and it is thought they date from the 9th century BC. The foundations were dug into the rocks and the holes into which support poles were placed can still be seen today. The huts themselves were probably made of wood with straw roofs. The floor was lower than the surrounding ground. One of the foundations of the largest hut is about 5 metres (16 feet) in length and has two smaller holes at its entrance, probably for a porch.

The inhabitants of these huts on the Palatine were shepherds and peasants whose main activity, however, was robbing the travellers as they crossed the ford. Other groups of people lived on the nearby hills of Esquiline, Viminal and Quirinal. These shepherd-bandits of the Palatine Hill were the first Latins

Right: Archaeological remains, much older than the oldest Roman remains, have been discovered on the Palatine Hill near the remains of the house where the first Roman Emperor, Augustus, probably lived, but which is known as Livia's House (Livia was his wife). These remains were the foundations of huts belonging to the Iron Age. This illustration depicts these 'first Romans' in their village. Notice the wooden framework of the huts and their small porches. They were ready to attack anyone who entered their territory (marshland with malaria-carrying mosquitos) in order to cross the River Tiber at the ford of Tiberina Island, seen in the distance. Prehistoric cemeteries have been discovered near this ford. The tombs contain urns in the shape of huts, probably similar to the huts found in the village. The marshland around the hills was drained in the sixth century BC, probably by the Etruscan kings, with the construction of the Cloaca Maxima drainage system.

and they later joined forces with the groups on the other hills and a unified city began to emerge. Roman legends attribute the foundation of Rome on the Palatine Hill to Romulus and Remus in 753 BC.

We know very little of this early Rome. Facts have been distorted by legends. However, we are able to see how social life was organized by reading the descriptions left by the historians of the time and, from the same source, we can deduce a little information on Etruscan life. In Rome the king was chosen according to the wishes of the gods. The will of the gods was interpreted by the priests who 'read' the bones of sacrificed animals and the flight of birds, as was done in Etruria. The king was a political, military, reli-

gious and judicial head. He was helped by a group of elderly men, known as the Senate, and by a group of priests. The citizens had to work for the government and fight in the frequent military campaigns. They could voice their opinions through a tribunal. The Etruscans, who actually ruled Rome for a period in the 6th century BC, changed this system a little and gave the citizens particular duties in military matters. This became the Law of Servius Tullius, who was really an Etruscan prince called Macstarna.

Thus, Rome grew as an Etruscan centre, but eventually the Etruscans were expelled and from then on their influence on the development of Roman civilization was ignored.

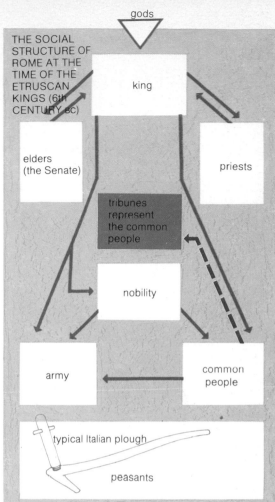

THE SOCIAL STRUCTURE OF ROME AT THE TIME OF THE ETRUSCAN KINGS (6th CENTURY BC)

gods

king

elders (the Senate)

priests

tribunes represent the common people

nobility

army

common people

typical Italian plough

peasants

Opposite: View of the River Tiber. The name of this river reminds us of the close relationship between the ancient Romans and the Etruscans. *Tibur* is an Etruscan word and roughly means mountainous. We know that the word Rome also comes from an Etruscan word, *Rumon*, meaning the settlement by the ford.

Below: The Ploughman of Arezzo, an ancient clay model discovered in Tuscany. Notice the plough (which has been copied in the diagram above).

299

8. Man and Civilization

The Faults of Civilizations

Having summed up the events and characteristics of some of the ancient civilizations, we will now try to clarify our research a little.

We began with basic facts such as the actual presence of man on Earth and his need for food in order to survive. These facts are also true for all other living things. But man has efficiently used his ability, skill and power of organization in a way that no other animal has been able to do. On the other hand, we have also seen that in many cases men have become involved in complicated methods of production which have caused them to argue amongst themselves. They still managed to survive, but in order to do so they had to force other people to suffer even more than they did.

We have been able to recognize the solutions which the various cultures and civilizations developed in order to live in their particular surroundings. However, we must, at this point, ask whether there was always only one solution. Would it have been possible to have made a different choice? In very many cases a different solution would not have been possible. The civilizations could only have developed in that particular way, but many mistakes were made later on. For example, working together towards a single goal and facing the various problems created by the environment was indeed the right thing to do. But was changing a system of production involving many people into a community which elevated a small number of men into a ruling class the only way of organizing society? Was war really necessary in acquiring new lands for production, or was it a sign of a flaw in these civilizations?

Man's Virtues

We have been able to find faults and mistakes, but can we learn anything from these civilizations of the past? There are many ways of looking at these cultures. We can see them as objects in a museum, a collection of dead things, or as information which needs to be catalogued. Or we can bring them back to life. During the last century, and at the beginning of our own century, a great deal of information has been produced from historical and archaeological discoveries. But even today some people put forward fantastic explanations for proven archaeological facts. Haven't we all read 'explanations' of how Stonehenge or the Egyptian pyramids were built by extra-terrestials?

If we really want to understand civilizations, we can use this information about those of the past and learn from it. If, for example, we try to find out what actually worked in any particular period of history, we will quickly discover that it was co-operation between people. Successful communities made use of their natural surroundings without destroying, spoiling or exterminating it or their neighbours. It is still possible for people to work together.

Many people today still do not know how to read or write, but many others are able to do so and, indeed, must teach those who are ignorant. Today, methods of communication are excellent, but they must be properly used. For example, television is able to encourage its audiences to buy things which are often useless, but it can also

educate, explain and make information available to help people choose the best course of action. The same may be said of books, newspapers, the cinema and radio, and even of art and music. Today, communication, the sending and receiving of information, is a task which does, and must, involve everybody. A very important job is that of the teacher. A good teacher passes on 'culture', helps his or her pupils

Above: Detail of the head of the she-wolf in the Capitoline Museum in Rome. This famous bronze statue was created by Etruscan craftsmen in the late sixth century BC. The curls on the animal's coat are features of a particular style of Etruscan art. The she-wolf is suckling the babies Romulus and Remus, the mythical founders of Rome. So this Roman statue is really Etruscan. We can rarely say that one civilization is the offspring of another. Different civilizations have often fought each other, and one of the most common forms of contact between (and thus influence on) civilizations has been through war.

develop and grow up, and works with them to create a civilization.

Are We Civilized?

The study of the past can help us in our present-day life, but it can also help us in the future. In this book we have tried to look inside the ancient civilizations and understand how they worked. We can do the same for our own civilization and study our mistakes.

We have many advantages that the people of these ancient civilizations did not have. Above all many of us have the ability to choose. We know that we do not have to believe political propaganda; we know how to ask for more

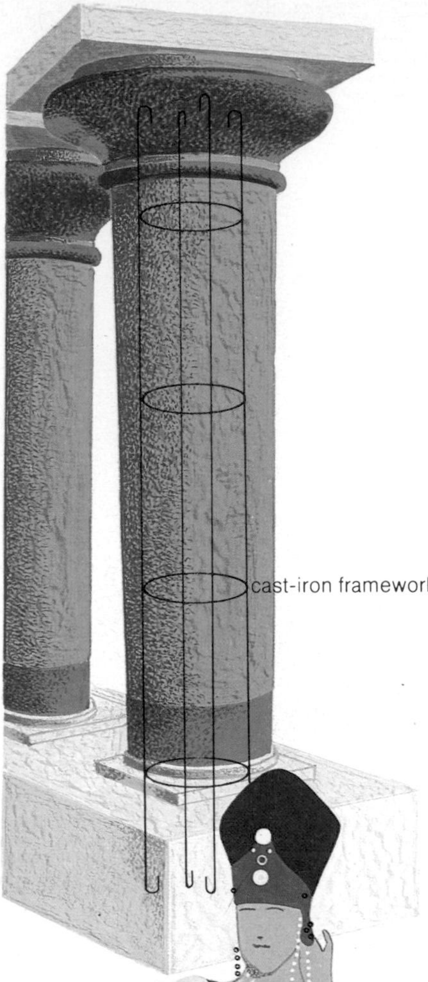

Right: The discoveries of the ancient world have been absorbed by modern society, but sometimes evidence from the past has not been fully understood. This has resulted in a variety of anomalies and misconceptions, some examples of which are illustrated here. Ancient buildings have been restored using modern techniques; for example, Sir Arthur Evans strengthened the columns of the palace of Knossos with reinforced concrete. The events and characters of history have been rewritten as fiction producing some odd discrepancies; for example, the character of the Carthiginian queen Salammbo in the French novelist Gustave Flaubert's book was based on an historical character but behaves like a 19th century heroine (or *femme fatale*). The Italian composer Verdi's opera *Aida* is set in Ancient Egypt, but as in this photograph from a 1920s production at La Scala opera house in Milan, Italy, the sets often include 20th century elements such as the triumphal arch as well as genuinely Egyptian items such as the statue of Ramses II.

Many 19th and 20th century buildings have incorporated features of ancient architecture, sometimes mixing them together; for example, in Italy, Milan railway station's odd mixture of styles has been jokingly called an example of the 'Assyrian-Milanese' style. And ancient monuments have sometimes been thought to provide evidence of visits by extra-terrestrial beings. The Temple of Inscriptions in the ancient Mayan city of Palenque in Mexico has the figure of a god on the lid of a coffin. This figure has been thought to be the detailed plan of a space ship, and that the imposing creations of ancient civilizations could only have been the work of aliens, not mere humans.

The columns of the Minoan palace at Knossos on Crete

cast-iron framework

Salammbo the Carthiginian queen of Flaubert's novel

1920s production of *Aida*

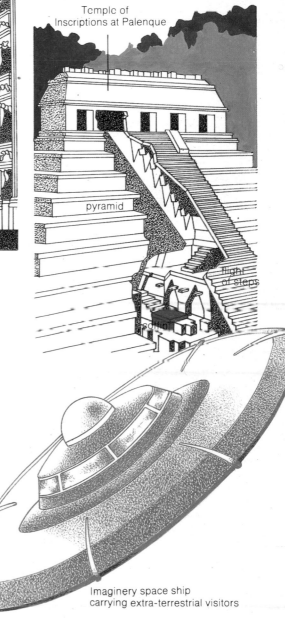

Temple of
Inscriptions at Palenque

pyramid

flight
of steps

coffin

Imaginery space ship
carrying extra-terrestrial visitors

Milan's central railway station

Below: Civilizations have developed a number of varied characteristics which have been and may continue to be used for better or for worse. Some of these controversial aspects of civilization are illustrated here. City life, upon which civilizations are largely based, has created divisions between classes of people according to their roles. Some roles, and thus classes of people, are more powerful than others. Reading and writing divides people between those who can and those who cannot, as they are instruments of power. Today, information, and hence the knowledge which could change civilization, can be made widely available to those who can read through libraries. Civilizations have continued to wage war, but on an increasingly large scale, using much more powerful weapons. The stability of civilizations has often been dependant on the share of the wealth which has been paid to their workers, the majority of their people.

information about what we are told by those in power; we can be aware of prejudiced attitudes towards other people, and try to get rid of them; and we know that we are all equal, that there are no divine men or god-like rulers. We know that even those in authority make mistakes and that we must often pay for their errors. We have learnt to read and write, a gift which we have received from the ancient civilizations. Thus we are able to communicate, to assess our situation and choose how to behave. We can recognize mistakes and implement changes which will help to bring about a better civilization.

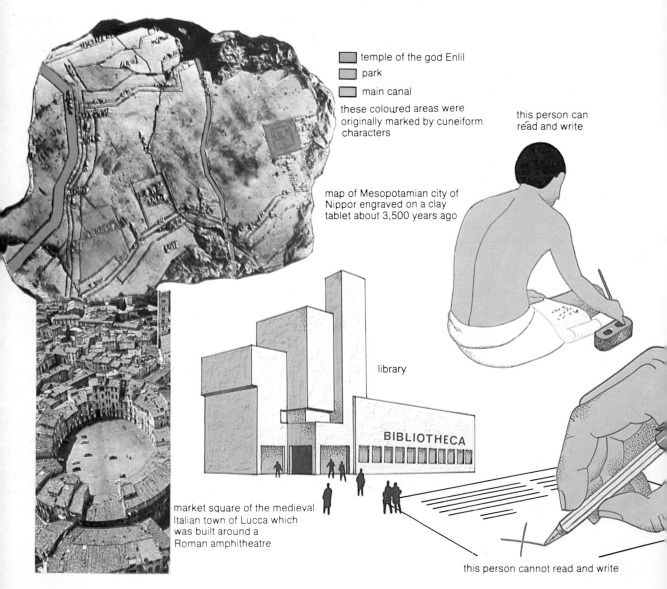

temple of the god Enlil
park
main canal

these coloured areas were originally marked by cuneiform characters

map of Mesopotamian city of Nippor engraved on a clay tablet about 3,500 years ago

this person can read and write

library

BIBLIOTHECA

market square of the medieval Italian town of Lucca which was built around a Roman amphitheatre

this person cannot read and write

We know that civilizations are born, grow and die, and that they can die painfully. We must make our civilization grow, because every person can and must reach complete maturity and become truly civilized.

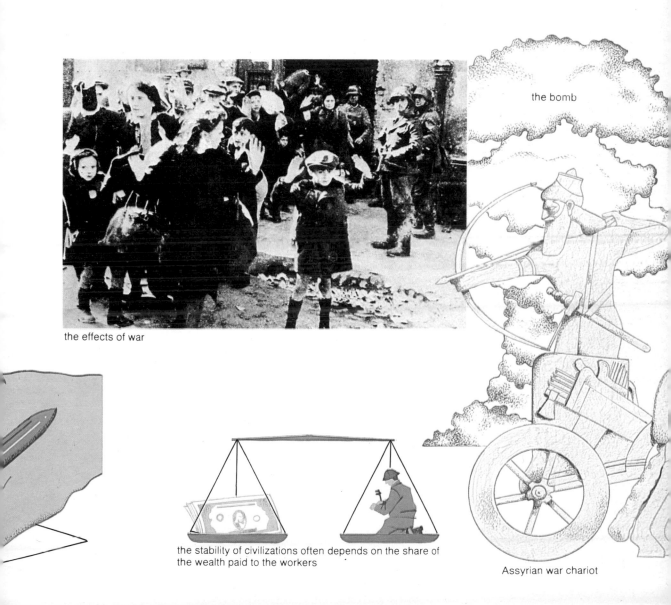

the bomb

the effects of war

the stability of civilizations often depends on the share of the wealth paid to the workers

Assyrian war chariot

REGION	4000	3800	3600	3400	3200	3000	2800	2600	2400	2200	2000	1800	1600	1400

SOUTHERN MESOPOTAMIA — Sumerians — Akkadians — Babylonians

BABYLONIA — Sumerians — Babylonians

ASSYRIA

unified Egypt — Old Kingdom — Middle Kingdom — New Kingdom

Indus Civilization — Indo-Europeans

GREECE — Minoans

GREECE — Minoans

MACEDONIA

ANATOLIA — Hittites

PHOENICIA/ NORTH AFRICA

PERSIA

PALESTINE

Shang

people of the megaliths

Taken from Ron Carter, *L'Alba della Civilta*, Vallardi

306

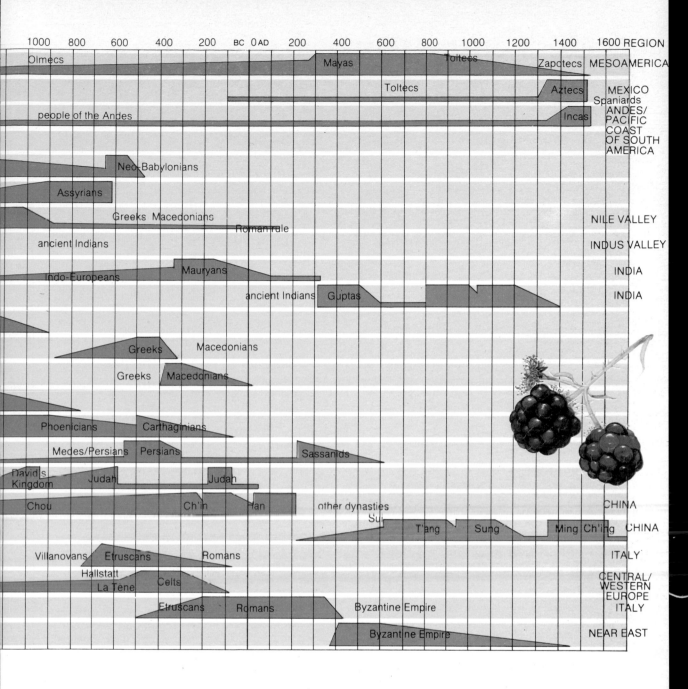

| 1000 | 800 | 600 | 400 | 200 | BC 0 AD | 200 | 400 | 600 | 800 | 1000 | 1200 | 1400 | 1600 | REGION |

Olmecs — Mayas — Toltecs — Zapotecs — MESOAMERICA

Toltecs — Aztecs — MEXICO

Spaniards

people of the Andes — Incas — ANDES/PACIFIC COAST OF SOUTH AMERICA

Neo-Babylonians

Assyrians

Greeks Macedonians — Roman rule — NILE VALLEY

ancient Indians — INDUS VALLEY

Indo-Europeans — Mauryans — INDIA

ancient Indians — Guptas — INDIA

Greeks — Macedonians

Greeks — Macedonians

Phoenicians — Carthaginians

Medes/Persians — Persians — Sassanids

David's Kingdom — Judah — Judah

Chou — Ch'in — Han — other dynasties — CHINA

Sui — T'ang — Sung — Ming Ch'ing — CHINA

Villanovans — Etruscans — Romans — ITALY

Hallstatt — Celts — CENTRAL/WESTERN EUROPE

La Tene

Etruscans — Romans — Byzantine Empire — ITALY

Byzantine Empire — NEAR EAST

Above: Civilizations come and go, they flower and mature, then decay. This chart summarizes the histories of the major civilizations of the world, showing their relationships to each other in time. Like the branch of a blackberry bush with its fruit in various stages of ripeness, civilizations at any given time have existed together in various states of maturity.

307

Voices from the Past

For seven days now / I have not seen
my loved one.
A sickness has fallen upon me; / my
limbs have grown heavy,
My very body have I forgotten. / If
doctors come to see me,
Their remedies will not relieve my
suffering. /
No wise man can find a solution:
My sickness stays hidden from the
world.
When I hear them say: 'Here she
comes!'
I spring to life; / her name revives
me.
My loved one is the best of all
medicines to me. /
. . . When I see her,
I am restored to health. / When she
opens her eyes, /
She makes my heart grow young;
when she speaks / it grows strong.
When I embrace her, / the sickness
goes away. /
And only seven days has she been
away from me.

Egyptian poem from the New Kingdom,
late second millennium BC

'I am tired of standing here in the
mine: even my sweat is getting saltier!
I need a change: I will stand just
outside near the cauldrons of brine'.
'Try changing your breeches:
they're soaking wet! Have some apple
wine and stoke up the fire a little. We
must hurry! The salt wagons are
ready and they expect us to fill them
up . . .'

Imagined conversation between
two salt miners in Hallstatt,
Austria, 7th century BC

The great wind begins to blow, / and
the clouds are setting sail.
My empire now extends throughout
the whole universe /
And now I am returning to my native
land. / And how to find
The heroes who should be standing
guard / over all my frontiers?

Song of the Great Wind by
Liu Pang, first Emperor of
the Chinese Han dynasty,
247–195 BC

'Come up here on to the balcony of
the tower. Can you see them there,
on the horizon? Those shadows, it's
them coming to attack us. And our
walls will not be strong enough to
hold them at bay; they will come and
plunder our granaries and kill us and
our children.'
'Yes, it's them, I can see them
clearly now. I'll call the others. We
must kill those grain thieves. They
think it's easier to steal food than
grow it themselves and spill their
sweat on the soil!

Imagined conversation between
two sentries on the walls of
Jericho, 8th millennium BC

O City, your name is famed but still
you are destroyed.
O City, whose walls once rose
proudly into the sky, now you and
your lands are in ruins.
My City, a caring mother whose
sheep have been snatched away,
O Ur, you are like a mother goat
whose kids are now no more.

Lamentation on the Destruction
of Ur, a Sumerian text, about
2000 BC

'I know that we will leave this place one day: the earth is growing less fertile, we cannot live off ash from the trees. And the yellow maize needs rich soil, soil which is nutritious. One day we will depart.'

'What are you talking about, old man? I know that if I burn down the trees to make room for the yellow maize, and in a year burn more down, then as long as the gods are with us it will go on this way.'

'I know what I'm talking about, boy! Our houses will not last for ever; we will abandon them eventually, and perhaps the great staircases in the temples will be abandoned too.'

Imagined conversation between an old man and a young one at the Mayan city of Tikal in Central America, 6th century AD

O grant us help against the foe,
   for vain is the help of man!
With God we shall do valiantly;
   it is he who will tread down our foes.

Last two verses of Psalm 60 from the *Bible*, 10th century BC

I have seen how the seeds that fall on the earth grow into new grass; I have seen this so many times. And I said to myself: perhaps the earth restores to life anything placed in it? So this is why I have placed my child, my dear little child, who has only just been born and now is dead, in the earth and covered him with it. The wolves will not eat you, little one, and the earth will bring you back in strength and greatness.

Imagined speech of a mother at her son's burial, La Ferrassie, a cave in France inhabited by Neanderthal Man 50,000 to 60,000 years ago

This temple and this statue are dedicated to Uni-Astarte, the lord Thefarie Velianas placed them here.

Dedication on one of the Etruscan plaques at Pyrgi, Italy, early 5th century BC

'Pass me the long pole, we'll put it in this hole and use it to take a sighting on the big stones. The longest night of the year is the day after tomorrow.'

'When does the moon rise? We should be able to tell from the position of the other poles. Is it tomorrow we're having the great feast?

Imagined conversation between two 'astronomers' at Stonehenge, England, about 3,500 years ago

Let me tell you what an unhappy man a soldier is. He has many people above him: generals, captains, standard-bearers, commanders, quartermasters. They get their orders from the royal tent and then they shout: 'Rouse yourselves! Wake up!' The soldier wakes up after barely an hour's sleep and they keep him busy from dawn till dusk. When he's so hungry his belly hurts, they give him his rations, but they're disgusting.

His wife and children are waiting for him back in the village. And what happens if he dies? He'll never come back. If he survives, he'll be totally worn out. If he runs away and deserts, his family is thrown into jail.

Egyptian text from the late New Kingdom, 13th–12th centuries BC

'The earth is shaking! People say that underneath in the palace cellars there is a great monster called the Minotaur who keeps bumping into the foundations. Don't you believe it?'

'They're just stories. There's nothing down there. It's just the earth shaking, like a woman giving birth. It has something in it which rages and roars like a bull. And sometimes it explodes: it always happens when that mountain there starts smoking.'

Imagined conversation between two Cretans before a volcanic eruption, 2nd millennium BC

The streams that come cascading down from the Caucasian Mountains are the tears of Sewsereq. They glide along, and in the murmuring sound they make as they go, you can hear these words: 'As I no longer have the strength to help Mankind, at least my tears will succour them!'

Scythian myth preserved in Caucasian oral folklore, 1st millennium BC

'Come along the beach with me. I've found some fertile land. And I've also discovered why it's so fertile: it's the seabirds that do it. There's lots of it.

'And we have to take this stuff and put it on our fields?'

'Look at my field, look at my maize!'

Imagined conversation between two peasants on the seashore at the foot of the Nazca valley, Peru, 3rd–2nd millennium BC

Suddenly a hole appeared in the
 earth. / The spirit of Enkidu
Flew out like an escaping wind. /
 They embraced
And kissed each other; / they
 whispered to each other:
'Tell me, my friend! Tell me, my
 friend, / tell me
What the land is like from whence
 you came.' / 'I will not tell you, my
 friend,
I will not tell you. / If I told you what
 it is like where I come from,
You would sit down and weep' (said
 Enkidu).
'Well, I will sit down and weep' (said
 Gilgamesh)
'The friend you were touching, his
 body is now but dust.'

Twelfth tablet of the Assyrian version of the Mesopotamian story of Gilgamesh, 1st millennium BC. The hero, Gilgamesh, is a semi-god. Enkidu is his human friend. Here they are talking about the land of the dead where Enkidu now is, and from which he has been recalled in spirit form.

'Bricks, bricks, always bricks! We never do anything but make bricks! Will these granaries never be finished?'

'Do you know what I think? If we carry on burning wood to bake bricks and make granaries to keep our grain in, we will end up destroying the forest and there will be no more animals to hunt and no more birdsong to listen to.'

Imagined conversation between two workers at Harappa, on the Indus River, late 3rd millennium BC

The matting is falling apart on the
 floors / of the huts
The makeshift huts / in the autumn
 ricefields /
And the dew is seeping through,
 seeping through on to my hands.

Poem by the Japanese Emperor Tenchi (662–671 AD) written during a visit to some peasant hovels (the 'dew' is tears)

'Do what I'm doing, boy: hit the bottom wheel with your foot, look how the table moves round, the clay is moulded by your hands and the vase takes shape.'

'So it does. But you manage to make it turn the way you want it to; I'm kicking too hard and the table's not turning properly.'

'Don't kick it: imagine it's a cow you're pushing. Start off very gently and then speed up; do you see?'

> Imagined conversation between two potters, one young, one old, in a shop in the Mesopotamian city of Uruk, late 4th millennium BC

'Milk that cow! Hurry up: the shepherd's due any minute'!

> One milk-thief to another

'Come on, my friend, eat your bread!'

> Cowherd giving bread to a sick calf

'Row, row harder, comrade! Faster!
'I am rowing, but everyone keeps saying 'row harder!'

> Two oarsmen

'Here's some good grass! Eat!'

> Boy offering a forkful of hay to his animals

> Captions found on wall paintings in common people's tombs from the Egyptian sixth dynasty, about 22nd century BC

These are voices speaking to us from the past; some have come from written texts, others are an attempt to imagine the words that might have been exchanged between people whose remains and artefacts have been found on archaeological sites.

The texts quoted here and elsewhere in the book are taken or adapted from the following books:

L'alba della civiltà ed Sabatino Moscati, UTET, Turin 1976
Annone *Il periplo* (L Del Turco) Sansoni, Florence 1958
Silvio Curto *L'arte militare presso gli antichi Egizi* Museo Egizio di Torino, Turin 1969
Sergio Donadoni *La letteratura egizia* Sansoni Accademia, Florence, 1967
Georges Dumézil *Storia degli Sciti* Rizzoli, Milan 1980
Iscrizioni latine arcaiche ed Carlo Carena, Sansoni, Florence 1954
Letteratura e poesia dell' Antico Egitto ed Edda Bresciani, Einaudi, Turin 1964
Miti babilonesi e assiri ed Giuseppe Furlani, Sansoni, Florence 1958

Antonio Pagliaro and Alessandro Bausani *La letteratura persiana* Sansoni Accademia, Florence 1968
Popl Vuh ed Adrian Recinos and Lore Terracini, Einaudi, Turin 1960
Georges Posener et al *Dizionario della civiltà egizia* Il Saggiatore, Milan 1961
Giovanni Rinaldi and Ferdinando Luciani *Le letterature antiche del Vicino Oriente* Sansoni Accademia, Florence 1968
Fujiwara Teika *La centuria poetica* Sansoni, Florence 1950
Testi religiosi egizi ed Sergio Donadoni, UTET, Turin 1970
Testi sumerici e accadici ed Giorgio R Castellino, UTET, Turin 1977

Bibliography

Branigan, Keith *Prehistory* (*History as Evidence* series) Kingfisher Books, London 1984

Cootes, R J and Snellgrove, L E *The Ancient World* (Longman Secondary Histories series) Longman, Harlow 1970

The Emergence of Man (20 vols) Time Life Books, London 1973–1976

Fagg, C, Chamberlain, N and Dear, B *Ancient Rome* (*Great Civilizations* series) Longman, Harlow 1978

Gobineau, J A de *The World of the Persians* John Gifford, London 1971

Henrikson, A *Through the Ages* Orbis Publishing, London 1983

Jellicoe, G A & S *Landscape of Man* Thames and Hudson, London 1975

Kleibl, Josef *The Hamlyn Book of Early Man* Hamlyn, London 1976

Knox, R, Dear, B and Dear, C *Ancient China* (*Great Civilizations* series) Longman, Harlow 1978

Lansing, Elizabeth *The Sumerians* (*Cassell's Early Culture* series) Cassell, London 1974

Last Two Million Years: Reader's Digest History of Man Reader's Digest, London 1973

McCord, Anne *Early Man* (*The Children's Picture Prehistory* series) Usborne, London 1977

McLellan, Elizabeth *Minoan Crete* (*Aspects of Greek Life* series) Longman, Harlow 1976

MacNamara, Ellen *Everyday Life of the Etruscans* Batsford, London 1973

Millard, Anne *Ancient Civilizations* Kingfisher Books, London 1982

Millard, Anne *Ancient Egypt* (*Great Civilizations* series) Longman, Harlow 1978

Millard, Anne *Incas* (*Great Civilizations* series) Longman, Harlow 1980

Millard, Anne *Pocket Handbook to the Ancient World* Usborne, London 1982

Millard, Anne and Vanags, Patricia *Children's Encyclopedia of History* Usborne, London 1977

Mitchell, James (ed) *History and Culture 1* (*The Mitchell Beazley Joy of Knowledge Library*) Mitchell Beazley, London 1977

Prescott, William H *The World of the Aztecs* John Gifford, London 1970

Reid, Jane (ed) *The Ancient Greeks and Romans* (*The Open Book* series) Hodder & Stoughton, London 1984

Roberts, J M *The Earliest Men and Women* (*An Illustrated World History* series No 1) Penguin Books, London 1980

Roberts, J M *The First Civilizations* (*An Illustrated World History* series No 2) Penguin Books, London 1980

Salt, J and Purnell, F *From Early Man to Norman Times* (*Discovering History* series) Oliver & Boyd, Edinburgh 1970

Unstead, R J *Egypt and Mesopotamia* A & C Black, London 1977

Walsh, Jill Paton *The Island Sunrise – Prehistoric Britain* (*The Mirror of Britain* series) Andre Deutsch, London 1975

Whitlock, Ralph *Everyday life of the Maya* Batsford, London 1976

Index

Entries in italic type refer to illustrations or charts.

318

Picture Acknowledgements

Antikvarisk-Topografiska Arkivet, Stockholm (ATA) 153 top right, 165 bottom; F Arborio Mella, Milan 278 (Museo Archeologico Nazionale, Cagliari), 292 left (Museo Etrusco, Chiusi), 292 right (Museo Archeologico, Florence), 293 left (Museo Etrusco, Chiusi), 293 right (Museo Archeologico Nazionale, Palermo); Archivio Mondadori, Milan 13, 15 (Motto), 20, 21, 29 top right (Motto), 36 right, 40–41 (Archaeological Museum, Ankara), 54, 64, 82 bottom (Ashmolean Museum, Oxford), 86, 91 top (National Museum of Iraq, Baghdad), 105 bottom left, 107 (National Archaeological Museum, Athens), 122 (British Museum, London), 123 top (British Museum, London), 136–7, 167 top right, 224, 224–5, 225, 227, 237, 264 (Louvre, Paris), 268 (National Museum, Aleppo), 282–3, 290; Bibliotheque Nationale, Paris 238; Boitier-Connaissance des Arts – TOP 279 top (Louvre, Paris); Lee Boltin, New York (courtesy of University Museum, University of Pennsylvania) 97, 245 top; Aurel Bongers, Recklinghausen 244 (Ermitage, Leningrad); R Emmett Bright, Rome 145 right (National Museum of Pakistan, Karachi), 145 left (National Museum of Iraq, Baghdad), 147 (National Museum of Pakistan, Karachi); British Museum, London 124 bottom centre, 126–7, 272–3, 277, 279 bottom; A Broglio, Ferrara 21 top left; G Coato, Verona 80–81, 87 top, 110–11 bottom, 118, 198–9, 206–7, 209, 214, 214–15, 217 bottom, 262; Jones Colin, London 242 (Ermitage, Leningrad); C Colombi, Brescia 219; Colorphoto Hans Hinz, Basle 27 top; P Cozzaglio, Brescia 123 bottom (drawing); M De Biasi, Milan 36 left; A Durazzi-Dufoto, Rome 136 (National Museum of Iraq, Baghdad); Ermitage, Leningrad 246–7 top (inset photo); A Fedini, Milan 120–21, 154–5; Fiore, Turin 123 bottom, 234 top; U Fronk, Verona 19; G Gerster, Zurich frontispiece, 29 bottom, 63, 68, 69, 70, 70–71, 74, 74–5, 75 right, 78, 79, 88–9, 91 bottom, 135, 196, 197, 210, 217 top, 248–9, 254–5, 270, 271; F Ghiringhelli, Milan 12–13, 20–21, 23, 24–5, 29 top left, 30, 32, 33 bottom, 34–5 top, 42–3, 44, 45 bottom, 46, 52–3, 55, 56 left, 59, 62, 65, 66–7, 75 left, 83 bottom, 87 bottom, 89, 90–91, 94–5, 99 bottom, 101 top, 102, 109, 110–11 top, 115 top, 121, 124 top, 125 top, 129, 131 top, 133 top, 137, 142, 145 top, 150–51, 164, 165 top, 166, 171 left, 176–7, 178–9, 184, 191 bottom, 192 bottom, 194, 202, 203, 208, 220–21, 222–3, 226, 231, 232, 234 bottom, 235, 245 bottom, 246–7 bottom, 251, 258 bottom, 259 top, 261 top, 272 bottom, 282 top, 291, 299 top, 302–3, 304–5, 306–7; Giraudon, Paris 273 (Louvre, Paris); G Guerreschi, Milan 154; Ava Güler, Istanbul (Museum of Archaeology, Ankara) 39, 45 top, 47 top; Hirmer Fotoarchiv-Hirmer Verlag, Monaco 126 left (National Museum, Damascus), 139 (Museum of Archaeology, Ankara), 269 bottom (National Museum, Aleppo); M Holford, London 275 (British Museum, London); © Holle Verlag, Baden-Baden (drawing) 246–7 top; Istituto di Etruscologia e Antichita Italiche, University of Rome 287, 294 top (S Moscati); Jericho Excavation Fund, London 49 left, 50; Kazuteru Saionji 101 bottom; Kodansha Ltd, Tokyo 56 right (Museum of Yugoslavia), 80 (Egyptian Museum, Cairo), 82 top (Egyptian Museum, Cairo), 83 top (Egyptian Museum, Cairo), 103 right (National Museum, Tokyo), 104 right (Museum of Yugoslavia), 105 right (Museum of Yugoslavia), 108, 110 (Egyptian Museum, Cairo), 112 (Egyptian Museum, Cairo), 113 left, 113 right (Egyptian Museum, Cairo), 114 (Egyptian Museum, Cairo), 115 (Egyptian Museum, Cairo), 119 (Egyptian Museum, Cairo), 128 centre (Louvre, Paris), 131 bottom (Louvre, Paris), 133 bottom (Louvre, Paris), 140 (British Museum, London), 162 (Museum of Yugoslavia), 163 (Museum of Yugoslavia), 174 (Museum of Yugoslavia), 174–5 (Museum of Yugoslavia), 180–81 (Museum and Collection, Athens), 185 (Museum and Collection, Athens), 188 (Museum and Collection, Athens), 189, 192 bottom (Museum and Collection, Athens), 193 (Museum and Collection, Athens), 198 (National Museum of Anthropology, Mexico City), 199, 200, 201, 204, 205, 207, 212, 213 (National Museum of Anthropology, Mexico City), 215, 221 top (Minneapolis Institute of Arts, Minneapolis), 228 (National Museum, Tokyo), 228–9, 229 (National Museum, Tokyo), 230 (National Museum, Tokyo), 233, 236–7, 248 top, 248 bottom (Metropolitan Museum of Art, New York), 250–51 (British Museum, London), 252 (British Museum, London), 252–3 (British Museum, London), 253 (British Museum, London), 254 (Egyptian Museum, Cairo), 255 (Egyptian Museum, Cairo), 258 top (Egyptian Museum, Cairo), 259 bottom (Egyptian Museum, Cairo), 261 bottom (Egyptian Museum, Cairo), 262–3 (Egyptian Museum, Cairo), 263 (Egyptian Museum, Cairo), 265 (Louvre, Paris), 266–7, 269 top (Louvre, Paris), 301 (Palazzo dei Conservatori, Rome); from 'Gli antecedenti della civilta dell' Indo' by J F Jarrige and R H Meadow in Le Scienze no 146, October 1980, p 76 (reproduced by kind permission) 98, 99 top; Linden Museum, Stuttgart 216; Magnum, Milan (Eric Lessing) 140–41 (Louvre, Paris), 142–3, 152 left (Danish National Museum, Copenhagen), 171 right (courtesy of Naturhistorisches Museum, Vienna), 172 (courtesy of Naturhistorisches Museum, Vienna), 173 (courtesy of Naturhistorisches Museum, Vienna); Mandel-Dimt, Milan 33 top; Marka, Milan 104 left (Saint-Germain-en-Laye-Musée des Antiquités-Giraudon), 152 left (Schweizerisches Landesmuseum, Zurich); G Martini, Verona 76–7; Matsuyama Art Center, Matsuyama 100, 221 bottom; J Mellaart, London 51 bottom; The Metropolitan Museum of Art, New York 128 bottom left, 260; T Micek, Innsbruck 179; Musee de l'Homme, Paris 43; Museo Archeologico, Florence 288; Museo Nazionale di Villa Giulia, Rome 283, 285, 295; Published with the permission of the Danish National Museum, Copenhagen – photography L Larsen 153 top left, 153 centre left, 159; Museum of Far Eastern Antiquities, Stockholm 223; Museum für Vor-und Frühgeschichte Preussischer Kulturbesitz, Berlin – photography J Liepe 105 top left; Oriental Institute, University of Chicago 96 bottom; A Panicucci, Milan 77, 108–9; D Pellegrini, Milan 72, 73, 194–5, 195; Pictor, Milan 31, 48, 49 left, 184–5, 190–91; The Pierpont Morgan Library, New York 124 bottom right; M Pucciarelli, Rome 191 top (Museum and Collection, Athens), 286, 288, 289; F Quilici, Rome 282 bottom (Museo Nazionale di Villa Giulia, Rome); Realités, Paris 242–3 (Ermitage, Leningrad); Réunion des Musées Nationaux, Paris 126 right; L Ricciarini, Milan 280 top (Archivio B – Musée National du Bardo, Tunis, 281 (Archivio B – Archeological Museum, Carthage), 128 top (Bevilacqua), 130 (Bevilacqua – Louvre, Paris), 266 (Bevilacqua – Louvre, Paris), 280 bottom (Bevilacqua – Museo Archeologico Nazionale, Cagliari), 138 (Borromeo-Archaeological Museum, Ankara), 146 (Borromeo), 81 (Simion – Louvre, Paris), 103 left (Simion – Museo Nazionale de'Arte Orientale, Rome), 128 bottom (Simion – Louvre, Paris), 299 bottom (Simion – Museo Nazionale di Villa Giulia, Rome), 298 (Tomsich); A Ripamonti, Milan 54–5, 84–5, 106–7, 116–17, 211, 257; Scala, Florence 125 bottom (Oriental Institute, University of Chicago), 145 bottom (National Museum of India, New Delhi), 153 bottom, 294 (Museo Archeologico, Florence); Sergio, Milan 14–15, 16–17, 18, 22, 34–5 bottom, 37, 40, 50–51, 57, 61, 93, 149, 157, 161, 169, 182–3, 187, 239, 240–41, 276–7, 296–7; J E Sjöberg, Gothenburg 167 left, 167 bottom right; J R Solecki, Department of Anthropology, Columbia University, New York 12; G Tortoli, Florence 134; J Vertut, Paris 17 top right, 17 bottom, 27 bottom (Musée de Préhistoire, Les Eyzies); The Walters Art Gallery, Baltimore 96 top, 136.